Vancouver Cooks 2

JOAN CROSS
JAMIE MAW
ANDREW MORRISON

EDITORS

Vancouver Cooks 2

CHEFS' TABLE SOCIETY OF BRITISH COLUMBIA

Douglas & McIntyre
D&M PUBLISHERS INC.
Vancouver/Toronto/Berkeley

Douglas & McIntyre
An imprint of D&M Publishers Inc.
2323 Quebec Street, Suite 201
Vancouver BC Canada V5T 4S7
www.douglas-mcintyre.com

Library and Archives Canada Cataloguing in Publication
Vancouver cooks 2 / Chefs' Table Society of British Columbia ;
edited by Joan Cross, Jamie Maw and Andrew Morrison;
foreword by Vicki Gabereau.
Includes index.
Recipes from members of the Chefs' Table Society of British Columbia.

ISBN 978-1-55365-534-3 (bound).—ISBN 978-1-55365-261-8 (pbk.).

1. Cookery, Canadian—British Columbia style. 2. Cookery—
British Columbia—Vancouver. 3. Cookery—British Columbia.
I. Cross, Joan, 1939– II. Maw, Jamie, 1952– III. Morrison, Andrew,
1973– IV. Chefs' Table Society of British Columbia.
TX715.6.V3653 2009   641.59711′33   C2009-900944-7

Editing by Saeko Usukawa
Cover and text design by Peter Cocking
Cover photograph by Shannon Mendes
Photography by John Sherlock and Shannon Mendes
Printed and bound in Canada by Friesens
Printed on acid-free paper
Distributed in the U.S. by Publishers Group West

We gratefully acknowledge the financial support of the Canada
Council for the Arts, the British Columbia Arts Council, the Province
of British Columbia through the Book Publishing Tax Credit and
the Government of Canada through the Book Publishing Industry
Development Program (BPIDP) for our publishing activities.

Contents

Foreword

When I was a kid in the 1950s, Vancouver had few restaurants, except for coffee shops of the greasy spoon variety with 7-Up signs shouting "Western and Chinese Food Served Here," and fish-and-chip joints. In my neighbourhood of Kerrisdale there were only three places to eat out: the Ding-Ho drive-in, the Avenue Grill (then owned by Sam Feldman's granddad) and the Yorkshire Inn, which served roast beef, puffy puddings, a medley of seasonal canned vegetables and gravy.

Farther afield there was Vie's, a joint on Union near Main and Hastings where they served skillet-fried steaks and you took your own booze, pre-licencing. Downtown you could find Oscar's at the corner of Burrard and Georgia, a place famous for its running bet: eat the 32-ounce steak (and a baked potato the size of Idaho) and it was free. Fail, and your dad would be instantly broke.

Back then, "fine dining" was restricted to hotels and golf clubs. Hotels had dining rooms and even wine lists. So if you were having a big night out, The Georgia, The Devonshire and the Hotel Vancouver (the Panorama Roof Ballroom offered Dal Richards' big band music to work off your stroganoff) were your front-running choices. The fare from one to the other differed not at all: the chefs were from Europe so you could count on imported escargot doing the backstroke in garlic butter and frozen Icelandic scampi in cream-of-cream sauce, all washed down with wine from France.

Most of my friends never went to a restaurant at all, not just because there was nowhere to go but because it wasn't yet part of the culture—everyone was home for dinner at 5:30. But my parents were newspaper people, well-acquainted with the soft underbelly of the city, and they liked places off the beaten path. At home my mother even cooked with garlic that didn't come in a jar and she wasn't even Italian. While we went to White Spot, the great drive-in chain, for their Bar-B-Q chicken burger—now lamentably discontinued but then sublime to my nine-year-old palate—we also went to Chinatown. The Ho Inn and the On On leap to mind, and it was there I saw my first fingerbowl; my friend drank from it.

How things have changed. In the early '60s, independent restaurants could finally get liquor licences, which encouraged citizens—at long last—to dine out. (Ironically, it was the teetotalling W.A.C. Bennett who unwound the hotels' booze monopoly). Hy's, for instance, made you think you were in New York City or one of its better suburbs. The original William Tell, a Swiss restaurant with fondue and wine bottles suspended on cast-iron holders, was the height of sophistication. There you would find the charming owner, Erwin Doebeli, regaling guests such as Jayne Mansfield, who dispensed with the bread cubes and drank her molten fondue—laced with about a ton of Gruyère and riesling—from an out-sized serving spoon and then went and performed at The Cave nightclub.

The immigration booms of the late '60s and the late '80s peppered the town with exciting new dining opportunities. Those new Canadians who joined the table changed not just what we eat, but *how* we eat it: sharing plates (the small plates phenomenon was invented right here), but mainly just casually meeting up at restaurants (by the late seventies, Vancouverites were outspending Torontonians almost two-to-one in restaurants). Puccini's was where writers and TV people and cops went for steaks and spaghetti *con aglio e olio*. The waiters were pretty *olio* too. Then a French place called Le Petit Montmartre opened in an old house on Broadway, the chef a real French guy. There was no salt and pepper on the tables—what a drama over that, but the best pepper steak in the city, before or since. In Gastown, Jean-Claude Ramond opened la crêperie (all lower case like the '70s in general), catering to Shaughnessy matrons' French clubs and forlorn backpackers, and Joel Thibault fired up Chez Joel in Blood Alley. And brunch at Chez Victor on Seymour Street was the height of '70s cool: we ordered French press coffee and ate shirred eggs with gravlax through contrails of Gauloise cigarettes.

And then the city's restaurant options began to expand and grow up just as the government created the agricultural land reserves that preserved farmland around the city. Francesco Alonghi showed up, as did Umberto Menghi then John Bishop. The first two took Italian dining from the gingham tablecloth and raffia Chianti candlestick era to an entirely new place. And it took John Bishop, a Brit, to tell us that the foodstuffs right at our doorstep were better than Seafood Newburg, vol-au-vents and Steak Diane. Now the produce of our valleys stays at home, as does much of our fishery, but we don't—we're a food-crazed town.

The campaign to use local produce and wines has drawn the food-obsessed from around the world. Asian ingredients are now second nature on western menus, and vice versa—especially in our wild and crazy izakaya-yas. (It is entirely possible that the best sushi can be had right here. I am not necessarily saying it is better than in Japan but it's a lot cheaper.) And the DNA from all those cultures has woven into a distinct local cuisine so you know you could only be eating here.

I am a restaurant frequenter, and I love the experience no matter how toney or not-so-toney. I love Yang's—once at Main and 26th, now on Kingsway—and I would crawl over hot coals to eat their Screaming Chicken. But I'm equally at home at West or Bishop's or Cioppino's, where I am obsessed with the rotisserie chicken.

Vancouver is now undeniably a culinary hotspot and it will continue to be long after I've pushed back from the table. What is it that makes this place unique? The province's farmers and growers provide fresh, local, seasonal, sustainable food that means we can taste where we live. Talented chefs from here and around the world add their home-grown flavours and techniques and continuously refuel the mix. Those chickens that I love so much come from Polderside Farms in the Fraser Valley and, recently, our city councillors said it's possible to raise chickens in our backyards again. Can't get more local than that.

Writing this is making me hungry. After thumbing through the proofs of this fine cookbook, I'm getting ready to do a little shopping and chopping. Care to tag along?

VICKI GABEREAU

Introduction

Collectives achieve results that no individual could attain alone, and the Chefs' Table Society is no different. A collaboration of British Columbia's outstanding chefs and culinary professionals—each dedicated to eagerly sourcing local, seasonal and sustainable ingredients—the society meets ten times a year to discuss in depth both the challenges and the sheer joy of cooking here. Time and again, this free exchange of ideas sparks new ones and creative solutions that enrich both the group as a whole and our culinary community at large.

The runaway success of our first cookbook, *Vancouver Cooks*, has led us to back to the well once again. While the original amply chronicled the very best of what we eat and made the recipes accessible to the home cook, this one probes even deeper into our gastronomic code by sourcing signature recipes pulled from our best restaurant menus. Not only do we plate the works of our innovators, we also introduce the next generation, and celebrate those who brought new flavours to these shores from around the world.

Since its inception in 2003, the Chefs' Table Society has helped to finance and launch many important initiatives. One of our chief tenets is to nurture and mentor ascendant talent. Accordingly, a number of apprenticeships and bursaries have been granted to emerging local chefs, including one in partnership with Les Clefs d'Or, which awards an annual bursary to outstanding culinary students demonstrating financial need. And in a spirited competition, where student chefs took part in the society's first Culinary Challenge, a $5,000 scholarship was awarded to Vancouver Community College for its team's sophisticated take on local ingredients. A children's culinary education program—Project Chef—has been underwritten to introduce Vancouver elementary school students to inspired cooking and good nutrition. The society has also partnered with the Terranova Schoolyard Project, a community-based garden project that engages troubled children and teens.

In one of its strongest leadership roles, the Chefs' Table Society has formed another collaboration, this time with local spot prawn fishermen. The Spot Prawn Festival has encouraged and supported the use of this fine local product in BC restaurants, while also educating the consumer as to its sustainability and fine flavour. The same is true for the society's other bonds, now forged clear across the province, with farmers, foragers, ranchers and fishers.

Putting together this feast was possible only because of a lengthy list of volunteers and culinary professionals. We thank them all, a highly dedicated and directed group. I would like to recognize the special efforts of several. Logistical support was provided by the intrepid Tiffany Soper and my wife, Michelle Sproule. Sid Cross, whose nose for marrying food and wine is justifiably legendary, and who has educated many budding palates across the province, begat the wine pairings along with Tim Ellison of the Pacific Institute of Culinary Arts. And through the lenses of photographers John Sherlock and Shannon Mendes, plates of glorious food leap off the page.

We would also like to acknowledge the efforts of another strong collaboration, the extraordinary team at Douglas & McIntyre, our publisher. It was Lucy Kenward who was the unfailing and patient back-stop who pushed this book ever forward and whose final edit ensured a read as clear and enjoyable as the finished dishes. Saeko Usukawa worked closely with Joan Cross to shape and edit the recipes and ancil-lary text, and it is Peter Cocking's design (and coordination with our photographers) that illuminates our words. Chris Labonté graciously handled the business side of our contract.

But I reserve special thanks for my co-editors, Jamie Maw and Joan Cross. Jamie—co-founder of the society and a 2009 inductee to the BC Restaurant Hall of Fame—shepherded every aspect of this book, from liaising with many of its contributing chefs to editing its every word and contributing a good many of his own. The always gracious Joan Cross worked in concert with executive chef and program director Julian Bond of the Pacific Institute of Culinary Arts. Julian's students tested many of the recipes, but it was the vigilant Joan who further tweaked them for the home cook—for she is a skilled one. The testing protocols comprise the heftiest workload of any cookbook; Julian and Joan ensured that these recipes would be enjoyable to shop for and prepare at home and that the results would be deeply flavourful. They are.

The Chefs' Table Society needs to be sustainable too. That's why the sale of this cookbook is fundamental to the programs that will be under-taken in the years ahead. We encourage you to buy a few copies—it's a wonderful corporate or personal gift, and certainly a terrific memento for visitors to our province.

So here we share with you the fruits of our collaboration and trust that the joy and the passion of these pages will soon reach into your very own kitchen.

Now eat this book!

ANDREW MORRISON

List of Recipes

Minestrone Verde with
Extra-virgin Olive Oil *129*

Spring Pea Soup with Hand-peeled
Shrimp and Tarragon Crème
Fraîche *141*

Melon Almond Gazpacho with
Dungeness Crab Salad and
Basil Oil *146*

Fanny Bay Oyster Soup *174*

Barbecued Peking Duck Soup and
Homemade Won Tons with Lime, Chili,
Ginger and Green Onion *180*

Salads

Hamilton Street Cobb Salad *21*

Fresh Herb Salad with
Cucumber, Radish and Feta *49*

Poached Pear and Pecan Spinach
Salad with Warm Goat Cheese *57*

Seafood Sashimi Salad *92*

Glorious Organics "Celebration"
Greens with Sapo Bravo Peach and
Tarragon Vinaigrette *116*

Candied Bull Kelp Salad *161*

Salade de Homard Printanière *203*

Fish and Shellfish Entrees

Halibut with Curry Salt, and Pea
and Bacon Purée *14*

Terrine of Sardines, Heirloom
Tomatoes, Zucchini and Basil *17*

Smoked Trout Rillettes with Endive
and Blue Cheese Salad *25*

Qualicum Bay Scallops with Big
Leaf Maple–candied Leeks, Foraged
Mushrooms and Wild Boar Bacon *29*

Halibut with Morels and Brown Butter
Sauce, Parsley and Garlic Pommes
Purée, Braised Lettuce and Peas *32*

Sablefish Marinated in Venturi-
Schulze Balsamic Vinegar, with
Venturi-Schulze Brut Sabayon,
Organic Pear and Carrot Salad with
Toasted Walnuts *46*

Jack's Sooke Ruby Trout, Garden
Herb Purée, Walla Walla Onion
and Chorizo Tart *53*

Grilled Wild Salmon with
Porcini Agnolotti and Tarragon
Beurre Blanc *74*

Baja-style Fish Tacos with Jicama
Slaw and Chipotle Aïoli *80*

Albacore Tuna Togarashi with
Buckwheat Soba Noodles and Candied
Ginger–Three Citrus Vinaigrette *82*

Gindara (Sablefish) *89*

Arctic Char à la Provencal *101*

Halibut Cheek Congee with
Lemon Zest Salt *108*

Qualicum Bay Scallops with Wild Rice,
Radish and Shiitake Mushroom Sauté,
Santa Rosa Plum Glaze *114*

Grilled Ahi Tuna with Spinach, Pickled
Shiitake Mushrooms and Dashi *117*

Seared Spring Salmon with Artichokes,
Swiss Chard and Herb Purée *119*

Crispy Professor Albright Trout, Warm Dungeness Crab, Spot Prawn and Mushroom Salad with Westbank Walnut Emulsion *121*

Prosciutto-wrapped Albacore Tuna with Creamy Polenta and Tomato Olive Vinaigrette *173*

Potato-crusted Lois Lake Steelhead with Celery Root Purée and Cabernet Reduction *182*

Pan-seared Ling Cod with Truffle Chanterelle Purée, Sauté of Sugar Pumpkin and Baby Zucchini with Bacon Emulsion *188*

Hamachi, Foie Gras and Barbecued Eel with Soy-Mirin Glaze *192*

Terrine of Smoked Trout Bellies with Pickled Root Vegetables and Thyme Crème Fraîche *208*

Tojo's Sablefish *217*

Meat and Poultry Entrees

Pulled Pork Sandwiches with Spicy Barbecue Sauce *22*

Roasted Nicola Valley Fallow Venison with Glazed North Arm Farm Beets and Chocolate Jus *39*

Thiessen Farm Squab Breast with Bulgar Wheat, Apple and Fireweed Honey Salad, Sautéed Fiddleheads and Feta *60*

Rabbit in Two Mustards *69*

Chicken Karaage *91*

Vitello Tonnato *95*

Tagliata di Manzo *96*

Butterflied Leg of Lamb with Herb Jus *97*

Chicken Breasts and Thighs in Clove, Black Cardamom and Yogurt Curry *104*

Su Dong Po Pork *107*

Smoked Cheddar Bison Burgers with Roasted Garlic Mayonnaise *124*

Moroccan Spiced Lamb Chop with Cucumber, Olive and Sheep's Milk Feta Salad, Yogurt-Garlic Dressing *133*

Berkshire Pork Duo: Tenderloin and Crispy Belly with Sauerkraut, Horseradish Coleslaw and Mustard Pork Jus *137*

Dry-aged Rib-eye Steak with Morels, Nugget Potatoes and Gentleman's Butter *145*

Organic Confit Pork Belly with Apricot Purée, Red Quinoa, Shiitake Mushrooms, Plums and Chocolate Mint *149*

Oven-braised Venison Ragout with Juniper Berries and Fresh Herbs— A Christmas Recipe *176*

Roast B.C. Bison Tenderloin with Bison Goulash *179*

Boneless Cornish Hens with Bread Stuffing and Escargot Ragout *185*

Red Wine-braised Oxtail with Sugar Pumpkin Gnocchi, Shallots and Pancetta *196*

Joues de Veau Braisées, Brunoise aux Potirons, Pappardelle et Sauce Pinot Noir *204*

Grain, Pasta and Vegetarian Entrees

Blue Heron Farm Squash Agnolotti
with Chestnuts, Brown Butter
and Sage 35

Linguine di Mare 87

Red Bell Pepper and Shallot Curry 103

Chicken Orecchiette with
Double-smoked Bacon and
Parmesan Cheese 126

Dungeness Crab Tagliarini with
Chili, Garlic and Parsley 130

Savoury Mushroom Tart with
Aged White Cheddar, Oloroso Sherry
and Balsamic Glaze 135

Carnaroli Risotto on Heirloom
Tomato and Basil Salad 143

Late Summer Vegetable Lasagna 159

Pine Mushrooms en Papillote 195

Chanterelle Open-faced Ravioli
with Crisp Berkshire Bacon 207

Duck Confit Ravioli with Cipollini
Onion and Chestnut Chutney 210

Accompaniments

"Signature" Cinnamon Sugar Yam
Fries with Mint Aïoli 31

French Sorrel Apple Sorbet 48

Grilled Whole Wheat Flatbread 50

Hot Spiced Wine 71

Desserts

Lavender Honey Nougatine Glacée 27

SoBo's Fresh Blackberry Pie 45

Frozen Crème Brûlée with Honey
Sponge Cake and Port-roasted
Grapefruit 62

Strawberry Sablé with Raspberry
Coulis and Vanilla Panna Cotta 76

Roasted Peach Tart 84

Grand Marnier Soufflé 98

White Chocolate and Passion Fruit
Mousse with Sesame Tuiles 142

Westham Island Farm Strawberries
with Venturi-Schulze Balsamic
Zabaglione, Agassiz Hazelnut Oil 164

Vila Gracinda Chocolate and
Quebec Maple Syrup Cone, with
Whiskey, Sorrento Nut and Vanilla
Milkshake 171

Parisienne Chocolate Mousse
and Vanilla-poached Pear with
Pear Gelée 200

Lavender-crusted Shortcake and
Summer "Thyme" Macerated Fruit and
Berries with Vanilla Cream 212

Pear Almond Tart with Black
Currant Jam 214

Double Chocolate Chip Cookies 216

Local,
Seasonal &
Sustainable

VANCOUVER IS ONE of the most exciting gastronomic centres in the world. Our culinary heritage, enriched by more than a hundred mother cuisines, offers both diversity and assimilation at the table. Although those mother cuisines are well preserved throughout the city, over the past decade their presence has contributed to an entirely new regional food culture. That culture has been made possible and enhanced by the extraordinary quality and variety of ingredients delivered from British Columbia's fisheries, ranches, farms and fields.

In this first section, we introduce many influential chefs who champion this ingredient-driven gastronomy while helping to ensure the sustainability of its resources. Their collaborations with local growers are showcased on plates across the city daily. Now we invite you to make these delicious dishes at home.

Squash Blossoms
Stuffed with Three Cheeses and Served over Eggplant Purée

Squash Blossoms

1 medium potato

12 squash blossoms, with or without fruit attached

¼ cup soft goat cheese

¼ cup grated Moonstruck White Grace cheese or 2- or 3-year-old white cheddar

2 Tbsp grated Parmesan cheese

Olive oil for deep-frying

Eggplant Purée

1 large globe eggplant

Kosher salt

2 cloves garlic, thinly sliced

2 sprigs thyme

¼ cup olive oil

2 lemons, juice of

2 Tbsp toasted pine nuts for garnish

Extra-virgin olive oil for garnish

Tempura Batter

2 egg yolks

1 cup ice water or San Pellegrino

2 cups all-purpose flour

Squash blossoms are a treat. They are generally not available except to home gardeners, but they are sometimes available at farmers' markets. These stuffed squash blossoms are delicious on their own or as a side dish. *Serves 4 to 6*

Squash Blossoms Cook potato in a small pot of boiling water on high heat. Remove from the heat, drain and allow to cool, then peel and rice through a food mill.

Cut off stems of blossoms if they are too long. If there is fruit attached to the blossoms, trim off the end of the fruit and slice it once lengthwise to help it cook. Carefully open the blossoms, then remove and discard the stamens, dirt or insects.

Blend together riced potato, goat cheese, Moonstruck cheese and Parmesan in a small bowl. Season lightly with salt and pepper. Place the cheese mixture in a warm place to soften, then spoon it into a piping bag. Gently place the piping tip inside one blossom, fill three-quarters of the blossom with the cheese mixture, then twist the top of the blossom closed to keep the filling inside. Repeat for each blossom. Place stuffed blossoms on a tray and refrigerate.

Eggplant Purée Preheat the oven to 375°F. Cut eggplant in half lengthwise, sprinkle the cut sides liberally with kosher salt and allow to stand at room temperature for 30 minutes to draw out moisture. Use paper towels to wipe off the salt and excess moisture. Score the flesh side of the eggplant, making lengthwise cuts ¼-inch deep and 1 inch apart. Insert garlic and thyme into the cuts.

Drizzle an ovenproof dish with olive oil. Place eggplant, flesh-side down, in the dish. Bake in the oven for 35 to 45 minutes, or until soft. Remove from the oven and allow to cool enough to handle. Scrape out the eggplant flesh, including garlic and thyme. Discard the skins. Purée eggplant flesh and lemon juice in a food processor. Pass through a fine-mesh sieve to remove seeds and thyme branches. Place sieved eggplant flesh in a covered container and refrigerate.

Tempura Batter Place egg yolks and ice water in a stainless steel bowl and mix lightly. Add flour and mix lightly with a fork, just to combine (be careful not to overmix the batter or the coating will not be crisp).

To Finish Squash Blossoms Place 2 to 3 inches of oil in a wok, or place oil in a deep fryer to the marked line, or half-fill a tall-sided heavy pot on the stovetop and heat to 330°F. Dip squash blossoms in tempura batter to coat fully. Fry in three batches, for about 2 to 3 minutes each, or until light gold and crispy. Drain on paper towels. Season with salt and pepper.

To Serve Place a small mound of chilled eggplant purée on each plate and top with two or three squash blossoms. Garnish with pine nuts and a drizzle of extra-virgin olive oil.

Wine Wild Goose Vineyards Riesling

Halibut with Curry Salt
and Pea and Bacon Purée

Pea and Bacon Purée

4 Tbsp unsalted butter

1 small white onion, finely chopped

2 oz double-smoked bacon, in ¼-inch dice

1 cup peas, thawed if using frozen

6 Tbsp chicken or vegetable stock

1 medium potato, peeled, in ½-inch dice

1 sprig mint

1 sprig thyme

3 Tbsp half-and-half cream

Halibut with Curry Salt

1 tsp curry powder

1 Tbsp kosher salt

2 Tbsp grapeseed oil

4 fillets halibut, each 5 oz, boneless, skinless

Pea shoots for garnish

1 Tbsp extra-virgin olive oil for garnish

Curry salt adds a spicy fragrance to the savoury purée of peas and bacon placed under the halibut. *Serves 4*

Pea and Bacon Purée Melt 2 Tbsp of the butter in a pot on medium heat. Add onion and bacon, then sauté for 4 to 5 minutes, or until light golden. Add ½ cup of the peas, stock, potato, mint and thyme. Turn up the heat to high and bring to a boil. Season with salt and pepper. Turn down the heat to low and simmer gently for 12 to 15 minutes, or until potato is tender. Remove and discard mint and thyme. Add the remaining ½ cup of peas and the remaining 2 Tbsp of butter, then cook for 2 minutes, or until just done. Transfer to a blender or food processor and pulse until you have a rough purée, then stir in cream. (Or use a potato masher or a fork to achieve a textured purée.)

Halibut with Curry Salt Combine curry powder and salt in a small bowl, mixing thoroughly. Season halibut liberally with this curry salt.

Heat grapeseed oil in a large frying pan on medium-high heat. Place fish, presentation-side down, in the pan, and sauté for 3 to 4 minutes, or until golden brown. Gently flip over fish and cook for 3 to 4 minutes, or until done (the fish should be soft to the touch and still slightly opaque in the centre).

To Serve Place a small mound of pea and bacon purée in the centre of each warmed plate, then top with a piece of halibut. Garnish with pea shoots and a drizzle of extra-virgin olive oil.

Wine Blasted Church Vineyards Hatfield's Fuse White Blend

Terrine of Sardines, Heirloom Tomatoes, Zucchini and Basil

Tarama is salted cod roe that is sold in Greek grocery stores. It adds flavour and helps to bind the layers of the terrine. If you cannot find fennel pollen, substitute 1 tsp ground fennel seeds. *Serves 6 to 8*

Terrine of Sardines Scale, gut and rinse each sardine. On each fish, make an incision behind both sides of the head to expose the spine. Place the sardine on its back, then pull the head slowly upward, towards the tail (you should be able to pull out the spine with most of the tiny bones attached, although you will probably not get all of them). Cut off the fins and the tails. Discard the heads, spines, fins and tails.

Dissolve salt in water in a large bowl. Add sardines and allow them to sit in this brine for 10 minutes. Take sardines out of the brine and pat dry with paper towels.

Preheat the oven to 350°F. Brush sardines with 2 Tbsp of the olive oil and sprinkle lightly with fennel pollen. Place fish on a parchment paper–lined baking sheet and roast in the oven for 2 to 3 minutes. Lift out the parchment paper and transfer sardines to a clean baking sheet, then refrigerate for at least 10 minutes.

Butterfly the sardines by cutting them down the centre, cutting almost but not completely through, then open and flatten.

Preheat the grill to high. Brush zucchini slices with 2 Tbsp of the remaining olive oil and grill on each side for 2 to 3 minutes, or until light grill marks are visible. Season with salt and pepper, then drain on paper towels.

Fill a bowl with ice water. Bring a medium pot of water to a boil on high heat. Add tomatoes, blanch for 10 seconds, drain, then plunge them into the ice water. Peel tomatoes and quarter them; remove and discard the seeds. Drain tomatoes on several layers of paper towel.

Take out bread from water and gently press out the moisture. Purée bread, tarama, garlic and lemon juice in a blender or food processor. With the motor running, slowly add canola oil and the remaining ½ cup of olive oil in a thin steady stream until emulsified.

Continued overleaf

Terrine of Sardines

6 medium sardines, total weight 3 lbs

2 Tbsp salt

2 cups water

½ cup + 4 Tbsp olive oil

1 tsp fennel pollen

2 medium zucchini, cut lengthwise into ⅛-inch thick slices

3 large heirloom tomatoes

4 slices white bread, crusts removed, soaked in 1 cup water

4 Tbsp tarama

1 small clove garlic, finely chopped

1 lemon, juice of

½ cup canola oil

1 cup dry white wine

2 shallots, minced

5 leaves gelatin, softened in cold water

1 cup whipping cream

1 cup whipped cream

16 leaves basil

7 oz baby arugula for garnish

Sprigs of fennel for garnish

Place wine and shallots in a small pot on medium heat, then simmer for about 5 minutes, or until liquid is reduced by half. Strain through a fine-mesh sieve into a bowl and discard solids. Remove gelatin leaves from the water, gently squeeze out any excess water and stir into the warm wine reduction until they dissolve. Whisk this mixture into the tarama mousse until well blended. Stir in whipping cream, then gently fold in whipped cream.

Lightly oil the inside of a terrine mould that is 10 × 3½ inches and 4 inches deep. Line the mould with plastic wrap, leaving 4 inches of plastic hanging over on each side. Spoon a ½-inch layer of tarama mousse into the bottom of the terrine pan, then top it with four tomato quarters, side by side. Cover with a thin layer of tarama mousse and place four basil leaves on top, pressing them down gently so that they are submerged. Arrange a layer of grilled zucchini slices on top, then cover with another thin layer of tarama mousse. Top with two butterflied sardines, tail ends at the centre of the terrine, then cover with another thin layer of mousse. Continue layering tomatoes, basil, zucchini and sardines, with intervening thin layers of mousse, until everything is used up. Finish with a ½-inch layer of mousse. Fold the overhanging plastic wrap over the top and refrigerate for 24 hours.

Fennel Vinaigrette Extract the fennel juices in a juicer. (If you do not have a juicer, cut up the fennel, purée in a food processor with ½ cup of water, then strain through cheesecloth.) Place fennel juice in a bowl and whisk in lemon juice and oil until well emulsified, then season with salt and pepper.

To Serve Unmould the terrine onto a cutting board, leaving the plastic wrap in place for easier handling. Use an electric knife to cut slices ¾-inch thick, then place one slice in the centre of each chilled plate. Remove and discard the plastic wrap. Surround each terrine slice with fennel vinaigrette, then garnish with baby arugula and sprigs of fennel.

Wine Peller Estates Riesling Private Reserve

Cold Uni Chawan Mushi
(Cold Uni Egg Custard)

Mitsuba is Japanese wild parsley, sold in specialty food stores. If you cannot find it, use blanched snow peas cut in half. Similarly, if you cannot find the katakuri-ko, a Japanese starch traditionally made from the corm of lilies but now often from potatoes, use potato starch. This dish is traditionally made in chawan mushi cups; if you do not have any, use small ramekins. *Serves 4*

Dashi Wipe kombu gently with a moist paper towel to remove any loose impurities. Place kombu and water in a pot on medium-high heat and bring to a simmer. When kombu rises to the surface, remove it from the pot and discard. Turn off the heat, stir in bonito flakes and allow to infuse for 30 seconds. Use a spoon to skim off any impurities from the surface.

Fill a large bowl with ice. Strain the dashi immediately through a fine-mesh sieve into a bowl and discard the solids. Set the bowl of dashi on the bowl of ice and allow to cool to room temperature. Refrigerate in an airtight container. Makes more than you will need for the recipe. Will keep in the refrigerator for up to 1 week.

Uni Chawan Mushi Whisk together eggs and the 1²/₃ cups of the dashi in a bowl. Stir in 4 tsp (or to taste) of the soy sauce, ¼ cup (or to taste) of the mirin and a pinch of salt. Pass the mixture through a fine-mesh sieve and discard the solids. Divide the mixture among four chawan mushi cups. Cover the cups with their lids and cook in a steamer placed over a pot of boiling water for 5 to 6 minutes. Remove the cups from the steamer and allow to cool to room temperature. Refrigerate for at least 30 minutes, or until cold.

Meanwhile, combine the remaining ½ cup of the dashi, the remaining 1 tsp of soy sauce and the remaining 1 tsp of the mirin in a pot on medium heat, then simmer for 10 minutes. In a small bowl, mix katakuri-ko with 1 Tbsp cold water until smooth, then stir it gradually into the dashi and continue cooking until the mixture thickens and becomes smooth. Remove from the heat and allow to cool. Refrigerate for at least 10 minutes, or until cold.

Fill a small bowl with ice water. Bring a small pot of water to a boil on high heat. Add mitsuba and blanch for 1 minute, then drain and plunge it into the ice water. Drain, then add mitsuba to the dashi sauce.

To Serve Place a chawan mushi cup on each chilled plate. Place two pieces of uni on top of each serving, then drizzle with dashi sauce.

Wine Burrowing Owl Estate Winery Pinot Gris or Masa Shiroki Sake

Dashi

1 piece kombu (dried seaweed), about 6 inches long

4 cups water

1 cup bonito flakes (Japanese dried smoked bonito)

Uni Chawan Mushi

2 eggs

1²/₃ cups + ½ cup dashi

5 tsp light soy sauce

¼ cup + 1 tsp mirin (Japanese sweet cooking rice wine)

1 Tbsp katakuri-ko

8 sprigs mitsuba, stems only, in ¾-inch segments

2 uni (sea urchins), each cut into 4 pieces

Hamilton Street Cobb Salad

A variation of the original salad created in 1937 at the Holly-
wood Brown Derby restaurant, this tasty, colourful Cobb
salad features local spot prawns instead of chicken breast.
Serves 1 as an entrée

Dijon Mustard Vinaigrette Combine vinegar, mustards, honey
and salt in a food processor or a blender and whip at high speed for
30 seconds. With the motor running, slowly add the canola and
olive oils in a steady stream, then process for another 30 seconds
after all the oil has been added. Refrigerate until needed. Will
keep in the refrigerator, tightly covered, for up to 3 days.

Cobb Salad Preheat the broiler or a barbecue to 450°F. Place the
prawns about 4 inches from the heat and grill until they are just
firm and pink, 1½ to 2 minutes. Remove from the heat and allow
to cool. Shell prawns, leaving tails on.

Peel the avocado and cut into ½ inch slices.

In a large bowl, gently toss salad greens with the vinaigrette.

To serve Arrange the salad greens on an oval-shaped serving
plate. Keeping each ingredient separate, lay neat rows of blue
cheese, tomatoes, avocado, spot prawns, egg and bacon on top
of the greens. Serve immediately.

Wine Blue Mountain Pinot Gris or Inniskillin Dark Horse
Chardonnay

Dijon Mustard Vinaigrette

2 Tbsp white wine vinegar

1 Tbsp + 1½ tsp grainy
Dijon mustard

1½ tsp smooth Dijon mustard

1 Tbsp honey

½ tsp salt

⅓ cup canola oil

⅓ cup olive oil

Cobb Salad

3 spot prawns, shells on
but heads removed

½ avocado

3 cups organic mixed
salad greens, chilled

2 Tbsp Dijon mustard vinaigrette

2 oz Poplar Grove Tiger
Blue cheese or your favourite
blue cheese, room temperature,
crumbled

1 large heirloom tomato, in
¼-inch dice, or 12 teardrop
or grape tomatoes

2 large eggs, hard-boiled and
peeled, in ¼-inch dice

4 slices bacon or pancetta,
diced and cooked until crisp

Pulled Pork Sandwiches
with Spicy Barbecue Sauce

Barbecue Sauce

1 Tbsp vegetable oil

½ white onion, in ¼-inch dice (about 1 /2 cups)

1 Granny Smith apple, peeled and cored, in ¼-inch dice

2 cloves garlic, chopped

2 bottles (each 15 oz) of your favourite barbecue sauce

2 cups apple cider vinegar

Pork Rub Mixture

6 Tbsp salt

4 Tbsp sugar

4 Tbsp brown sugar

4 Tbsp ancho chili powder

4 Tbsp freshly ground black pepper

2 Tbsp cayenne pepper

¾ cup sweet Hungarian paprika

¼ cup smoked paprika

2 Tbsp garlic salt

Pulled Pork Sandwiches

1 pork shoulder roast, about 8 lbs, blade bone in or out

1 cup prepared yellow mustard

2 cups apple juice

15 to 20 white bread buns (1 per sandwich), cut in half

These delicious sandwiches are a variation on a method I learned while I was a member of Canadian National BBQ Champion Rockin' Ronnie Shewchuk's competitive team, the Butt Shredders. It's a recipe that makes a lot of meat, so plan to serve it when you're feeding a crowd, or freeze any leftover meat in sealed containers for up to a month. Serve the juicy pulled pork with crispy onions or coleslaw. *Serves 15 to 20*

Barbecue Sauce Heat oil in a large pot on medium heat. Add onions and cook, stirring, until they are a rich, caramelized golden brown, 20 to 25 minutes. Add apple and garlic and continue to cook, stirring occasionally, for 10 minutes. Add barbecue sauce, then pour vinegar into the empty bottles to rinse them and add to the sauce. Stir well. When the sauce is hot, reduce the heat to low and cook for 20 minutes. Will keep refrigerated for up to 1 week. Makes about 5½ cups.

Pork Rub Mixture Combine all ingredients in a small bowl and set aside. Will keep in an airtight container for up to 6 months.

Pulled Pork Sandwiches Start making this recipe the day before serving so you can cook the meat overnight. Preheat the oven to 225°F and place a perforated rack in a large roasting pan.

Pat dry pork shoulder with a towel and slather all over with mustard, then coat completely with the rub mixture (reserve any extra rub for another use, perhaps with spare ribs or chicken legs). Set pork in the roasting pan, pour in apple juice and cover with a lid or aluminum foil. Place in the oven and cook for 10 to 12 hours, or until tender (195°F on a meat thermometer). Remove from the oven and allow to rest for 45 minutes. The blade bone, if it is still in, will slide out easily once the meat is cooked. Discard the bone and any liquid in the pan.

Using your hands or two forks, pull or shred the warm meat into a large bowl, mixing in 3 cups of cold barbecue sauce as you shred. Once all the meat has been pulled, add more barbecue sauce to taste. Refrigerate the pulled pork and any excess sauce until needed.

To Serve Place 4 to 5 oz of pulled pork in a microwave-safe container and heat on high for 30 seconds, or until warm but not hot. Arrange the pork on the bottom half of a white bread bun, then top with the other half. Repeat with the remaining pork and buns until you have 15 to 20 sandwiches. Serve immediately.

Wine Misconduct Wine Company's The Big Take (a blend of Merlot, Cabernet Sauvignon and Cabernet Franc)

Cauliflower, Celery Root and Jerusalem Artichoke Soup
with Black Truffle Cream and Fried Sage

Soup
½ cup + 2 Tbsp butter
1 medium cauliflower, in florets
1 large celery root, in ½-inch dice
12 Jerusalem artichokes, in ½-inch dice
1 large onion, chopped
4 leaves sage
2 sprigs thyme
Freshly grated nutmeg to taste
1⅔ cups fino sherry
1⅔ cups dry white wine
2 cups whipping cream
4 cups chicken or vegetable stock

Truffle Cream and Sage
1 black truffle
1 Tbsp vegetable oil
18 to 24 leaves sage
½ cup whipping cream
3 Tbsp sour cream
1 tsp black truffle oil + for garnish

Jerusalem artichokes, also known as sunchokes, are the root of a perennial sunflower. Their delicious flavour marries well with the cauliflower and celery root in this winter soup. *Serves 6 to 8*

Soup Melt butter in a large non-reactive pot on medium heat. Add cauliflower, celery root, Jerusalem artichokes, onion, sage and thyme. Season lightly with salt, pepper and nutmeg to taste. Cook, stirring, for about 15 minutes, without allowing vegetables to take on colour. When vegetables start to release liquid and soften, stir in sherry, wine, cream and 2 cups of the stock. Bring to a boil on medium-high heat, then turn down the heat to low and simmer for 45 to 60 minutes, or until vegetables have collapsed and released their starches. Remove and discard sage and thyme.

Remove the pot from the stove and allow the soup to sit at room temperature for 1 hour; while still warm, purée in batches in a blender (not a food processor). The soup should have the consistency of heavy cream; if necessary, use the remaining stock to adjust the consistency. Season with salt and pepper.

Truffle Cream and Sage Cut truffle in half. Finely slice one-half of truffle and reserve. Finely chop the remaining half truffle and reserve.

Heat vegetable oil in a small frying pan on medium-high heat until nearly smoking. Add sage leaves and fry for only a few seconds, or until crisp. Drain on paper towels.

Place whipping cream, sour cream, truffle oil and finely chopped truffle in a bowl, then whip until the mixture holds soft peaks.

To Serve Heat soup and ladle into warmed bowls. Top each with 1 Tbsp of the truffle cream, two or three fried sage leaves, two truffle slices and a tiny drizzle of truffle oil.

Wine Inniskillin Okanagan Vineyards Winery Discovery Series Chenin Blanc

Smoked Trout Rillettes
with Endive and Blue Cheese Salad

You can make this tasty appetizer a day or two ahead of a dinner party to take some of the pressure off cooking and hosting.
Serves 6

Trout Rillettes Preheat the oven to 400°F. Sprinkle a little water on a parchment paper-lined rimmed baking sheet and arrange trout, skin-side down, on it. Season with salt and white pepper. Roast in the oven for about 7 minutes, or until trout is opaque in the centre. Remove from the oven and allow to cool.

Remove and discard the skin from trout and flake the flesh into a bowl. Add crème fraîche, tarragon, chives, lemon zest and juice, then blend it all together using a spatula (or your hands), just until a coarse paste forms. Do not overprocess.

Line each of six ramekins, 2½ inches in diameter, with smoked salmon. Fill each ramekin with the trout mixture and fold over the excess smoked salmon to form a tight parcel. Cover and refrigerate for at least 1 hour. Will keep in the refrigerator for up to 2 days.

Salad To make the dressing, whisk together oil, mustard, honey and lemon juice in a bowl. Slice endive into fine strips and add to the dressing, along with cheese. Toss gently.

To Serve Turn the rillettes carefully out of the ramekins onto individual chilled plates. Arrange salad on the side.

Wine Arrowleaf Cellars Gewürztraminer

Trout Rillettes
4 fillets trout, skin on

⅓ cup crème fraîche or sour cream

1 Tbsp finely chopped fresh tarragon

1 Tbsp finely chopped chives

1 lemon, zest and juice

14 oz smoked salmon, thinly sliced

Salad
2 Tbsp olive oil

1 Tbsp Dijon mustard

1 Tbsp honey

1 lemon, juice of

12 spears endive

3 oz Poplar Grove Tiger Blue or other blue cheese, crumbled

Lavender Honey Nougatine Glacée

The combination of nougatine glacée and lavender always takes me right back to the south of France, especially Provence, and all of its glory. This elegant dessert can be frozen in different shapes and garnished with a variety of nuts, berries and sauces.
Serves 6 to 8

Nougatine Place sugar and water in a pot on medium-high heat and bring to a boil. Do not stir. Cook until syrup thickens and starts to caramelize. As the sugar begins to caramelize, shake and swirl the pan gently to prevent sugar from burning in any one spot. Stir in almonds, then pour evenly onto a parchment paper–lined baking sheet. Allow to cool, then crush.

Italian Meringue Combine sugar, honey and water in a pot on medium-high heat and bring to a boil without stirring.

Place egg whites in the bowl of a stand mixer fitted with a whisk or in a bowl with a hand-beater at the ready. When the sugar syrup reaches 240°F on a candy thermometer, begin beating egg whites to soft peaks. When the sugar syrup reaches 249°F, remove it from the heat. With the stand mixer or hand-held beater on high speed, add the hot sugar syrup to the beaten egg whites in a slow, steady stream, until completely incorporated. Once the sugar syrup is all added, leave the mixer running on high until the thick meringue is cool to the touch.

Crème Anglaise Beat together ¼ cup of the sugar and egg yolks in a pot until pale yellow.

In another pot on medium heat, combine vanilla bean, milk and cream with the remaining 1 Tbsp of the sugar, then bring to a boil. Remove from the heat, cover and allow to infuse for 30 minutes, then strain through a fine-mesh sieve and discard the solids.

Fill a bowl with ice. Whisking continuously, pour the vanilla milk into the egg yolks in the pot. Place the pot on medium heat and cook, stirring, until the mixture reaches 170°F on a candy thermometer or coats the back of a wooden spoon. Strain immediately through a fine-mesh sieve into a clean bowl, then place on the bowl of ice to cool. Discard the solids. Refrigerate the crème anglaise until needed.

Continued overleaf

Nougatine
1 cup sugar
¼ cup water
1 cup almond flakes

Italian Meringue
1¾ cups sugar
2 Tbsp lavender honey
⅓ cup water
6 egg whites

Crème Anglaise
¼ cup + 1 Tbsp sugar
6 egg yolks
½ vanilla bean
½ cup milk
½ cup whipping cream

Nougatine Glacée

1 cup chopped candied fruit of your choice

1 Tbsp Kirsch

2½ cups whipping cream

1 recipe nougatine

1 recipe Italian meringue

1 recipe crème anglaise

Crushed pistachios for garnish

Fresh berries for garnish

Caramel Leaves

⅔ cup sugar

2 Tbsp water

Nougatine Glacée Place candied fruit and Kirsch in a bowl and allow to soak for 30 minutes.

Place cream in another bowl and whip until it becomes thick with soft peaks. Gently fold in candied fruit, nougatine, Italian meringue and crème anglaise. Pour into small containers of your choice or into a long narrow loaf pan, then place in the freezer. Will keep frozen for up to two weeks.

Caramel Leaves Grease a large piece of parchment paper. Bring sugar and water to a boil in a pot on medium-high heat, without stirring (swirl the pot), until it becomes a pale caramel colour. Spread this over the prepared parchment paper to a thickness of ⅛ inch. Allow to harden, then break into decorative pieces (leaves).

To Serve Unmould nougatine glacée (or cut into slices 1½-inches thick if in a loaf pan) and place on individual chilled serving plates. Garnish with a sprinkle of crushed pistachios, fresh berries and caramel leaves.

Wine Hawthorne Mountain Vineyards See Ya Later Ranch Ehrenfelser Icewine

Qualicum Bay Scallops
with Big Leaf Maple–candied Leeks,
Foraged Mushrooms and Wild Boar Bacon

Qualicum Bay on Vancouver Island is the source of highly sought-after scallops that are large, juicy and flavourful. They lend themselves to many garnishes, such as the ones in this dish. *Serves 6*

Maple-candied Leeks Combine brown sugar, water and maple syrup in a small pot on medium heat. Bring to a boil and simmer for 2 minutes. Add leek and bring back to a boil, then turn down the heat to low and simmer for 2 minutes. Remove from the heat and allow leek to cool in the liquid.

Sea Asparagus Bring a large pot of water to the boil on high heat. Add sea asparagus, blanch for 1 minute, drain and pat dry.

Melt butter in a frying pan on medium-high heat. Add sea asparagus and sauté for 3 to 4 minutes. Stir in lemon juice and remove the pan from the heat.

Scallops If mushrooms are small or medium, leave them whole, but if they are very large, cut so they are a similar size but still recognizable.

Heat 1 Tbsp of the oil in a frying pan on medium-high heat. Add bacon and sauté for about 5 minutes, or until slightly crisp. Add butter, mushrooms and wine. Cook, stirring, for 2 to 4 minutes, or until liquid evaporates and mushrooms are tender. Remove from the heat.

In a separate frying pan on medium-high heat, heat the remaining 1 Tbsp of the oil until it begins to smoke. Add scallops and cook on one side for 1 to 2 minutes, or until caramelized (check the edges for browning about a quarter of the way up the sides). Flip over scallops, add all but 2 Tbsp of the candied leek with one or two spoonfuls of its cooking liquid, then sauté scallops for 1 to 2 minutes, or until they start to caramelize (do not overcook). Remove from the heat.

To Serve Divide the mushroom mixture among the warmed plates and top each serving with a scallop. Drizzle with pan juices and garnish with reserved candied leek on top. Garnish with sea asparagus (optional).

Wine Calona Vineyards Artist Series Chardonnay

Maple-candied Leeks
½ cup brown sugar

⅓ cup water

6 Tbsp Big Leaf maple syrup

1 leek, white and light green parts only, julienned

Sea Asparagus (optional)
1 cup sea asparagus

2 tsp unsalted butter

Dash of lemon juice

Scallops
1 cup wild mushrooms (oyster, chanterelle, lobster, pine)

2 Tbsp canola oil

3½ oz wild boar bacon

1 tsp butter

1 to 2 Tbsp dry white B.C. wine

6 medium scallops

"Signature" Cinnamon Sugar Yam Fries
with Mint Aïoli

This is a colourful, tasty dish to share, with the accompanying mint aïoli a surprise for the palate. *Serves 6 to 8*

Mint Aïoli Process mint, lemon zest and lemon juice in a food processor or blender until mint is finely chopped. Add mayonnaise, honey and salt, then blend thoroughly.

Cinnamon Sugar Yam Fries Place oil in a deep fryer to the marked line or half-fill a tall-sided heavy pot on the stovetop and heat to 350°F.

Peel yams and cut into wedges ¼-inch wide. Whisk together cornstarch and water in a large stainless steel bowl. Add yams and toss until completely coated with the cornstarch mixture. Deep-fry yam wedges in batches for about 3 minutes, occasionally using tongs to separate them so they don't stick to each other.

Use a slotted spoon to remove yam wedges from the oil and allow to rest for 2 minutes on trays lined with paper towels. Deep-fry yam wedges again for 2 minutes, or until crisp. Use a slotted spoon to remove yam from the oil and place on paper towel–lined trays.

Mix together sugar and cinnamon in a small bowl.

To Serve Arrange yam wedges on a warmed serving platter, then sprinkle them with salt and the cinnamon-sugar mixture. Serve the mint aïoli in a bowl on the side.

Wine Twisted Tree Vineyards & Winery Tempranillo

Mint Aïoli
¼ cup mint leaves, stems removed
½ lemon, zest and juice of
2 cups mayonnaise
2 Tbsp fireweed honey
Pinch of salt

Cinnamon Sugar Yam Fries
Vegetable oil for deep-frying
8 medium-large yams
2 Tbsp cornstarch
¼ cup water
2 Tbsp sugar
2 Tbsp cinnamon
Pinch of salt

Halibut with Morels and Brown Butter Sauce
Parsley and Garlic Pommes Purée, Braised Lettuce and Peas

Brown Butter
1 lb butter, unsalted

Parsley and Garlic Pommes Purée
4 cups milk
½ cup olive oil
6 cloves garlic, peeled
4 medium Yukon Gold potatoes, peeled, in 1-inch dice
3 Tbsp finely chopped Italian flat-leaf parsley

Lettuce and Peas
1 Tbsp butter
3 oz smoked bacon, in ¼-inch dice
12 pearl onions, blanched and peeled
1 yellow carrot, blanched, in ¼-inch dice
1 orange carrot, blanched, in ¼-inch dice
2 small gem lettuces, cut in half
2 sprigs thyme
½ cup chicken stock
½ cup frozen peas

Halibut
4 fillets halibut, each 6 oz, cut into 2 escalopes each
Flour for dredging
4 Tbsp olive oil
1 Tbsp butter

Halibut, with its snowy white, non-oily flesh, is a perfect foil for the morel and brown butter sauce. *Serves 4*

Brown Butter Melt butter in a small, deep, heavy-bottomed pot on low heat. Stir constantly and be careful not to let it burn; wait patiently for about 10 minutes for butter to become a deep rich hazelnut brown. Decant the clear brown butter carefully, leaving behind the dark debris at the bottom of the pot. Strain through a fine-mesh sieve into a clean container and discard solids. Cover and refrigerate. (You will not need all of the brown butter for this recipe, but it will keep refrigerated longer than unsalted butter because the milk solids have been eliminated. Brown butter is delicious on steamed vegetables.)

Parsley and Garlic Pommes Purée Place milk, oil and garlic in a large pot on medium heat and bring to a boil. Turn down the heat to low and cook for 10 to 12 minutes, or until garlic is soft. Add potatoes and cook for 15 to 20 minutes, or until soft. Drain potatoes and reserve the cooking liquid.

While potatoes are hot, mash them vigorously, then whip in a stand mixer (or with a hand-held beater), adding back enough of the reserved cooking liquid to make the potato mixture soft but not runny. Pass the potato mixture through a fine-mesh sieve for extra smoothness, if desired. Season with salt and pepper to taste. Fold in parsley just before serving.

Lettuce and Peas Preheat the oven to 425°F. Melt butter in a wide, shallow ovenproof frying pan on medium-high heat. Add bacon, onions, and yellow and orange carrots, then sauté for 1 minute. Add lettuces, thyme and stock, then bring to a boil. Cover the pan with aluminum foil and bake in the oven for 15 to 20 minutes, or until carrots are tender.

Return the frying pan to the stovetop on medium heat, add frozen peas and cook for 2 to 3 minutes, or until done. Drain and discard any excess liquid. Remove and discard thyme. Season with salt and pepper to taste.

Halibut Season fish with salt and pepper. Lightly dredge fish in flour, then shake off the excess. Heat oil and butter in a large non-stick frying pan on medium heat, just until butter begins to brown. Add fish and sauté gently for 2 to 3 minutes on each side, or until just done (the fish should be soft to the touch and still slightly opaque in the centre.)

Brown Butter Sauce Make this sauce at the last minute. Heat ¼ cup of the brown butter in a frying pan on medium-high heat. Add morels and sauté for several minutes, or until soft. Stir in lemon juice, soy sauce and veal jus. Bring to a boil, then add the remaining ⅔ cup of the brown butter, and boil again to emulsify. Season to taste with salt and pepper.

To Serve Place pommes purée in the centre of each warmed plate and top with two pieces of fish. Arrange vegetables around the edge, keeping within the rim of the plate. Garnish with a drizzle of brown butter sauce.

Wine Nk'Mip Cellars Qwam Qwmt Chardonnay

Brown Butter Sauce

¼ cup + ⅔ cup brown butter, plus extra for garnish

1 lb morel mushrooms, halved

½ cup fresh lemon juice

1 Tbsp soy sauce

½ cup brown veal jus or dark chicken stock (made with roasted bones)

Blue Heron Farm Squash Agnolotti
with Chestnuts, Brown Butter and Sage

Agnolotti are similar to ravioli, except that they are round or semicircular in shape. You can make the squash filling a day ahead. *Serves 8*

Squash Filling Preheat the oven to 325°F. Melt ½ cup of the butter in a roasting pan on the stovetop on low heat, then stir in maple syrup and combine well. Add squash, toss to coat evenly with the maple syrup mixture and roast in the oven for 30 to 40 minutes, or until squash begins to soften, sweat and give out moisture. Remove from the oven.

Melt the remaining 1½ cups of the butter in a large pot on medium-low heat. Add onions, garlic, ginger, cinnamon, cloves, nutmeg and thyme; cook for about 30 minutes, or until very soft and aromatic. Add squash and cook until soft. Remove from the heat and allow to cool a little. Purée in a high-powered blender and pass through a fine-mesh sieve, discarding solids. Allow to cool completely, then cover and set aside. Makes 4 cups of filling. Any left over can be used as a vegetable accompaniment to a meal.

Chestnut Pasta Dough Place all-purpose flour, chestnut flour and salt in the bowl of a stand mixer fitted with a dough hook and combine. In another bowl, whisk together egg yolks, eggs and oil. Add egg mixture all at once to the dry ingredients in the stand mixer. Start the mixer on low speed and add water, if needed, to achieve a dough that feels dry to the touch and forms a ball, then knead on medium-high speed for 7 minutes. Wrap the ball of dough in plastic wrap and allow to rest for at least 1 hour.

To Assemble Divide the dough in half. Rewrap one portion while you work with the other. Roll out the dough on a lightly floured surface to a thickness of ½ inch, then roll through a pasta machine until you reach the finest setting and have smooth, thin sheets.

Scoop the squash filling into a piping bag with a ½-inch hole. Cut the dough into strips 4 inches wide. Pipe a line of filling lengthwise from end to end, ¼ inch in from the edge of the dough. Brush water about ½-inch wide, down the length of the opposite edge. Fold the pasta over the filling, pressing down with your fingers to seal the edges. Use your fingers to form a line of pillow-shaped squares by pressing across the length at intervals of 2 inches. Use a fluted cutter to trim away ¼ inch from the filling along the length, then cut between each pillow to make separate agnolotti.

Continued overleaf

Squash Filling

2 cups butter

¾ cup maple syrup

2 organic squash (butternut, kurri, acorn), peeled, in 1-inch dice

2 onions, in 1-inch dice

1 head garlic, chopped

2-inch piece ginger, finely chopped

1 tsp ground cinnamon

1 tsp ground cloves

1 tsp nutmeg

1 tsp chopped thyme

Chestnut Pasta Dough

4½ cups all-purpose flour

1 cup chestnut flour (from a specialty food store)

1 tsp salt

10 large egg yolks

2 large eggs

1 Tbsp extra-virgin olive oil

Garnishes

1 cup butter

2 cups frozen peeled chestnuts, thawed in refrigerator, or fresh peeled chestnuts (also available peeled in vacuum-packed bags)

24 leaves sage

⅓ cup toasted pumpkin seeds

Garnishes Prepare these while the water is coming to a boil for the pasta (see below). Melt butter in a large frying pan on medium-high heat, stirring occasionally, for about 5 minutes, or until it turns brown. Add chestnuts and cook for 2 to 3 minutes, or until golden brown; use a slotted spoon to transfer them to a plate and reserve. Add sage leaves to the frying pan and cook for 20 to 30 seconds; use a slotted spoon to transfer them to a paper towel–lined plate and reserve. Return chestnuts to the frying pan, add enough water to half cover them and cook for about 15 minutes, or until the water is almost evaporated and the chestnuts are soft. Remove from the heat.

To Serve Place a large pot of salted water on medium-high heat and bring to a boil. Carefully drop in the agnolotti and cook at a gentle boil for about 4 minutes, or until al dente. Drain pasta, place in a bowl and toss gently with chestnuts, sage leaves and pumpkin seeds. Divide among individual heated bowls.

Wine Kettle Valley Winery Reserve Pinot Noir or Road 13 Vineyards Jackpot Chardonnay

Roasted Sunchoke Soup
with Smoked Sablefish Brandade and Meyer Lemon

Sunchokes are also known as Jerusalem artichokes. Meyer lemons were first imported into the United States from China in 1980. They taste like a cross between a lemon and a tangerine, and are prized for their low acidity and juiciness. *Serves 6 to 8*

Sunchoke Soup Melt butter in a large pot on medium-high heat, stirring occasionally, for 8 to 10 minutes, or until it reaches the foamy nut-brown stage. Add onion, garlic, ginger, curry powder and turmeric; sauté, stirring frequently, for 10 to 12 minutes, or until onion is caramelized. Add sunchokes and cook for about 5 minutes, or until they begin to take on colour. Add wine and deglaze the pan, then add vanilla bean, bay leaf and thyme. Cook for 2 to 3 minutes, or until the pan is almost dry, then add milk. Turn down the heat to medium and simmer for 15 to 20 minutes, or until sunchokes are soft enough that they can be squashed against the side of the pot with a wooden spoon. Remove from the heat. Take out and discard vanilla bean, bay leaf and thyme. Allow to cool a little, then purée in a blender. For a silky smooth consistency, pass the soup through a fine-mesh sieve and discard solids. Season to taste with salt and pepper.

Sablefish Brandade Segment and remove the membranes from two of the lemons for garnish and place in a small bowl. If the lemon segments are too acidic, stir in a pinch of sugar. Zest the remaining lemon and reserve the zest and lemon.

Preheat the oven to 375°F. Heat a heavy-bottomed ovenproof frying pan on medium-high heat. Add 3 Tbsp of the oil, sunchokes, garlic and lemon zest, then toss gently. Roast in the oven for about 30 minutes, or until sunchokes are soft. Remove from the oven.

Heat 3 Tbsp of the remaining oil in an ovenproof frying pan on high heat. Add fish and sear for about 2 minutes on each side. Place the pan in the oven and roast fish for 5 to 7 minutes, or until the flesh flakes easily. Remove from the oven and squeeze the juice from the zested lemon over the fish.

Combine the sunchoke mixture, fish (with pan juices) and parsley in a bowl. Crush with a large fork, leaving the mixture fairly chunky. Taste the brandade and season with salt and pepper.

To Serve Heat the remaining 1 tsp of the oil in a non-stick frying pan on medium heat, add the brandade and heat until warm. Heat the soup. Arrange brandade in the centre of each warmed bowl and pour the soup around. Garnish with lemon segments.

Wine Gray Monk Estate Winery Pinot Auxerrois

Sunchoke Soup
½ cup butter

1 large onion, in ¼-inch dice

5 cloves garlic, chopped

1 tsp chopped ginger

2 tsp Madras curry powder

Pinch of turmeric

26 oz sunchokes (Jerusalem artichokes), in ½-inch dice

5 Tbsp Viognier, Riesling or Pinot Gris

½-inch piece vanilla bean, split lengthwise

1 bay leaf

3 sprigs thyme

6 cups milk

Sablefish Brandade
3 Meyer lemons

6 Tbsp + 1 tsp extra-virgin olive oil

8 to 10 large sunchokes (Jerusalem artichokes), peeled

2 cloves garlic, roughly chopped

8 to 10 oz piece smoked sablefish (smoked black cod)

1 bunch Italian flat-leaf parsley, stemmed, chopped

Roasted Nicola Valley Fallow Venison
with Glazed North Arm Farm Beets and Chocolate Jus

Due to the lack of inner muscle fat on venison, it should be served rare for optimum tenderness. The chocolate adds a depth to the sauce that enhances the mild flavour of the meat. The balsamic vinegar is from Venturi-Schulze Vineyards on Vancouver Island. *Serves 6*

Venison Clean venison, removing all the sinews, and reserve the trimmings for the chocolate jus. Refrigerate venison and trimmings until needed.

Chocolate Jus This sauce can be made ahead of time and gently reheated. Melt chocolate in a heatproof bowl placed over a pot of simmering water (a bain-marie), then mix in softened butter. Remove from the bain-marie, allow to cool and refrigerate chocolate butter until needed.

Heat oil in a medium frying pan on medium-high heat. Add venison trimmings and sear for 3 to 4 minutes, or until golden. Add onion and garlic, then cook for 5 minutes. Add wine and deglaze the pan, then turn down the heat to medium-low and simmer until reduced by two-thirds. Stir in demi-glace and thyme, then simmer for 5 minutes. Skim, then strain through a fine-mesh sieve and discard solids. Return to the heat for 15 to 20 minutes, or until reduced and thick enough to coat a spoon.

Cut 3 Tbsp of the chocolate butter into small cubes (you will have some left over) and whisk into the reduced liquid in the frying pan. Season to taste with salt and pepper, then stir in vinegar. Refrigerate if not using right away. (Use the chocolate butter in any wine-based sauce for meat to vary the flavour. Will keep in the refrigerator for 2 weeks, in the freezer for 3 months.)

Glazed Beets Wash and trim beets, leaving on ½ inch of the stem. Reserve the beet greens.

Combine vinegar and water in a large pot on high heat and bring to a boil. Add beets and cook until tender (if using different coloured beets, cook them separately to preserve their individual colours). Drain and allow to cool.

Peel beets. Set aside two of the purple beets to purée. Cut the remainder of the beets into quarters.

Purée the two purple beets and 2 tsp of the butter in a blender, adding a little water, if needed, to achieve a spreadable consistency. Season to taste and reserve in a warm place.

Continued overleaf

Venison

4 lbs Nicola Valley venison loin

¼ cup sifted cocoa powder

2 tsp olive oil

1 Tbsp butter

2 sprigs thyme

1 bay leaf

Chocolate Jus

2 oz chocolate
(55% cocoa), chopped

¼ cup unsalted butter, softened

2 tsp vegetable oil

Reserved venison trim

1 Walla Walla or other
sweet onion, sliced

1 clove garlic, sliced

1 cup Shiraz or other
full-bodied spicy red wine

1¼ cups veal demi-glace

1 sprig thyme

2 Tbsp Venturi-Schulze
balsamic vinegar

Glazed Beets

18 North Arm Farm small beets
(preferably a mix of Chioggia,
golden, white, purple) with their
greens or spinach or red chard

¼ cup vinegar or fresh lemon juice

2½ cups water

1 Tbsp + 4 tsp butter

1 tsp fireweed honey

2 Tbsp Venturi-Schulze
balsamic vinegar

To Finish Venison Remove venison from the refrigerator half an hour before cooking to allow it to come to room temperature. Season with salt and pepper. Use paper towels to remove excess moisture from venison, then coat with cocoa, shaking off the excess.

Preheat the oven to 350°F. Heat a large ovenproof frying pan on medium for a few minutes before adding oil. Sear venison on all sides until evenly browned, then roast in the oven for 12 to 18 minutes, until rare (135°F on a meat thermometer). Remove from the oven and add butter, thyme and bay leaf, then spoon over venison many times. Allow to rest in a warm place for 10 minutes. Carve into thin slices.

To Finish Beets While the venison is resting, finish the beets. Melt 1 Tbsp of the butter in a frying pan on medium heat until it starts to foam. Add quartered beets and sauté for 2 minutes. Pour off excess butter, stir in honey, evenly coat beets and return the pan to the heat. Add 1 Tbsp of water and balsamic vinegar, then deglaze the pan. Season to taste and keep warm.

In another frying pan on high heat, melt the remaining 2 tsp of the butter. Add beet greens and sauté for 5 minutes, or until soft. Season to taste and keep warm.

To Serve Heat chocolate jus. Draw a pattern on each warmed plate with the warm beet purée, then arrange carved venison, quartered beets and beet greens on each plate. Finish with a drizzle of chocolate jus.

Wine Township 7 Vineyards & Winery Syrah

Dungeness Crab Spoons

with "Swift Aquaculture" Wasabi Emulsion and Vancouver Island Sea Asparagus

Dungeness crab, the pride of the West Coast, is the perfect beginning to any meal. *Serves 6*

Court Bouillon Combine all of the ingredients in a stockpot on medium-high heat, bring to a simmer and keep hot.

Crab Place crab in a bowl large enough to hold it and the court bouillon. Pour the hot court bouillon over crab, then cover the bowl with plastic wrap. Allow to stand for 10 minutes, then remove crab and allow to cool slightly.

Cut off crab legs and the top, then clean the rest of the body. Use a pair of kitchen scissors to cut off one end of each section of leg and remove the meat. Remove meat from the claws. Refrigerate crabmeat until needed. Discard court bouillon.

Wasabi Emulsion Fill a bowl with ice water. Bring a pot of water to the boil on high heat. Add wasabi leaves, blanch for 30 seconds, drain and plunge into the bowl of ice water. Drain wasabi leaves and reserve.

Combine egg yolks, mustard and vinegar in a blender. With the motor running, add oil in a thin steady stream to form an emulsion. Add wasabi leaves and blend for 30 seconds, then strain through a fine-mesh sieve and discard the solids. Refrigerate until needed.

Sea Asparagus Place sea asparagus in a bowl of water to cover and soak for 10 minutes to remove excess salt. In the meantime, heat oil in a frying pan on medium heat. Add shallot and sauté for 2 to 3 minutes, or until softened slightly. Drain sea asparagus, add to the pan and sauté for 2 minutes. Season with freshly ground black pepper and vinegar to taste; do not add salt.

To Serve Season crabmeat with chives, salt and a small amount of the wasabi emulsion. Check for and remove any bits of shell in the mixture as you do so.

Draw a line of wasabi emulsion on each chilled Chinese ceramic soup spoon. Top with crabmeat and garnish with sea asparagus.

Wine Lake Breeze Vineyards Pinot Blanc or Little Straw Sauvignon Blanc

Court Bouillon

16 cups water

2 Tbsp white wine vinegar

4 black peppercorns

10 coriander seeds

1 bay leaf

3 sprigs thyme

1/3 cup salt

Crab

1 Dungeness crab, about 3 lbs

1/4 cup chopped chives

Wasabi Emulsion

8 oz wasabi leaves
(Japanese food store)

3 egg yolks

1 tsp smooth Dijon mustard

1 Tbsp white wine vinegar

1 cup canola oil

Sea Asparagus

8 oz sea asparagus

2 tsp olive or vegetable oil

1 shallot, in 1/8-inch dice

1/2 tsp or to taste
white wine vinegar

Risotto Bullets

3 cups assorted mushrooms
(morel, chanterelle,
shiitake, portobello),
sliced or in ¼-inch dice

½ cup olive oil

6 to 8 cups vegetable stock

½ cup minced leeks

2 Tbsp minced shallots

2 Tbsp minced garlic

3 cups arborio rice

½ cup dry white wine

2 tsp salt

1 Tbsp ground black pepper

1½ cups finely grated Asiago
cheese, plus extra for garnish

2 Tbsp butter

8 oz fontina cheese

7 to 10 egg whites

5 to 7 cups panko
(Japanese bread crumbs)

Snipped chives for garnish

These little bullets are a cross between a jalapeño popper and a risotto cake. If the process of rolling out the risotto is too daunting, you can form it into balls, sink a cube of cheese in the centre of each, and call them risotto balls. They make a satisfying appetizer or a lovely side dish. *Makes 30 pieces*

Preheat the oven to 400°F. Toss mushrooms with 2 Tbsp of the oil, lay them on a rimmed baking sheet and roast in the oven for 20 minutes. Remove from the oven.

Heat stock and keep warm. Heat 1 Tbsp of the oil in a heavy medium-sized pot on medium-high heat. Add leeks, shallots and garlic, then sauté, mixing with a wooden spoon, for about 5 minutes. Add rice and toast it lightly, stirring constantly, for 3 to 5 minutes. Add wine and stir until it is absorbed by the rice. Add one-third of the hot stock and stir gently until most of it has been absorbed by the rice. Continue to slowly add stock, stirring constantly, until most of it has been absorbed. (This process should take between 25 and 30 minutes. When complete, the rice should be al dente and the texture should be slightly creamy.) Season with salt and pepper to taste. Add mushrooms, Asiago cheese and butter. Carefully fold the mixture together.

Line a rimmed baking sheet with a piece of parchment paper 15 × 17½ inches, then spread the risotto mixture on it in an even layer. Place the baking sheet on a rack and allow risotto to cool to room temperature, then refrigerate for 1 hour.

Cut risotto lengthwise into five strips, each 3 inches wide. Cut fontina cheese into strips 3½ × ¼ × ¼ inch. Take one strip of risotto and place it on a sheet of parchment paper 6 × 17½ inches. Lay one-fifth of the fontina pieces lengthwise down the centre of the risotto strip. Lift the two lengthwise edges of the parchment paper and bring them together at the top. Gently lift the whole thing and mould the risotto around the cheese. Once the risotto has been moulded into a long, rounded shape, roll it up in the parchment paper. Repeat for each strip of risotto. When complete, place the risotto rolls in the freezer for about 45 minutes, or until frozen.

Cut risotto rolls into pieces 2 to 3 inches long. Remove the parchment paper. Place egg whites and panko crumbs in separate shallow dishes. Take one risotto bullet, coat it in egg white, then lightly and evenly coat it in panko. Repeat until each piece has been coated.

Heat the remaining 5 Tbsp of the oil in a frying pan on medium heat. Add risotto bullets and cook for 5 to 6 minutes, or until heated through and a light golden brown. Be careful not to over-cook them, or the cheese will begin to ooze out.

To Serve Arrange the risotto bullets on a warmed serving platter. Garnish with chives and grated Asiago.

Wine Blue Mountain Vineyard & Cellars Pinot Noir

SoBo's Fresh Blackberry Pie

Wild blackberries abound in August and make for a fun day of picking. It makes sense to freeze some for winter treats. Fresh is best, but frozen berries will work. *Serves 8 (one 9-inch pie)*

Pastry Combine flour and sugar together in a large bowl. Add butter, and with clean hands, rub it into the dry mixture until pea-size bits form, with some larger pieces. Add ice water all at once, tossing the mixture with your hands until a loose dough forms.

With dry, floured hands, divide dough and form two discs, one just a little bit larger than the other. Wrap each disc in plastic wrap and refrigerate for 1 hour, or until well chilled.

Roll out the larger disc of pastry on a lightly floured surface to form a 13-inch diameter circle about ⅛-inch thick. Fit the dough into a 9-inch pie plate, then trim even with the rim of the plate.

Blackberry Filling Gently toss together blackberries, sugar, cornstarch, salt and cinnamon (optional) in a large bowl.

To Assemble Preheat the oven to 425°F and set the rack in the bottom third of the oven. Pour blackberry filling into the pastry shell.

Roll out the remaining disc of pastry on a lightly floured surface to form an 11-inch circle about ⅛-inch thick, then drape it over the filled pie. Trim the pastry, leaving a ¾-inch overhang. Fold the overhang under the bottom pastry rim. Seal and flute the edge, then cut steam vents in the centre of the top.

Whisk together egg yolk and water in a cup, then brush this glaze over the top of the pastry. Bake the pie in the oven for 15 minutes, then turn down the heat to 350°F and bake for another 35 to 45 minutes, or until the fruit is tender, the filling has thickened and the pastry is golden. (If you use frozen berries, you will need to bake for a further 10 to 15 minutess.) Remove from the oven and allow to cool on a rack.

To Serve Cut the pie into eight slices. It is delicious served warm with vanilla bean ice cream.

Wine Fort Wine Company Wild West Blackberry Port or Cherry Point Vineyards Cowichan Blackberry Port

Pastry

2½ cups all-purpose flour

1 Tbsp sugar

1 cup unsalted butter, cold, in ½-inch cubes

¾ cup ice water

Blackberry Filling

7 cups local blackberries

1 cup sugar

¼ cup cornstarch

¼ tsp salt

½ tsp cinnamon (optional)

1 egg yolk for glaze

1 Tbsp water for glaze

Sablefish Marinated in Venturi-Schulze Balsamic Vinegar

with Venturi-Schulze Brut Sabayon, Organic
Pear and Carrot Salad with Toasted Walnuts

Sablefish
½ cup Venturi-Schulze
balsamic vinegar
½ cup water
4 pieces sablefish, each 5 to 6 oz
2 Tbsp sunflower seed
or grapeseed oil

Pear and Carrot Salad
8 walnut halves
1 pear, Anjou, Bosc or Bartlett
1 medium carrot

Sabayon
3 egg yolks
¼ cup non-alcoholic pear cider
3 Tbsp Venturi-Schulze
Brut Naturel or other
dry sparkling white wine

Marinating the sablefish in the Venturi-Schulze balsamic vinegar (locally produced on Vancouver Island), will maximize the flavour of the finished dish. *Serves 4*

Sablefish Start this dish the day before serving. Combine vinegar and water in a non-reactive rectangular dish that will hold the fish in one layer. Add fish, cover and marinate for 12 hours in the refrigerator, turning over fish after 6 hours.

Remove fish from the marinade and drain on a plate lined with paper towels. Transfer fish, flesh-side down, to a clean plate, then cover and refrigerate until needed.

Pear and Carrot Salad Preheat the oven to 325°F. Place walnuts on a small baking sheet and toast for 6 to 7 minutes, or until golden and fragrant. Crush lightly and reserve.

Core and julienne pear. Peel and julienne carrot the same size as pear. Place pear and carrot in a small bowl, toss together gently, and reserve.

To Finish Sablefish Preheat the oven to 400°F. Heat oil in a large ovenproof frying pan on medium-high heat for 3 to 4 minutes. Arrange fish, flesh-side down, in the frying pan, and roast in the oven for 7 to 9 minutes, or until the flesh starts to flake. Remove from the oven.

Sabayon Bring a pot of water to a boil on high heat, then turn down the heat to medium or low to keep the water at a simmer. In a stainless steel bowl that fits over the pot, combine egg yolks, pear cider and wine, whisking vigorously over the simmering water for 3 to 4 minutes, or until soft peaks form. Remove from the heat.

To Serve Place a piece of sablefish in each warmed bowl and pour 2 Tbsp of the sabayon over it. Place a small amount of pear and carrot salad on top of the sabayon. Sprinkle with toasted walnuts.

Wine Venturi-Schulze Vineyards Siegerrebe blends of Estremi or Millefiori

French Sorrel Apple Sorbet

2 cups peeled, cored, chopped, organic apples (Braeburn, Granny Smith or Fuji)

2 cups organic apple juice

2 cups firmly packed organic French sorrel leaves

French sorrel leaves are available where fresh herbs are sold and lend an appealing tang to the sweetness of the apple in this sorbet. *Serves 4 to 6*

Place apples and apple juice in a stainless steel pot on high heat and bring to a boil. Turn down the heat to medium and simmer for 25 to 35 minutes. Pour the apple mixture into a bowl and refrigerate for about an hour, or until cold.

Place the cold apple mixture and sorrel leaves in a blender on high speed and process until smooth. Refrigerate for 3 hours, or until well chilled.

If you have an ice-cream machine, process the apple mixture according to the manufacturer's directions, then place in the freezer. Otherwise, place the mixture in a non-reactive casserole dish, 9 × 11 inches, and freeze for 2 to 3 hours, stirring occasionally as it freezes. Will keep frozen for 2 to 3 days, though it tastes best served the day it is made.

To Serve Scoop into balls and serve in small fruit cups or glasses.

Wine Elephant Island Orchard Wines Crab Apple or Gehringer Brothers Estate Winery Late Harvest Riesling

Fresh Herb Salad
with Cucumber, Radish and Feta

We love this summer salad paired with grilled whole wheat flatbread (page 50). *Serves 6 to 8*

To make the salad, slice cucumber into quarters lengthwise, then cut into ½-inch pieces and place in a large serving bowl. Add radishes, basil, parsley, cilantro, chives and mint.

To make the dressing, whisk together honey, salt and lemon juice in a small bowl. Gradually whisk in oil.

To Serve Pour the dressing over the salad and toss lightly. Add feta and toss lightly. Season to taste with freshly ground black pepper. Serve with grilled whole wheat flatbread on the side.

Wine Pinot Gris from Saturna Island Family Estate Winery or Lang Vineyards

1 English cucumber, ends removed

12 radishes, thinly sliced

1 cup loosely packed basil leaves

1 cup Italian flat-leaf parsley, coarse stems removed

1 cup cilantro, coarse stems removed

1 cup 1-inch pieces chives

½ cup mint, coarse stems removed

1 tsp liquid honey

¼ tsp sea salt

1 Tbsp lemon juice

3 Tbsp extra-virgin olive oil

1 cup crumbled goat's milk feta cheese

Freshly ground black pepper to taste

Grilled Whole Wheat Flatbread

¼ cup water at room
temperature (68°F)

2 tsp olive oil

¼ cup yogurt

½ tsp dry instant yeast

1¼ cups stone-ground
whole wheat flour

½ tsp sea salt

Flour for dusting

Olive oil to grease the bowl

1 tsp salted butter, softened

Use a local stone-ground whole wheat flour such as Anita's Organic Grain & Flour Mill's fine grind whole wheat flour or look for stone-ground Red Fife wheat at a farmers' market. *Makes 8 flatbreads*

Whisk together water, oil and yogurt in a large bowl. Mix in yeast, flour and salt by hand, until the dough comes together. Turn out the dough onto a lightly floured surface and knead for 5 to 6 minutes, until a smooth ball forms. Grease the bowl with oil, then return the dough to the bowl and cover with plastic wrap. Leave the dough to rise in a warm, draft-free place for 2 hours.

After the dough has risen, it can be rolled out and grilled immediately or refrigerated for up to 24 hours before rolling out. (If you refrigerate the dough, remove from the refrigerator 30 minutes before rolling out so it can warm up.)

Preheat the barbecue to medium-high. Turn out the dough onto a lightly floured surface, divide it into 8 equal portions and hand roll into balls. Use a small rolling pin to roll each ball of dough into a thin oval about 4 inches by 6 inches. Place the rolled-out dough on a lightly oiled baking sheet.

Turn down the barbecue to medium heat and place the flatbreads on the surface of the grill. Grill with the lid up for about 1 minute, until the dough starts to bubble and puff up. Use tongs to turn the flatbreads over, close the lid of the barbecue and bake for 45 seconds. Use tongs to transfer the flatbreads to a cloth-lined serving tray. Brush each flatbread with ⅛ tsp butter and stack one on top of another. Wrap the cloth around the stack of flatbreads to keep them warm and soft until ready to serve.

Wine Syrah from either Nichol Vineyards and Estate Winery or Sandhill Small Lots

Jack's Sooke Ruby Trout

Garden Herb Purée, Walla Walla Onion and Chorizo Tart

We have been using rainbow trout from Sooke on Vancouver Island for many years. Trout cooks very quickly and is best cooked in a hot pan. The herbs for the sauce come from our own organic kitchen garden, and we encourage you to have your own herb garden to enhance your food. *Serves 6*

Pastry Place flour on a clean work surface or in a mixing bowl, then make a well in the centre. Place butter, beaten egg, salt and sugar in the centre of the well. Slowly draw the flour into the centre of the well, until all of the ingredients are almost mixed together. Add milk and gather the mixture into a ball. Knead twice to form a smooth dough. Flatten into a disk and wrap with plastic wrap. Refrigerate for 1 hour before using.

Preheat the oven to 400°F. Roll out the dough on a lightly floured surface into an 11-inch circle, 1/8-inch thick. Use the pastry circle to line a 9-inch flan ring with a removable bottom. Refrigerate while you make the filling.

Onion and Chorizo Filling Heat oil in a large frying pan on medium-high heat. Add chorizo and cook, stirring all the while, for 5 to 6 minutes, or until crispy. Use a slotted spoon to remove chorizo from the pan and reserve. Turn down the heat to medium, add onion and fennel to the frying pan, and sauté for 12 to 15 minutes, or until tender and golden. Stir in brown sugar and the reserved chorizo. Season to taste with salt and pepper.

To Assemble Preheat the oven to 400°F. Spoon the onion and chorizo filling into the pastry-lined flan ring. Mix together egg and cream in a small bowl, then pour over the filling. Bake the tart in the oven for 35 to 40 minutes, or until golden brown (to check for doneness, shake the tart very gently—if the centre moves slightly, the tart is ready, as it will continue to cook in its own heat). Remove from the oven and allow to cool. Carefully remove the tart from the flan ring. Cut into six portions and leave at room temperature.

Continued overleaf

Pastry

1¾ cups flour

½ cup + 3 Tbsp butter, slightly softened, in ½-inch cubes

1 egg, beaten

1 tsp salt

1 tsp sugar

1 Tbsp milk, cold

Onion and Chorizo Filling

1 Tbsp olive oil

3½ oz chorizo sausage, in ¼-inch dice

1 large white onion, thinly sliced, Walla Walla or other sweet variety

1 bulb fennel, peeled and thinly sliced

2 Tbsp brown sugar

1 egg

¼ cup whipping cream

Herb Purée

1 cup spinach leaves

¼ cup basil leaves

3 Tbsp mint leaves

1 Tbsp + 2 tsp thyme leaves

1 Tbsp + 2 tsp oregano leaves

½ cup whipping cream

½ cup + 2 Tbsp cold butter, in ½-inch cubes

Trout

¼ cup butter

3 shallots, thinly sliced

2 cups very thinly sliced green cabbage

½ cup Riesling

2 cups spinach leaves

¼ cup crème fraîche or sour cream

½ cup canola oil

6 fillets rainbow trout, each 4 to 5 oz, pin bones removed

1 lemon, juice of

Sea salt

Herb Purée Fill a bowl with ice water. Bring a pot of water to a boil on high heat. Add spinach, basil, mint, thyme and oregano, then blanch for 30 seconds. Drain and plunge into the ice water. Drain, gently squeeze dry and place in a blender.

Heat cream in a small pot on medium heat, then pour into the blender over the blanched herbs and purée well. Season to taste with salt. Transfer to a small pot on low heat. Whisk in butter, piece by piece, until all of it is emulsified into the sauce. Keep warm until needed.

Trout Melt 2 Tbsp of the butter in a large frying pan on medium heat. Add shallots and sauté for 3 to 4 minutes, or until tender. Add cabbage and Riesling, then cook for 4 to 5 minutes, or until cabbage is tender. Add spinach and toss gently. Stir in crème fraîche and cook for 3 to 5 minutes, or until spinach wilts and the mixture is hot. Season to taste with salt and pepper.

Preheat the oven to 350°F. Heat the portioned onion and chorizo tart in the oven for 5 minutes.

While the tart is being warmed up, heat oil in a large frying pan on high heat until it starts to smoke. Turn down the heat to medium, add trout, skin-side down, and cook for 2 minutes. Flip over fish carefully, then add lemon juice and the remaining butter. Baste trout with the pan juices as it cooks for another 2 minutes. Just before serving, season fish with sea salt.

To Serve Spread herb purée on one half of each warmed plate and top with a portion of the cabbage mixture. Arrange trout on top of the cabbage and place a slice of the onion and chorizo tart on the side.

Wine Mission Hill Family Estate Winery Reserve Riesling

Cool Heirloom Tomato Gazpacho
with Olive Oil and Carmelis Chevry Sorbet

This is one of our most popular starters in August, when the Okanagan is experiencing its hottest temperatures. As it happens, all the vegetables are at their best then as well. The savoury sorbet is a nice contrast to the Chevry fresh goat cheese from Carmelis, a local dairy. *Serves 6*

Gazpacho Begin this recipe the day before serving. Place all of the ingredients in a non-reactive container and mix well. Cover and refrigerate overnight for the flavours to blend.

Place in a blender and purée on high speed until smooth. Adjust the seasoning, if necessary (cold food usually requires more). Pass through a fine-mesh sieve, using a rubber spatula to push the mixture through, and discard the solids. Refrigerate until needed.

Sorbet Mix together water and sugar in a small pot on medium-high heat, bring to a simmer, then remove from the heat at once. Quickly transfer this hot syrup to a blender, add egg whites and purée well. With the blender running on low speed, slowly add olive oil and lemon juice in a thin stream. Slowly add goat cheese and blend until smooth. Refrigerate for 30 minutes, or until chilled.

Place sorbet in an ice-cream machine and follow the manufacturer's directions. Store in the freezer. Will keep frozen for 1 or 2 days.

To Serve Ladle gazpacho into chilled bowls and place a scoop of sorbet in the centre. Drizzle extra-virgin olive oil around the sorbet.

Wine Mission Hill Family Estate Winery Reserve Sauvignon Blanc or Ganton & Larsen Prospect Winery Council's Punch Bowl Sauvignon Blanc

Gazpacho

6 very ripe Cascade or Roma tomatoes, in ½-inch dice

1 red bell pepper, in ½-inch dice

1 medium cucumber, in ½-inch dice

1 small fennel bulb, in ½-inch dice

4 shallots, sliced

2 cloves garlic, minced

1 tsp chopped thyme

1 slice white bread, ¾-inch thick, no crust, in crouton-size pieces

¼ cup + 2 tsp aged sherry vinegar

½ cup sparkling water

½ cup extra-virgin olive oil

1 Tbsp honey

1 tsp fine sea salt

Sorbet

1¼ cups water

½ cup sugar

3 egg whites

1½ cups olive oil

½ cup + 2 Tbsp fresh lemon juice

8 oz Carmelis Chevry or other fresh young goat cheese

Extra-virgin olive oil for garnish

Poached Pear and Pecan Spinach Salad
with Warm Goat Cheese

We created this salad to showcase the baby spinach from Susan Davidson's organic farm, and we serve it from May to the end of October, when the spinach is at its best. *Serves 4*

Maple Syrup–candied Pecans Preheat the oven to 300°F. Place sugar and water in a pot on medium-low heat, then bring to a boil. Do not stir. Cook until it turns a nice caramel colour. As the sugar begins to caramelize, shake and swirl the pan gently to prevent the sugar from burning in any one spot. Remove from the heat, then add pecans and maple syrup, mixing together well. Pour onto a baking sheet and bake in the oven for 20 minutes (the sugar will candy-coat the pecans). Remove from the oven and allow to cool before using. Will keep for several weeks in an airtight container.

Port Dressing Place port in a small pot on medium heat and simmer for about 10 minutes, or until reduced by half. Place reduced port, honey, vinegar and oil in a blender (or whisk by hand), then combine until emulsified. Refrigerate in a covered container. Will keep in the refrigerator for up to 2 weeks.

Poached Pears Cut a circle of parchment paper to fit inside a medium pot. Place wine, water, lemon juice and cinnamon in the pot on high heat and bring to a boil. Turn down the heat to medium-low, add pears and cover them with the parchment paper circle. Simmer gently for 25 minutes, or until pears are tender but still hold their shape. Remove from the heat and allow pears to cool in the cooking liquid.

Pear and Spinach Salad Place spinach, pears and port dressing in a bowl and toss to lightly coat.

Goat Cheese Rounds Divide goat cheese into four portions and shape into flat round disks about ¹/₂-inch thick. Set up three separate shallow bowls for flour, beaten eggs and panko. Dredge cheese rounds in flour, then beaten eggs and then panko.

Heat oil in a frying pan on medium-high heat. Add cheese rounds and brown for 2 minutes on each side. Remove from the pan.

To Serve Divide salad among plates and arrange four pear pieces on each serving. Scatter candied pecans around the salad and top with a warm round of goat cheese.

Wine Rigamarole Winery Sauvignon Blanc

Maple Syrup–candied Pecans
½ cup sugar
¼ cup water
1½ cups pecan halves
¼ cup maple syrup

Port Dressing
¾ cup ruby port
2 Tbsp honey
2 Tbsp raspberry vinegar
½ cup olive or canola oil

Poached Pears
2 cups dry white wine
2 cups water
1 lemon, juice of
1 cinnamon stick
4 Bosc pears, cored, peeled and quartered

Pear and Spinach Salad
4 cups fresh baby spinach
1 recipe poached pears
½ cup port dressing

Goat Cheese Rounds
8 oz goat cheese or chèvre in a log shape
½ cup flour
2 eggs, beaten
½ cup panko (Japanese bread crumbs) or other dried bread crumbs
2 tsp olive oil

Bouillabaisse du Pacifique

Fish Broth

¼ cup olive oil

½ tsp fennel seeds, crushed

2 cups sliced leeks,
white part only

2 cups sliced onions

3 cloves garlic, crushed

¼ cup tomato paste

2½ lbs halibut bones,
coarsely chopped and rinsed

1 lb salmon bones
(excluding head), coarsely
chopped and rinsed

1 cup dry white wine

6 fresh Roma tomatoes
or a 14-oz can of whole plum
tomatoes including liquid

2 Tbsp roughly chopped thyme

2 Tbsp roughly chopped parsley

2 Tbsp roughly chopped basil

½ tsp saffron

12 cups water

½ tsp salt

½ tsp freshly ground pepper

Bouillabaisse

1 recipe fish broth

6 small new potatoes, skins on,
cooked to fork-tender and halved

1 medium fennel bulb, julienned

6 large scallops

8 spot prawns

12 clams, scrubbed

12 mussels, scrubbed
and beards removed

1 lb mixed halibut and
salmon, in 2-inch cubes

Bouillabaisse looks hard to make, but it is easy. Go to your local fish market and select whatever is fresh in your area. We use seasonal local seafood: Salt Spring Island mussels, Savary Island clams, B.C. spot prawns, wild Pacific salmon and Pacific halibut. Rouille is a sauce traditionally served on toasted baguette slices to accompany fish soups; this one is made with saffron. Instead of making the rouille, you can mix 1 cup of store-bought mayonnaise with reduced stock, garlic and saffron. *Serves 4 to 6*

Fish Broth Heat oil in a stockpot on medium heat. Add fennel seeds and sauté, stirring, for about 30 seconds, or until fragrant. Add leeks, onions and garlic, then sauté for about 5 minutes, or until onions are soft. Stir in tomato paste, coating the leek and onion mixture well, and cook for 2 minutes. Add halibut bones and salmon bones, then cook for 5 minutes. Add wine and bring to a boil, then turn down the heat to medium-low and simmer for 5 minutes. Stir in tomatoes, thyme, parsley, basil, saffron and water. Turn up the heat to high and bring to a full boil, then turn down the heat to low and simmer for 25 minutes.

Strain the broth through a fine-mesh sieve, pushing with the back of a ladle to extract all the juices. Discard the solids. Skim off and discard excess oil from the top of the broth. Add salt and pepper.

Bouillabaisse Discard any mussels or clams with open shells that won't close tightly when tapped.

Set aside ½ cup of the broth for the saffron rouille. Place the remaining broth in a stockpot on high heat and bring to a boil. Turn down the heat to medium-low, then add potatoes, fennel, scallops, prawns, clams, mussels, halibut and salmon. Cover and simmer for 6 to 8 minutes. If any clams or mussels fail to open while cooking, discard them.

Saffron Rouille Place broth in a pot on medium-high heat and simmer until reduced by half. Place reduced broth, garlic, egg and egg yolk in a blender or food processor, then mix together. With the motor running, slowly pour in oil in a thin steady stream and blend until emulsified into a thick mayonnaise. Stir in salt and saffron. Makes 1 cup.

To Serve Place 2 Tbsp of saffron rouille on each slice of toasted baguette. Ladle the bouillabaisse into individual heated bowls and float a saffron rouille toast on each serving.

Wine Therapy Vineyards Pink Freud

Saffron Rouille

½ cup fish broth

2 cloves garlic, peeled and crushed

1 large egg

1 egg yolk

1 cup olive oil

Pinch of coarse salt

Pinch of saffron

4 to 6 thin slices baguette, toasted

Thiessen Farm Squab Breast
with Bulgur Wheat, Apple and Fireweed Honey Salad, Sautéed Fiddleheads and Feta

Fireweed Honey Dressing
2 tsp olive oil
1 tsp canola oil
½ tsp toasted pine nut oil
1½ tsp lemon vinegar
1 tsp fireweed honey

Bulgur and Apple Salad
1 cup bulgur wheat
2 Granny Smith apples, peeled, cored, in ¼-inch dice
2 Tbsp toasted pine nuts
6 mint leaves, julienned

Mint Leaf Garnish (optional)
Oil for frying
8 mint leaves

Fiddleheads and Feta
¾ cup fiddlehead ferns, well washed
1 tsp olive oil
4 oz feta cheese

Squabs
4 squabs, each 1 lb, cleaned and tied
1 Tbsp olive oil
1 Tbsp butter

Squab is a delicious, rich bird that is at its tenderest when cooked to the medium-rare stage. *Serves 8*

Fireweed Honey Dressing Make the dressing first. Combine olive oil, canola oil and toasted pine nut oil in a bowl. Whisk in vinegar and honey, then season with salt and pepper.

Bulgur and Apple Salad Place bulgur in a sieve and rinse under cold running water until the water runs clear. Bring 2 cups of salted water to a boil in a large pot on high heat, then stir in bulgur. Turn down the heat to low and simmer gently for about 15 minutes, or until bulgur is tender. Strain and refrigerate for about 2 hours, or until cold.

Combine bulgur, apples, pine nuts and mint in a bowl. Add some dressing, a little at a time, tossing to lightly coat the salad. Reserve the remaining dressing.

Mint Leaf Garnish Pour in enough oil to half-fill a small, tall-sided heavy pot on the stovetop and heat to 375°F. Add mint leaves, being careful not to let them split. Fry for 3 to 4 seconds, then use a slotted spoon to remove them and drain on paper towels.

Fiddleheads and Feta Fill a large bowl with ice water. Bring a pot of salted water to a boil on high heat. Add fiddleheads and blanch for 3 to 4 minutes, then drain and plunge into the ice water. Drain, then dry on paper towels.

Heat oil in a frying pan on medium heat. Add fiddleheads and sauté for 2 to 3 minutes, then transfer to a bowl. Crumble in feta and toss gently. Season to taste with salt and pepper.

Squabs Preheat the oven to 425°F. Season squabs all over with salt and pepper. Heat oil and butter in a heavy-bottomed, ovenproof frying pan on medium heat until nut brown. Add squabs and caramelize them all over. Place breast up in the pan and roast in the oven for 6 to 7 minutes.

Remove squabs from the oven and cut off the legs. Place legs back in the pan and roast with squabs in the oven for 5 to 6 minutes, or until cooked through. (Once cooked, the thigh bone can be removed fairly easily, making the leg easier to eat.) Remove from the oven and allow squabs to rest for at least 7 to 8 minutes before carving.

To Serve Place a 2-inch diameter ring mould in the centre of each
warmed plate. Place an eighth of the bulgur salad in each ring, using
a spoon to gently press into the ring. Remove the ring moulds, then
arrange the fiddlehead mixture around the outside.

Carve the breasts from squabs and place half a breast on top of
each portion of bulgur salad. Gently lean a leg against the bulgur,
then drizzle a little of the remaining dressing around each plate.
Garnish with fried mint leaves (optional).

Wine Quails' Gate Estate Winery Stewart Family Reserve Pinot Noir

Frozen Crème Brûlée

with Honey Sponge Cake and Port-roasted Grapefruit

**Port-roasted
Grapefruit**

1 cup ruby port

3 grapefruits, segmented,
membranes removed, with juice

Frozen Crème Brûlée

1 cup whipping cream

¼ vanilla bean

4 egg yolks

¼ cup sugar

1 tsp Cointreau or other
orange-flavoured liqueur

Serving this dessert in a bowl allows the cake to soak up the sweet juices from the port-roasted grapefruit. *Serves 6 to 8*

Port-roasted Grapefruit Start making this dessert the day before or the morning of serving. Preheat the oven to 350°F. Place port with grapefruit segments and juice in an ovenproof pan and roast in the oven for 10 minutes, or until hot. Remove from the oven and allow to cool. Refrigerate until needed.

Frozen Crème Brûlée Place cream and vanilla bean in a small pot on medium heat and bring to a boil, then strain through a fine-mesh sieve and discard solids.

Place egg yolks and sugar in a bowl and whisk together.

Fill a bowl with ice water. Place water in the bottom pot of a double-boiler, but leave room so that the water does not touch the bottom of the top pot. Bring the water to a boil on high heat, then turn down the heat to keep the water at a simmer, adjusting the heat as necessary to keep the water at a simmer; do not let it boil. Place the cream mixture and the egg yolk mixture in the top of the double-boiler, then whisk for about 15 minutes, or until very thick. Stir in Cointreau, then transfer the mixture to a bowl placed on the ice water to cool.

Wrap the bottom of a 6-inch metal ring with heavy foil (or use a 6-inch springform pan) and pour in the cooled mixture. Place in the freezer for about 6 hours or overnight, until frozen. Will keep frozen for two weeks in a covered container.

Honey Sponge Cake Preheat the oven to 350°F. Place a greased 6-inch metal ring (or a greased 6-inch springform pan) on a rimmed baking sheet.

Place water in the bottom pot of the double-boiler, but leave room so that the water does not touch the bottom of the top pot. Bring the water to a boil on high heat, then turn down the heat to keep the water at a simmer, adjusting the heat as necessary to keep the water at a simmer; do not let it boil. Place egg yolk, eggs, sugar and honey in the top of the double-boiler, whisking continuously, for 10 to 12 minutes, or until quite warm. Remove from the heat, then, using a stand mixer (or a hand-held beater), whisk until the mixture is cool, triple in volume, light and fluffy. When this consistency is achieved, add oil and whisk for 10 seconds. Remove from the mixer (or remove the beater), add flour and salt, then whisk by hand, using a folding motion. Make sure all of the flour is incorporated into the mixture.

Pour the batter into the prepared metal ring and bake in the oven for about 20 minutes, or until golden brown and spongy to the touch. Remove from the oven and allow to cool. Run a thin straight knife along the inside edge of the ring, then lift off the ring (or release the spring and remove the outer ring of the springform pan).

To Serve Unmould the frozen crème brûlée by running a straight knife along the inside edge of the ring. Place it on top of the sponge cake and cut into six to eight wedges. Return to the freezer for 30 minutes to harden.

Sprinkle the top of each wedge with sugar and caramelize using a domestic blowtorch. The frozen crème brûlée will start to melt at the edges, so work quickly.

Pour port-roasted grapefruit juice into each shallow serving bowl and place a wedge of the cake/frozen crème brûlée on top. The cake on the bottom will soak up some of the juice. Garnish with grapefruit segments.

Wine Sumac Ridge Estate Winery Vintage Pipe

Honey Sponge Cake
1 egg yolk
2 eggs
⅓ cup sugar
1 tsp honey
1 Tbsp vegetable oil
⅓ cup flour
⅛ tsp salt
2 Tbsp sugar for caramelizing

Innovative & International

FLAVOURS AND TALENTS from around the globe have done much to enrich Vancouver's restaurants. Whether they come from the late-night izakayas of Tokyo or were trained in strict European kitchens illuminated by Michelin stars, chefs from afar have long offered Vancouverites the opportunity to widen our culinary horizons.

In this section, we share those foreign accents through signature recipes fine-tuned to local ingredients. We also meet local chefs who have taken their knives travelling offshore to capture both inspiration and knowledge to create their own dishes. While these recipes have time-honoured roots, they are decidedly modern, and we home cooks are the beneficiaries.

Warm Caramelized Onion and Gruyère Tart

For a perfect light luncheon dish, serve these tarts with a tossed green salad. Be sure to use Swiss Gruyère cheese, as no other cheese will melt and provide the same flavour. *Makes six 3½-inch tarts*

Pâte Brisée Combine flour, salt and sugar in a food processor. Add butter and pulse for about 15 seconds, or until the mixture is coarse. With the motor running, pour in ¼ cup of the ice water in a slow, steady stream through the feed tube, until the dough just holds together when pinched between your fingers. Add some of the remaining ice water, if necessary. Do not process for more than 30 seconds.

Turn out dough onto a lightly floured work surface and gather into a ball. Divide dough into two equal pieces, flatten into disks and wrap with plastic wrap. Refrigerate for 30 to 60 minutes before using. (You can also freeze the dough for later use. Will keep in the freezer for up to 2 months; defrost in the refrigerator the day before using.)

Roll out dough on a lightly floured surface, one disk at a time, to a thickness of ⅛ inch. To prevent the dough from sticking to the work surface and to ensure uniform thickness, keep lifting it up and moving it a quarter turn as you roll (always roll from the centre outward to get uniform thickness). Cut into six rounds about 4½ inches in diameter. Press the pastry rounds gently to fill each 3½-inch diameter tart pan. Refrigerate until needed.

Onion Filling Preheat the oven to 400°F. Place onions on a rimmed baking sheet, add oil and toss to coat. Bake in the oven for up to 2 hours, stirring every 15 minutes, or until onions are very tender and a rich golden brown. (You can also caramelize onions in a heavy frying pan on the stovetop on low to medium-low heat, stirring frequently to prevent burning, for up to 2 hours, or until done.) Stir thyme leaves into onions, then remove from the oven.

Continued overleaf

Pâte Brisée

2½ cups all-purpose flour

1 tsp salt

Pinch of sugar

1 cup unsalted butter, chilled, in 1-inch cubes

½ cup ice water

Onion Filling

2 lbs onions, sliced

1 Tbsp olive oil

1 tsp thyme leaves

3 slices bacon, crisply cooked and crumbled (optional)

Béchamel Sauce

1 cup milk

2 Tbsp butter

2 Tbsp flour

½ tsp salt

4 oz Swiss Gruyère cheese, grated

3 eggs, beaten

Dash of freshly ground black pepper

Béchamel Sauce Heat milk in a pot on medium heat until hot and set aside.

Melt butter in a heavy-bottomed pot on low heat. Remove the pot from the heat and whisk in flour, mixing well. Place back on low heat and cook for 2 to 3 minutes. Add hot milk all at once, whisking constantly, and cook for about 2 minutes, or until the mixture is smooth and thick. Add salt to taste. Remove from the heat and place plastic wrap directly on the surface of the sauce to prevent a skin from forming. Allow to cool for about 10 minutes, then stir in cheese, beaten eggs and black pepper. Refrigerate until needed.

To Assemble Preheat the oven to 400°F and place the rack in the centre. Prick the bottoms of the tart shells all over with a fork. Line the tart shells with aluminum foil and fill with pie weights or dried beans. Place the tart shells on a rimmed baking sheet and bake in the oven for 10 to 12 minutes. Lift a corner of the foil to check that the pastry is partly baked. If it is, remove the aluminum foil and weights, then bake for 2 more minutes. Remove from the oven and set on a rack to cool. Leave the oven on.

Mix together the onion filling, bacon (optional) and béchamel sauce in a bowl. Divide this mixture among the half-baked pastry shells. Bake in the oven for 15 minutes, or until done. (The filling will form a dome when ready, and the centre of the tarts will move slightly when jiggled.) Allow to cool for a few minutes before serving.

To Serve Remove the tarts from their pans and place on individual warmed plates.

Wine Van Westen Vineyards Vivacious (mostly Pinot Blanc with a touch of Pinot Gris)

Rabbit in Two Mustards

Y ou can pretend that you're in Paris when you serve this classic rabbit dish, complete with cream and mustard sauce. *Serves 6*

Start this recipe the day before serving. Rub rabbit pieces with Dijon mustard, salt and pepper. Place rabbit in a non-reactive pan, cover with a damp cloth and rest overnight in the refrigerator.

Preheat the oven to 450°F. Heat oil in a large frying pan on medium-high heat. Add rabbit and sear until lightly browned. Turn down the heat to low, sprinkle flour over rabbit, stir and cook for 2 minutes to eliminate the taste of raw flour. Transfer rabbit to a dish, then add onion to the frying pan and sauté for 10 minutes. Add ¼ cup of the wine and deglaze the pan.

Turn down the oven temperature to 325°F. Arrange rabbit pieces in a large ovenproof pan, then add onions with their pan juices, bay leaves, garlic and thyme. Add the remaining wine to cover rabbit. Cover the pan with a lid or aluminum foil and bake in the oven for about 1½ hours, or until rabbit is tender.

To Serve Arrange rabbit pieces on a heated serving platter and cover with aluminum foil to keep warm. Stir cream into the pan juices and cook on medium-high heat for 10 or more minutes, until reduced so that the sauce coats the back of a spoon. Stir in grainy mustard. Season to taste with salt and pepper. Drizzle the sauce over rabbit.

Wine Cedar Creek Estate Winery Platinum Reserve Chardonnay

2 rabbits, have butcher cut each into 6 pieces (liver and kidney not used in this recipe)

½ cup Dijon mustard

¼ cup olive oil

2 Tbsp flour

2 onions, sliced

1 bottle (750 mL) dry white wine

2 bay leaves

3 cloves garlic

1 sprig thyme

2 cups whipping cream

1 Tbsp grainy mustard

Hot Spiced Wine

ot spiced wine is warming on a cold winter day and a perfect accompaniment to the richness of duck confit. *Serves 6 to 8*

Combine all of the ingredients in a pot on medium-high heat and simmer for 20 minutes.

To Serve Strain wine through a fine-mesh sieve and serve hot. Garnish individual glasses with a cinnamon stick.

1 bottle (750 mL) full-bodied red wine

3 Tbsp honey

2 sticks cinnamon

2 Tbsp cardamom pods

1 Tbsp coriander seeds

1 Tbsp black peppercorns

1 tsp cloves

1 orange, juice of

½ lemon, juice of

½ cup sugar

Cinnamon sticks for garnish

Pastry-wrapped Duck Confit

Duck Confit

3 Tbsp fleur de sel

4 cloves garlic, crushed

1 shallot, peeled and sliced

6 sprigs thyme

4 sprigs rosemary

1 Tbsp black peppercorns, crushed

1 Tbsp coriander seeds, crushed

3 cloves, crushed

4 duck legs, including thighs

8 cups rendered duck fat, more or less as needed

Pastry-wrapped Duck Confit

1 recipe duck confit

4 Tbsp diced (¼ inch) apple

4 tsp chopped walnuts, toasted

4 tsp snipped chives

4 tsp chopped parsley

4 Tbsp maple syrup

4 Tbsp ruby port

4 slices prosciutto

4 Tbsp unsalted butter, melted

4 large square sheets of spring roll wrapper, thawed

4 sprigs thyme

A new way to serve popular duck confit. Serve the pastry-wrapped duck confit packages uncut so that diners can discover the savoury surprises within. *Serves 4*

Duck Confit Start making this recipe a day or more before you plan to serve it. Mix together all of the ingredients, except for duck and duck fat, in a non-reactive container. Add duck and coat well. Cover and refrigerate for 12 to 18 hours.

Preheat the oven to 300°F. Remove duck from the refrigerator, rinse off seasoning and pat dry with paper towels. Place in an oven-proof pan, add enough melted duck fat to cover legs and thighs, then bake in the oven for 3 to 4 hours, or until meat is very tender and falling off the bone. Remove from the oven and allow legs and thighs to cool in the duck fat. Cover and refrigerate until needed. Will keep in the refrigerator for up to 3 months.

Pastry-wrapped Duck Confit Preheat the oven to 375°F. Remove duck from fat and use paper towels to wipe off the excess. Remove and discard skin. Pick meat from the bones in large pieces, then discard bones. (Melt duck fat, strain through a fine-mesh sieve, pour into clean jars and freeze for your next batch of confit or use some of it to cook potatoes. Will keep in the freezer for up to 3 months.)

Mix together duck meat, apple, walnuts, chives, parsley, maple syrup and port in a bowl. Season with salt and pepper. Divide mixture into four, then form each portion into an oval ball and wrap snugly with 1 slice prosciutto.

Brush melted butter onto spring roll wrappers. Place one portion of prosciutto-wrapped duck on one corner of a spring roll wrapper. Roll the wrapper over the prosciutto-wrapped duck, folding the sides in, and continue rolling to the opposite corner. Press together firmly to form a tight package. Use thyme sprigs like toothpicks to fasten the spring roll wrappers. Place the packages on a parchment paper-lined baking sheet and bake in the oven for 7 minutes.

To Serve Arrange pastry packages on a warmed serving platter.

Wine Hot spiced wine (page 71)

Grilled Wild Salmon

with Porcini Agnolotti and Tarragon Beurre Blanc

Porcini Agnolotti

8 oz fava beans, shelled

1 Tbsp olive oil

2 lbs fresh B.C. porcini mushrooms, in 1-inch pieces

3 shallots, chopped

2 cloves garlic, chopped

1 sprig thyme

1 fresh bay leaf

1 cup dry white wine

¾ cup mascarpone

¾ cup grated Parmesan cheese

3 Tbsp chopped Italian flat-leaf parsley

4 sheets of pasta dough, each 12 × 4 inches

Porcini are one of the meatiest mushrooms and taste spectacular when available fresh. Substitute any wild mushroom when porcini are not available. *Serves 4*

Porcini Agnolotti Fill a bowl with ice water. Bring a pot of water to a boil on high heat, add fava beans and blanch for 1 minute. Drain and plunge beans into the ice water. Allow to cool, then peel and chop.

Heat oil in a large frying pan on medium heat. Add mushrooms and cook for about 5 minutes, or until golden brown. Add shallots, garlic, thyme and bay leaf, then cook for 2 to 3 minutes. Add wine and deglaze the pan, then cook until all the liquid is absorbed by the mushrooms. Remove and discard bay leaf and stem of thyme.

Transfer the mixture to a food processor or blender and purée. Place the purée in a bowl and blend in mascarpone, Parmesan, parsley and fava beans. Season with salt and pepper to taste. Refrigerate for about 40 minutes, or until cool.

Place the cooled filling in a piping bag or use a spoon. On one pasta sheet, squeeze the stuffing to form five small mounds along the longest side. Brush the edges of the pasta and between the mounds with water, then fold over the pasta sheet lengthwise to cover the filling. Use your fingers to pinch the pasta closed every 1½ inches to form segments. Cut between the segments to yield five agnolotti. Repeat the process for each sheet to make twenty agnolotti in total.

Bring a large pot of salted water to a boil on high heat. Add agnolotti and cook for about 2 minutes. Use a slotted spoon to remove from the water.

Tarragon Beurre Blanc Mix together wine, vinegar and tarragon in a medium-sized heavy pot on medium heat. Cook for 6 to 8 minutes, or until reduced by four-fifths. Remove from the heat and whisk in butter cubes, one at a time, then strain through a fine-mesh sieve and discard solids. Add salt and lemon juice to taste. Keep warm. Just before serving, stir in chervil.

Wild Salmon Preheat a grill or a ridged grill pan on the stovetop to medium-high. Season salmon with salt and pepper, then drizzle each fillet with 1/2 tsp of the oil. Place fish on the grill and cook for 6 to 8 minutes, or to your preferred doneness.

Heat the remaining oil in a frying pan on medium heat. Add spinach and garlic, then sauté for 3 to 4 minutes, or until spinach wilts.

To Serve Centre a 3-inch ring mould on each warmed plate and pack it lightly with a quarter of the spinach. Remove the moulds and top each serving with a piece of grilled salmon. Arrange five agnolotti at the side of each serving and drizzle with the tarragon beurre blanc.

Wine Road 13 Pinot Noir or Jackpot Pinot Noir

Tarragon Beurre Blanc
2/3 cup dry white wine
1/4 cup Japanese rice vinegar
1 sprig tarragon, chiffonaded
1 cup butter, in 1/2-inch cubes
1/2 tsp lemon juice, or to taste
1 small bunch chervil, chopped

Wild Salmon
4 fillets wild Pacific salmon, each 5 oz
1 Tbsp olive oil
4 cups well-packed spinach
2 tsp finely chopped garlic

Strawberry Sablé

with Raspberry Coulis and Vanilla Panna Cotta

Sablé
2 cups all-purpose flour
¾ cup icing sugar
1¼ cups butter, in ½-inch cubes
1 Tbsp whipping cream
3 egg yolks
Icing sugar for garnish

Raspberry Coulis
4 cups frozen raspberries
⅔ cup sugar
24 small strawberries

Vanilla Panna Cotta
2½ leaves gelatin
2 cups whipping cream
⅔ cup sugar
½ vanilla bean, slit lengthwise
1 Tbsp dark rum

The sablé, a traditional French crispy shortbread cookie, is a perfect foil for the soft, chilled panna cotta. *Serves 8*

Sablé Sift flour and sugar together into a bowl. Add butter, cream and egg yolks, then mix by hand until everything is blended together. Gather the dough into a ball and flatten. Cover with plastic wrap and refrigerate for 1 hour.

Preheat the oven to 350°F. Roll out the dough on a lightly floured surface into a sheet about ¼-inch thick. Cut out eight 2-inch circles and place them on a non-stick baking sheet or one lined with parchment paper. Bake in the oven for 8 to 10 minutes, or until golden brown (watch closely as oven temperatures vary). Remove from the oven and allow to cool on racks. (You can re-roll the pastry scraps, cut them into shapes and bake; will keep in an airtight container for a week.)

Raspberry Coulis Place raspberries and sugar in a bowl, then toss together gently. Allow raspberries to thaw, then place in a blender and blend for 5 seconds. Pass through a fine-mesh sieve and discard solids.

Cut strawberries in half and glaze with a small amount of the raspberry coulis. Reserve the rest of the coulis. (Cut strawberries can macerate in the raspberry coulis, covered, in the refrigerator for a day before serving.)

Vanilla Panna Cotta Soak gelatin leaves in cold water for about 15 minutes. Fill a bowl with ice.

Combine cream, sugar and vanilla bean in a pot on medium heat and bring to a boil. Remove from the heat and strain through a fine-mesh sieve (discard solids) into a small bowl. Remove gelatin leaves from the water and gently squeeze out excess water. Use a spatula to fold gelatin leaves and rum into the cream mixture, stirring constantly (so the mixture does not set), until gelatin is dissolved and the mixture is smooth and thick. Place the bowl with the cream mixture on top of the ice to hasten cooling. Stir occasionally so that the mixture does not set around the edges.

Once the panna cotta has thickened, pour into eight moulds, each 2½ inches in diameter and 2 inches deep (or small glasses or ramekins) and refrigerate for 2 hours.

To Serve Use three sablés for each serving. Place one on each plate and cover with a circle of strawberry pieces, top with another sablé and another circle of berries. The third sablé goes on top and may be garnished with a light sprinkling of icing sugar passed through a sieve. The panna cotta may be unmoulded onto the plate beside the sablé stack or left in its container and set on the plate.

Wine Westham Island Estate Winery Strawberry or Tayberry

Charred Tomato Achiote Sopa
(Soup)

Azafran flor (sometimes called "false saffron") is a milder, cheaper version of saffron and is sold in Latino food stores.

Serves 8 or more

Tomato Achiote Sopa Combine all of the ingredients in a large, heavy-bottomed pot on medium heat and bring to a boil. Turn down the heat to medium-low and simmer gently, stirring occasionally, for 15 to 20 minutes, or until the flavours are fully integrated. Remove from the heat and allow to cool until warm.

Pour the mixture into a blender or use a hand-held blender and purée until it is mostly smooth. Season to taste with salt and a generous grind of black pepper.

To Serve Pour the soup into warmed bowls and serve with garnishes (optional) of fried tortilla strips, crumbled feta cheese, red onion and cilantro in separate side bowls.

Wine Stoneboat Vineyards Pinot Noir

Tomato Achiote Sopa

1 can (50 fluid oz) whole tomatoes, drained

12 Roma tomatoes, charred under the broiler

8 cups water

¼ cup achiote paste, crumbled

1 Tbsp Mexican oregano

1 tsp ground pasilla chili

½ tsp ground chipotle chili

2 Tbsp azafran flor

1 Tbsp + 2 tsp salt

1 Tbsp sugar

Garnishes (optional)

Fried tortilla strips

Crumbled feta cheese

Minced red onion

Minced fresh cilantro

Baja-style Fish Tacos
with Jicama Slaw and Chipotle Aïoli

Chipotle Aïoli
½ cup roasted
garlic cloves, puréed
½ egg, beaten
½ lime, juice of
2 chipotles in adobo sauce
(canned), finely chopped
1 Tbsp adobo sauce
¼ tsp honey
1 tsp salt
⅔ cup grapeseed oil
⅓ cup olive oil

Jicama Slaw
2 Tbsp red or white wine vinegar
1 Tbsp lime juice
3 Tbsp grapeseed oil
1 cup peeled and julienned jicama
½ romaine heart, shredded

Beer Batter
⅓ cup cornstarch
½ cup Maseca
instant corn masa mix
1 cup beer
½ tsp salt
A few grinds of black pepper

Fish Tacos
12 white or yellow
4- or 6-inch corn tortillas
1 Tbsp canola oil
½ lb snapper fillet, cut into
strips ½ × 2½ inches

You can prepare the components ahead of time so that you can assemble this dish quickly and have more time to spend with your guests. For the chipotle aïoli, you may mix 1½ cups of store-bought mayonnaise with garlic, lime juice, chipotles, adobo sauce and honey. *Serves 4 to 6*

Chipotle Aïoli Combine garlic, beaten egg, lime juice, chipotles, adobo sauce, honey and salt in a bowl. Very slowly stream in grapeseed oil and then olive oil, whisking aggressively until aïoli forms. Refrigerate until needed. Will keep in the refrigerator for up to 2 days.

Jicama Slaw Whisk together vinegar, lime juice and oil in a bowl. Season to taste with and salt and pepper. Three minutes before serving, add jicama and romaine to the dressing and toss gently.

Beer Batter Whisk together all of the ingredients in a bowl until they form a medium-thick batter.

Fish Tacos Preheat the oven to 325°F. Wrap tortillas in aluminum foil and warm in the oven for 10 minutes. While tortillas are being warmed, heat oil in a frying pan on medium heat. Dredge fish in the beer batter, lay gently in the hot oil and fry for 1½ minutes on each side, or until golden brown. Remove fish from the oil and set on a paper towel–lined tray to drain.

To Serve Top each warm tortilla with a small amount of jicama slaw, a dollop of chipotle aïoli and a piece of fish. Roll up the filled tortillas and serve on individual warmed plates.

Wine Mt Boucherie Estate Winery Gamay Noir

Sambal Drunken Prawns
B.C. Spot Prawns, Shaoxing Wine and Sambal Oelek

Big and luscious, the spot prawn is the largest locally harvested prawn. It's prized for its sweet, delicate flavour and firm texture. If you can't find Shaoxing wine (a Chinese rice wine), use dry sherry. *Serves 6*

Heat oil in a frying pan on medium-high heat. Add garlic and shallots, then sauté for 5 minutes, or until soft and aromatic. Add wine and deglaze the pan, then continue cooking for 1½ minutes. Stir in sambal oelek and sugar, then cook for another 30 seconds. Add prawns and cook for 1 to 1½ minutes; while they are cooking, add butter to emulsify the sauce. Once the prawns are cooked, transfer them to a warmed serving dish. Continue simmering the pan juices on medium heat for 3 to 4 minutes, or until reduced by half. Remove from the heat.

To Serve Pour the syrupy reduced pan juices over the prawns on the serving dish and garnish with cilantro.

Wine Sumac Ridge Estate Winery Steller's Jay Brut

1 Tbsp canola or extra-virgin olive oil

2 Tbsp chopped garlic

2 Tbsp chopped shallots

¼ cup Shaoxing wine

3 Tbsp sambal oelek

3 Tbsp sugar

18 B.C. spot prawns, shelled and deveined, tails on

1 Tbsp butter

Chopped cilantro for garnish

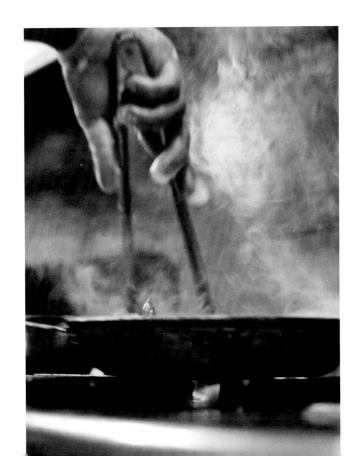

Albacore Tuna Togarashi
with Buckwheat Soba Noodles and
Candied Ginger–Three Citrus Vinaigrette

Soba Noodles
7 oz buckwheat soba noodles
2 tsp soy sauce
2 tsp sesame oil
1 tsp black sesame seeds
1 tsp white sesame seeds

Tuna Togarashi
6 oz albacore tuna loin,
sashimi grade
3 tsp shichimi togarashi
Pinch of sea salt
1 tsp canola oil
Enoki mushrooms for garnish
Pea sprouts for garnish

Citrus Vinaigrette
½ cup chopped candied ginger
1 tsp wasabi powder
1 lemon, juice of
1 orange, juice of
1 lime, juice of
½ cup extra-virgin olive oil

Shichimi togarashi is a dried mix of seven ingredients that vary from brand to brand. The most common ingredients include red chili pepper flakes, dried mandarin orange peel, black hemp seeds, white poppy seeds, nori seaweed bits, ground Szechuan pepper and white sesame seeds. *Serves 6*

Soba Noodles Bring a large pot of water to a boil on high heat. Add noodles and cook for 7 to 8 minutes, or until al dente. Remove from the heat. Drain noodles and place on a rimmed baking sheet, then add soy sauce, sesame oil, and black and white sesame seeds. Toss to coat the noodles evenly and refrigerate.

Tuna Togarashi Coat tuna with shichimi togarashi and salt. Heat oil in a frying pan on medium-high heat. Add tuna and sear on all sides, keeping the centre rare. Transfer tuna to a plate and refrigerate.

Citrus Vinaigrette Mix together candied ginger, wasabi powder, lemon juice, orange juice and lime juice in a small bowl. Whisk together while slowly adding oil. Season to taste with salt.

To Serve Use a long-tined fork to roll noodles into six small circular nests. Place a nest on each chilled plate and dress lightly with some of the vinaigrette. Cut tuna into six rounds and lay one round on top of each noodle nest. Garnish tuna with enoki mushrooms and pea sprouts, then finish with a light drizzling of the vinaigrette.

Wine Gray Monk Estate Winery Gewürztraminer

Roasted Peach Tart

Pastry

1 cup unsalted butter,
cold, in 1-inch cubes

½ cup sugar

1 cup all-purpose flour,
plus extra for dusting

1 cup pastry flour

Roasted Peaches

½ vanilla bean

3 Tbsp unsalted butter

6 large peaches, peeled,
pitted, in ½-inch cubes

2 Tbsp sugar

6 Tbsp mascarpone, softened,
for garnish (optional)

6 tsp B.C. honey for
garnish (optional)

Roasting adds another layer of flavour to the already delicious peach. This rustic tart is best eaten on the day it is made. *Serves 6*

Pastry Use a stand mixer or a hand-held beater to mix together butter and sugar until smooth. (If you use a food processor, you may need to work out a few lumps by hand.) Add all-purpose and pastry flours all at once, mixing just until the dough comes together. Form the dough into a disk, flatten and wrap tightly in plastic wrap. Refrigerate for a minimum of 1 hour.

Butter six tart rings, 3½ to 4 inches in diameter, with removable bottoms. Roll out the dough on a lightly floured surface to a thickness of ⅛ inch. Use a 4½- or 5-inch cookie cutter to cut out six or more rounds of dough. (The tart shells are delicate, so you may want to make an extra one or two in case of breakage.)

Transfer pastry rounds to a parchment paper–lined baking sheet and refrigerate for half an hour. Unbaked tart shells will keep frozen for up to a week. The remaining tart dough can be frozen or sprinkled with sugar and baked for snacks.

Preheat the oven to 375°F and place the rack in the bottom. Gently press each pastry round into a ring, making sure to fill the space. Trim off excess dough around the edges of the rings, then prick pastry all over with a fork. Place the tart rings on a baking sheet and bake in the oven, rotating the baking sheet halfway through baking, for about 15 minutes, or until golden all over. The tart shells will shrink slightly while baking. Remove from the oven and place on a rack to cool. When cool, gently release each pastry shell from its ring.

Roasted Peaches Preheat the oven to 450°F. Cut vanilla bean in half lengthwise and scrape out the seeds into a frying pan. Add vanilla bean and butter, then melt butter on low heat. Add peaches and toss lightly, then remove and discard vanilla bean.

Spread out peaches on a parchment paper–lined rimmed baking sheet and sprinkle with sugar. Roast in the oven, stirring every 5 minutes, until the edges of peaches begin to caramelize and juices begin to bubble (the peach pieces should keep their shape but yield easily when pressed). Remove from the oven and allow to cool.

To Assemble Divide peaches among six baked tart shells, evenly covering the bottom of each shell (you should have enough peaches to create generously rounded tarts).

To Serve Serve the tarts at room temperature or warm them up in a 350°F oven for 8 minutes. For a delicious garnish (optional), top the tarts with a dollop of mascarpone cheese and a drizzle of B.C. honey.

Wine Ehrenfelser from Cedar Creek Estate Winery or Summerhill Pyramid Winery

Linguine di Mare

Seafood and pasta both require little cooking time and are a tasty combination. *Serves 6*

Discard any mussels or clams with open shells that won't close tightly when tapped. Heat ¼ cup of the olive oil in a large pot on medium-high heat. Add the 3 smashed garlic cloves and sauté for about 2 minutes, or until golden. Add mussels and clams, cover and cook for 7 to 8 minutes, or until shells open. Use a slotted spoon to remove mussels and clams and set aside. If any mussels or clams fail to open while cooking, discard them. Strain the cooking liquid through a fine-mesh sieve, discard solids and reserve. Reserve the pot.

Place water and salt in a stockpot and bring to a boil on high heat. When the water comes to a rolling boil, add pasta and cook for 8 to 10 minutes (about 2 minutes less than the package directions).

While the pasta is cooking, wipe out the reserved pot with paper towels. Add the remaining ¼ cup of the olive oil and return to the stove on medium heat. Add onion, stirring frequently, and sauté for about 5 minutes, or until soft. Add the 6 sliced garlic cloves and sauté for 1 minute. Add prawns and scallops, then sauté for 1 minute. Add wine and simmer for about 2 minutes, or until prawns and scallops are cooked (opaque and barely firm to the touch). Remove prawns and scallops from the pot and reserve.

To the wine mixture in the pot, add the reserved cooking liquid from the clams and mussels, tomatoes and chili flakes. Cook on medium-high heat for about 5 minutes, or until reduced by half and thickened. Season to taste with salt. Add the reserved clams, mussels, prawns and scallops, then cook for 2 to 3 minutes to heat through.

At this point, the pasta should be cooked. Drain well and add to the seafood mixture. Cook the pasta in the sauce for another few minutes to allow it to absorb the flavours.

To Serve Add basil, oregano and parsley to the pasta. Toss gently. Transfer to a heated serving platter and arrange clams, mussels, prawns and scallops around the pasta. Drizzle with extra-virgin olive oil.

Wine Greata Ranch Vineyards Reserve Chardonnay

½ cup extra-virgin olive oil

9 cloves garlic, 3 smashed and 6 finely sliced

1 lb mussels, well scrubbed, beards removed

1 lb clams, well scrubbed

20 cups water

½ cup sea salt

1 package (500 g) linguine

1 cup finely sliced red onion

18 medium to large prawns, peeled and deveined

18 medium sea scallops, side muscle removed

1 cup Chardonnay or Pinot Grigio

1 cup drained canned whole tomatoes, hand crushed

1 tsp chili flakes

½ cup basil leaves, hand torn

¼ cup chopped oregano

¼ cup chopped Italian flat-leaf parsley

3 Tbsp extra-virgin olive oil for garnish

Gindara (Sablefish)

Sake has many uses in Japanese cuisine as tenderizer, a suppressor of saltiness and an eliminator of fishy taste. *Serves 4*

Start making this the day before you plan to serve it. Mix together miso, mirin, sake and sugar in a shallow dish. Add fish, cover and marinate for 11 to 12 hours in the refrigerator.

Preheat the oven to 500°F. Drain fish, rinse gently and pat dry with paper towels. Season fish with salt and pepper, then place on a rimmed baking sheet. Roast in the oven for 6 to 7 minutes, or until the flesh is barely opaque. Brown the tops quickly under the broiler, then remove from the oven.

To Serve Place each piece of fish on a warmed serving plate.

Wine Blasted Church Vineyards Chardonnay Musqué

2¼ cups white miso

1 cup mirin (Japanese sweet cooking rice wine)

½ cup sake

⅓ cup sugar

4 portions sablefish, each 5 oz

Renkon (Lotus Root) Gyoza

Ponzu Sauce
⅓ cup Japanese rice vinegar
¾ cup soy sauce
½ lemon, juice of
1 Tbsp sambal oelek

Lotus Root Gyoza
1 lb ground pork
1 Tbsp ground fresh garlic
1 Tbsp ground fresh ginger
1 dozen chives, finely chopped
2 Tbsp sesame oil
1 Tbsp sake
1 Tbsp salt
1 tsp sugar
1 egg
1 lb lotus roots

Tempura Batter
Vegetable oil for deep-frying
1 cup flour, plus extra for dredging
1 egg yolk
1 cup ice water

Lotus root, used in Japanese and Chinese cuisines for centuries, mixes well with other vegetables and is prized for its crunchiness. It also makes excellent pickles, chutneys and relishes. *8 to 10 gyoza*

Ponzu Sauce Combine all of the ingredients in a bowl and allow to rest.

Lotus Root Gyoza To make the filling, thoroughly mix together all of the ingredients, except for the lotus roots, in a bowl. Cut lotus roots into ⅛-inch thick slices and line them up in pairs.

To make a gyoza, place 2 Tbsp of the filling on one slice of a pair of lotus root slices. Place the other slice on top and press down, pushing the filling into the holes of lotus root. If the filling squeezes out from the sides, press it back inside. Repeat the process for each pair of lotus root slices.

Tempura Batter Place oil in a deep fryer to the marked line or half-fill a tall-sided heavy pot on the stovetop and heat to 350°F. To make the tempura batter, sift flour into a bowl. In another bowl, mix together egg yolk and ice water. Add flour to the egg mixture all at once and mix lightly. (The key to good tempura is not overmixing the batter. The batter should be lumpy, and there should be dry spots of flour on the inside of the bowl.)

Place a bowl of flour for dredging next to the tempura batter. Dredge each lotus gyoza in flour, shaking off excess. Dip each gyoza into the tempura batter, then deep-fry for about 3 minutes, or until golden. Use a slotted spoon to remove the gyoza and allow them to rest on a paper towel–lined tray.

Bring oil back up to 350°F. When the gyoza have rested a minimum of 3 minutes, deep-fry again for 5 minutes, or until golden brown. Use a slotted spoon to remove gyoza from the oil. Salt lightly.

To Serve Slice gyoza in half crosswise and arrange on a warmed serving platter. Serve with ponzu sauce in a bowl on the side.

Wine Nk'Mip Cellars Riesling

Chicken Karaage

This variation on the traditional chicken karaage, or sesame-fried chicken nuggets, is ideal for sharing. *Serves 3 to 4*

Make the marinade by mixing together sake, soy sauce, garlic, ginger, powdered fish broth and shichimi togarashi in a non-reactive bowl. Place chicken pieces in the marinade, rub in well, cover and refrigerate for 10 minutes.

Place oil in a deep fryer to the marked line or half-fill a tall-sided heavy pot on the stovetop and heat to 350°F. Place potato starch in a shallow bowl. Dredge marinated chicken pieces in potato starch and shake off excess. Deep-fry chicken for about 5 minutes, or until golden brown. Remove from the oil and drain on a tray lined with paper towels.

To Serve Arrange chicken pieces on a warmed serving platter. Garnish with lemon wedges, parsley and shichimi togarashi.

Wine Dunham & Froese Estate Winery Amicita White

1 Tbsp + 1 tsp sake

2 tsp soy sauce

¾ tsp shredded garlic

¾ tsp shredded ginger

1 tsp powdered fish broth
(no MSG, Asian food stores)

Pinch of shichimi togarashi
(page 82), plus extra for garnish

1½ lbs chicken thighs, boneless,
skin on or off, in 1-inch pieces

Vegetable oil for deep-frying

½ cup potato starch

Lemon wedges for garnish

Parsley, finely chopped,
for garnish

Seafood Sashimi Salad

Garlic Oil
¼ cup extra-virgin olive oil
10 thin slices garlic

Dressing
1 cup soy sauce
¾ cup rice vinegar
⅓ cup lemon juice
1 small onion, roughly chopped
⅓ carrot, peeled and roughly chopped
2 tsp sugar
½ tsp yuzu pepper paste
⅓ daikon radish, roughly chopped

Seafood Sashimi Salad
3 cups organic mixed salad greens (radicchio, red oak leaf lettuce, arugula, frisée)
9 thin slices of sashimi or other sushi-grade raw fish or smoked salmon
½ lemon, cut into 3 wedges, for garnish
½ cup pea shoots for garnish

Adapt the seafood ingredients to suit your tastes by using raw, cured or cooked fish. Yuzu pepper paste is a Japanese spicy, salty, citrus condiment, sold at Asian food stores. *Serves 3*

Garlic Oil Place oil and garlic in a small pot on medium heat and cook for 2 to 3 minutes, or until garlic is golden brown. Remove from the heat, strain through a fine-mesh sieve and discard garlic. Allow to cool to room temperature, then refrigerate immediately and use the same day. Note that garlic oil must be kept refrigerated.

Dressing Place all of the ingredients in a food processor or blender and purée until smooth.

Seafood Sashimi Salad Place salad greens in a large bowl. Add enough dressing to coat leaves lightly and toss gently.

To Serve Divide salad among chilled shallow serving bowls. Arrange three slices of fish on top of each serving and drizzle with garlic oil. Garnish with a wedge of lemon and pea shoots.

Wine Crowsnest Vineyards Family Reserve Riesling

Vitello Tonnato

This classic dish from northern Italy is at its best when you use a premium brand of canned tuna packed in olive oil in the sauce. Serve with crusty bread. *Serves 8*

Vitello Preheat the oven to 300°F. Rub salt and oil all over veal. Heat an ovenproof pan on high heat, add veal and sear until golden on all sides. Remove from the heat.

Lay rosemary on the bottom of a roasting pan, top with veal and roast in the oven for 30 to 45 minutes, or until medium-rare (135°F on a meat thermometer). Remove veal from the pan and allow to cool on a rack. Once veal has cooled, wrap in aluminum foil and refrigerate.

Tuna Sauce Drain tuna and reserve oil. Place tuna, capers, lemon zest and juice, anchovies and water in a blender on high speed or in a food processor, then purée until fairly smooth. With the motor running, slowly add the reserved tuna oil, then vegetable oil, until the mixture comes together like a milkshake. Season to taste with salt.

To Serve Slice cold veal as thinly as possible and arrange slices to cover the surface of a chilled serving platter or individual plates. Spoon tuna sauce over the veal to cover some of it and garnish with a few capers.

Wine Black Hills Estate Winery Nota Bene

Vitello

2 tsp olive oil

1¼ lbs veal, eye of round
(have butcher clean it up well)

Few sprigs of rosemary

Tuna Sauce

1 can (5 oz) of tuna in olive oil

1 Tbsp capers,
plus extra for garnish

½ lemon, zest and juice of

2 fillets anchovy

2 Tbsp water

¼ cup vegetable oil

Tagliata di Manzo

6 flatiron beef steaks,
each 5 to 6 oz, ½-inch thick

6 to 8 cups arugula

¼ cup balsamic vinegar

⅓ cup olive oil

½ cup pine nuts, toasted

7 oz Parmigiano-Reggiano

Coarse sea salt
for garnish (optional)

Use the best-quality balsamic vinegar that you have to finish this beef dish. *Serves 6*

Preheat a grill or a ridged pan on the stovetop on medium-high. Brush the grill surfaces with a little oil. Season steaks with salt and pepper, then grill for about 3 minutes on each side, or to the desired doneness. Remove from the grill and allow to rest for 10 minutes.

Place arugula and two-thirds of the vinegar in a bowl. Toss gently, add two-thirds of the oil and toss gently again. Season to taste with salt and pepper.

To Serve Slice steaks fairly thinly and arrange each on a warmed plate. Drizzle the remaining vinegar and the remaining oil over steaks. Place arugula beside the steak on each plate and sprinkle with pine nuts. Use a thin peeler to shave Parmigiano-Reggiano generously over each serving. Garnish (optional) with a sprinkle of coarse sea salt.

Wine Laughing Stock Vineyards Portfolio or Blind Trust red

Butterflied Leg of Lamb
with Herb Jus

Locally raised lamb cooked on the barbecue is perfect for stress-free summer entertaining. This dish goes well with baby roasted potatoes and seasonal vegetables. *Serves 8 or more*

Lamb Mix together rosemary, thyme, garlic, curry powder, oil, salt, black pepper and wine in a large non-reactive container. Add lamb and use your hands to rub the mixture evenly over the meat. Cover and marinate for a total of 2 hours, 1 hour in the refrigerator, then 1 hour at room temperature.

Preheat the barbecue to medium. Use paper towels to wipe off the marinade from lamb, then place lamb on the barbecue. Grill for 7½ minutes on each side, then turn down the heat to low, cover and continue to cook for about 40 minutes for medium-rare (125°F to 130°F on a meat thermometer). Remove from the barbecue and allow to rest on a carving board for 15 minutes.

Herb Jus Place stock, wine, thyme, rosemary and garlic in a pot on medium-high heat. Simmer for about 15 minutes, or until reduced by half.

Just before serving, reheat, stir in mint and whisk in butter, one cube at a time. Season to taste with salt and pepper.

To Serve Slice lamb thinly and serve with herb jus.

Wine Tinhorn Creek Oldfield's Collection Merlot

Lamb

3 Tbsp chopped mixed rosemary and thyme

8 cloves garlic, minced

1 tsp curry powder

¼ cup olive oil

1 Tbsp salt

2 tsp coarsely ground black pepper

1 cup dry red wine

6 to 7 lbs leg of lamb, boneless and butterflied

Herb Jus

½ cup veal stock

1 cup dry red wine

1 sprig thyme

1 sprig rosemary

1 tsp chopped garlic

2 sprigs chopped mint

¼ cup chilled butter, in ½-inch cubes

Grand Marnier Soufflé

Butter for greasing
Icing sugar for dusting
4 large eggs, separated
2 Tbsp Grand Marnier
½ tsp frozen orange
juice concentrate
¼ cup sugar
½ lemon, juice of

Serve this soufflé as is or with a sauce, such as ½ cup of crème anglaise with 1 Tbsp of Grand Marnier mixed in, or a dark chocolate sauce, or an orange sauce (cook 1 cup of apricot jam with ½ cup of water for 5 minutes, then stir in 1 tsp of orange zest and 2 Tbsp of Grand Marnier). *Serves 4*

Preheat the oven to 400°F. Butter a 4- to 5-cup soufflé dish very well and dust with icing sugar.

Whisk together egg yolks, Grand Marnier, frozen orange juice concentrate and 2 Tbsp of the sugar in a bowl.

Use a stand mixer or hand-held beater to whisk egg whites with the remaining 2 Tbsp of the sugar until medium peaks form. Beat in lemon juice. Fold the egg white mixture into the egg yolk mixture, then scoop into a soufflé dish. Bake in the oven for about 13 minutes, or until puffed and golden on top.

To Serve Dust soufflé with icing sugar and divide among warmed plates. Serve as is or with a sauce of your choice.

Wine Paradise Ranch Wines Chardonnay Icewine

Arctic Char à la Provencal

Arctic char is similar to trout and comes from cold northern waters. Here, we give it a southern French treatment. *Serves 6*

Toss tomatoes with a little salt in a bowl. Remove 2 thin slices from lemon, then cut each of those slices into small wedges that include the rind. Squeeze juice from the remaining lemon over tomatoes. Add lemon wedges, capers, garlic, anchovies, basil and ½ cup of the oil. Season to taste with salt and pepper. Set tomato sauce aside.

Score the fish skin to prevent it from curling while cooking, then season with salt and pepper. Heat the remaining 1 Tbsp of the oil in a large frying pan on medium-high heat. Add fish, skin-side down, and sear for 3 minutes, or until skin is crisp. Flip over fish and cook for about 3 minutes, until just opaque in the centre.

Place the tomato sauce in a clean frying pan on medium heat and cook until warm.

To Serve Place a fillet of arctic char on each warmed plate, top with tomato sauce and serve with your favourite pasta or rice.

Wine Viognier from La Frenz Winery or Mistral Estate Winery

4 medium to large tomatoes, peeled, seeded, in ½-inch dice

1 lemon

4 Tbsp capers

1 heaping tsp chopped garlic

3 fillets anchovy, chopped

1 bunch basil, coarsely chopped

½ cup + 1 Tbsp extra-virgin olive oil

6 fillets arctic char, each 4 oz

Oysters Gratinée

Clarified Butter

1 lb butter, salted or
unsalted, in 1-inch cubes

Oysters Gratinée

2 cups fine fresh bread crumbs

¾ cup very finely chopped parsley

¾ cup finely chopped basil

¾ cup finely chopped chives

⅓ cup finely chopped garlic

1 cup clarified butter

Pinch of salt

40 small beach oysters

Lettuce for garnish (optional)

Place the prepared oyster shells on a bed of rock salt on a rimmed baking sheet to keep them level while cooking and to make sure that the topping doesn't fall off. *Serves 8 as an appetizer*

Clarified Butter To make on the stovetop, place butter in a medium pot on medium heat. Once butter starts to melt, turn down the heat to low and keep stirring to make sure it does not burn; it will start to bubble but that will subside. Then after about 5 minutes, the butter will appear to separate. When this occurs, remove from the heat and allow to stand for 2 minutes. Skim off and discard the solids floating on top of the clarified butter. Carefully decant the clear butter into a container and discard the water at the bottom of the pan. (To make in the microwave, place butter in a glass microwave dish. Microwave on medium-high for 10 minutes. Remove from the microwave and allow to stand for 2 minutes, then continue as in the stovetop method.) Makes about 1 cup.

Oysters Gratinée Preheat the oven to 450°F. Mix together bread crumbs, parsley, basil, chives, garlic and ¾ cup of the clarified butter. Stir in salt.

Shuck oysters, detaching them from the shell but leaving them in the larger half of the shell. Drain and reserve juices. Place oysters in a roasting pan or on a rimmed baking sheet and brush with the remaining clarified butter. Drizzle oyster juices over oysters, then cover them with the bread crumb mixture and bake in the oven for 8 to 12 minutes, or until crispy on top.

To Serve Place five oysters on each warmed plate and garnish (optional) with lettuce.

Wine See Ya Later Ranch Brut

Red Bell Pepper and Shallot Curry

This dish is an excellent vegetable accompaniment to Chicken Breasts and Thighs in Clove, Black Cardamom and Yogurt Curry (page 104), as it goes well with the stronger spices in that dish. It is also delicious on its own with rice, chapatis or a baguette. This dish does have heat, so use the jalapeño peppers at your discretion. *Serves 6 to 8 as a side dish*

Slice green onions into thin rounds, keeping the white and green parts separate. Heat oil in a heavy pot on medium-high heat for 30 seconds. Add cumin seeds, and when they begin to sizzle in 30 to 45 seconds, immediately stir in shallots and the white part of the green onions. Cook, stirring occasionally, for 7 to 8 minutes, until golden. Add tomatoes, jalapeño peppers, salt, turmeric, paprika and black mustard seeds. Turn down the heat to medium and cook this masala for 10 minutes, or until you can see the oil separating and glimmering on top. Stir in red bell peppers, cover and cook for 5 minutes.

To Serve If serving immediately, stir in the green part of the green onions. Otherwise, stir them in after you reheat this curry and just before serving.

Wine Red Rooster Winery Merlot or Inniskillin Okanagan Discovery Series Zinfandel

1 bunch green onions

½ cup canola or other vegetable oil

1 Tbsp cumin seeds

8 shallots, thinly sliced

1 lb tomatoes, chopped

3 large jalapeño peppers, deseeded, finely chopped

1 Tbsp salt

1 tsp turmeric

1 tsp paprika

1 tsp ground black mustard seeds

3 to 4 red bell peppers, seeded, in 1-inch wide strips

Chicken Breasts and Thighs
in Clove, Black Cardamom and Yogurt Curry

Chicken Breasts

1½ lbs boneless chicken half breasts, trimmed of fat, skin on or off

⅓ cup canola oil

1 Tbsp salt

1 Tbsp ground cumin

1 Tbsp ground coriander

1 tsp ground cayenne pepper

1 Tbsp paprika

1 tsp ground dried ginger (optional)

Chicken Thighs

1½ cups yogurt, stirred well

1½ cups puréed canned tomatoes

1 Tbsp + 1 tsp salt

1½ tsp ground cayenne pepper

2 Tbsp ground coriander

3 Tbsp ground cumin

1 Tbsp + 1 tsp paprika

1 tsp ground dried ginger or 2 Tbsp + 2 tsp finely chopped fresh ginger

1 Tbsp celery seed

10 cloves

3 or 4 pods black cardamom, seeds only

7 large cloves garlic, finely chopped

2 tsp canola oil

1½ lbs chicken thighs, boneless, skinless, trimmed of fat

1 cup water

In this recipe, we cook the chicken two ways. We oven braise the chicken thighs, as the darker meat is juicier and soaks in the spices, as well as lending flavour to the broth. We marinate and grill the chicken breasts to retain the succulence of the white meat. Serve it with Red Bell Peppers and Shallot Curry (page 103) and basmati rice. Black cardamom is available at any Indian grocer. We prefer the optional dried ground ginger (known as soond) to fresh, if available; if you use soond, break any clumps into a powder. *Serves 6 to 8*

Chicken Breasts Toss together chicken with oil, salt, cumin, coriander, cayenne pepper, paprika and ginger. (Do not use fresh ginger in this part of the recipe, as it will burn when you grill the chicken later.) Cover and refrigerate for at least 3 hours.

Chicken Thighs Preheat the oven to 375°F. Mix together yogurt, tomatoes, salt, cayenne pepper, coriander, cumin, paprika, ginger, celery seed, cloves, black cardamom seeds, garlic and oil in a casserole dish. Add chicken thighs. Add water, mix well, cover and bake in the oven for about 40 minutes, or until chicken is tender and juices run a clear yellow. Remove from the oven and keep covered until ready to serve. If the thighs are very large, cut them in half to serve.

Once chicken thighs have been in the oven for 35 minutes, start grilling the chicken breasts.

To Finish Chicken Breasts Preheat a barbecue or a stovetop ridged grill pan on high. Oil the grill, then grill chicken for 4 to 5 minutes. Flip over and grill for another 4 to 5 minutes, or until juices run a clear yellow. Slice each half breast on the diagonal into three pieces.

To Serve Place a portion of basmati rice in the middle of each large warmed bowl. Arrange a chicken thigh and a piece of grilled chicken breast on top of the rice. Ladle ½ to ¾ cup of the Red Bell Pepper and Shallot Curry (page 103) around the chicken and rice.

Wine Sandhill Estate Vineyard Small Lots Barbera or Inniskillin Okanagan Discovery Series Malbec

Su Dong Po Pork

The exotic flavour combination of orange, tamarind and kecap manis works very well with the slow-cooked pork belly. Garnish this dish with pickled ginger and serve it with baby bok choy. *Serves 6*

Preheat the oven to 300°F. Heat oil in a large ovenproof braising pot (such as a Dutch oven) on medium-high heat on the stovetop. Add onions and sauté, stirring, for about 5 minutes, or until they begin to soften. Turn down the heat to medium, stir in ginger, season with salt and pepper, then cook for 30 to 45 minutes, or until onions are caramelized. Add sherry and deglaze the pan. Add pork and stir. Add oranges, sugar, tamarind, kecap manis, soy sauce, spice sachet and stock. Turn up the heat to high. When the liquid begins to boil, cover the pot and bake in the oven for 3½ to 4 hours, or until done (when ready, the pork should be soft and loose). Remove and discard oranges and sachet. Use a slotted spoon to remove pork and set aside. Bring the cooking liquid to a simmer on medium-high heat on the stovetop and cook, stirring constantly, for 5 to 10 minutes, or until reduced by a quarter. Return pork to the cooking liquid and stir to blend.

To Serve Serve pork and sauce over steamed rice.

Wine Domaine de Chaberton Estate Winery Bacchus

3 Tbsp canola oil
3 large onions, in 1-inch cubes
2 Tbsp minced ginger
¼ cup dry sherry or dry red wine
4 lbs pork belly, in 3-inch cubes
2 oranges, halved
½ cup maltose sugar or honey
1 Tbsp + 2 tsp tamarind extract
½ cup kecap manis
½ cup soy sauce
Spice sachet:
1 broken cinnamon stick, 3 cloves, 4 star anise and 2 green cardamom pods tied up in a piece of cheesecloth
8 cups chicken stock

Halibut Cheek Congee
With Lemon Zest Salt

Lemon Zest Salt

1 lemon

¼ cup sea salt or fleur de sel

Congee

1 cup jasmine rice (not rinsed)

8 cups fish stock

3 Tbsp rice vinegar

3 Tbsp mirin (Japanese sweet cooking rice wine)

2 tsp finely minced ginger

½ lb halibut cheeks

½ tsp sea salt or to taste

½ tsp white pepper

6 Tbsp finely chopped cilantro

1 cup pea shoots

½ cup julienned scallions, left in cold water to create a curl

Congee is a favourite street-food item in China, where it is eaten as a pick-me-up. The addition of halibut in this version is elegant and invigorating. *Serves 6*

Lemon Zest Salt Prepare the day before serving. Remove zest from half the lemon and chop finely (reserve the other lemon half for another use). Mix together lemon zest and salt in a small bowl. Spread out the mixture evenly on a baking sheet and allow to dry overnight.

Congee Combine rice, stock, vinegar, mirin and ginger in a heavy-bottomed pot on medium heat and bring to a boil. Cook for about 10 minutes, or until the mixture becomes cloudy and slightly thickened. Season halibut with salt and white pepper, then add to the pot at the 10-minute mark. When the rice is just cooked, 15 to 20 minutes from when you started, turn off the heat and leave the pot on the still warm element for 15 minutes. Taste and adjust the seasoning with salt and white pepper. When the congee has the consistency of porridge, it is ready.

Just before serving, use a slotted spoon to remove halibut, shred the flesh with a fork and stir back into the congee along with cilantro.

To Serve Ladle hot congee into warmed bowls, then garnish with pea shoots and drained scallions. Serve the lemon zest salt in a small dish on the side.

Wine JoieFarm Wines A Noble Blend

Spicy Curry Calamari

The spicy curry powder is also delicious on other fried foods such as prawns, any type of white fish or even french fries. The aonori (optional) is a type of Japanese dried green seaweed. *Serves 6*

Spicy Curry Powder Combine all of the ingredients in a small bowl, mixing well.

Spicy Curry Calamari Cleaned, prepared squid is available at fish stores. To prepare your own, place one hand on the head of the squid and the other on the base of the tentacles, then grasp the tentacles and pull gently. Remove the quill (the clear bone), then pull out and discard the guts. Cut away the tentacles just in front of the eyes, then squeeze out and discard the small hard beak. Rinse the body and the tentacles thoroughly with cold water, then pat dry with paper towels. Cut the body of the squid crosswise, about 2 inches wide, and cut the tentacles into two pieces each.

Place oil in a deep fryer to the marked line or half-fill a tall-sided heavy pot on the stovetop and heat to 375°F. Place flour in a shallow bowl and dredge squid in it, making sure all pieces are well coated. Remove from the flour and shake off excess. Deep-fry squid for about 1¹/₂ minutes. Use a perforated ladle or strainer to remove squid, straining off as much oil as possible. Drain on a paper towel-lined tray, then place in a bowl and sprinkle with lemon juice, spicy curry powder and aonori (optional), tossing to ensure calamari is well coated.

To Serve Arrange calamari on a warmed platter with garnishes (optional) of endive, radicchio and kale.

Wine Wild Goose Vineyards Mystic River Gewürztraminer

Spicy Curry Powder
2 tsp curry powder
2 tsp salt
¾ tsp cayenne pepper
¼ tsp garlic powder

Spicy Curry Calamari
2 Surume or other squid
Canola oil for deep-frying
2 cups all-purpose flour
½ lemon, juice of
1 recipe spicy curry powder
2 Tbsp aonori (optional)
2 pieces Belgian endive for garnish (optional)
2 pieces radicchio for garnish (optional)
2 pieces kale for garnish (optional)

Prosciutto Roll

Sushi Rice
1 cup Japanese rice vinegar
½ cup + 1 Tbsp sugar
1 Tbsp + 2 tsp salt
1 cup short-grain Japanese rice (such as Nishiki)

Soy-Mirin Reduction
3 Tbsp soy sauce
¼ cup mirin (Japanese sweet cooking rice wine)

Pesto
1 bunch basil
1 clove garlic
1 tsp soy sauce
3 Tbsp olive oil

Prosciutto Rolls
1 cup sushi rice
½ mango, peeled, in logs 3 × ¾ inches
¼ cup cream cheese, in logs 3 × ¾ inches
4 slices prosciutto
3 Tbsp soy-mirin reduction
4 Tbsp pesto

Japan meets Italy in this sweet and salty combination, a true balance of flavours. Instead of making sushi vinegar for the sushi rice, you may purchase it in an Asian food store. *Makes 32 pieces*

Sushi Rice To make sushi vinegar, combine vinegar, sugar and salt in a small pot on low heat, whisking until sugar and salt are dissolved. Remove from the heat and allow to cool.

Rinse and rub rice under cold water, repeating the process until the water runs clear. Drain rice in a sieve for about 10 minutes, then transfer to a rice cooker; add 1 cup of water and cook according to the manufacturer's instructions.

While the rice is still hot, transfer it to a Japanese wooden rice tub or a wide shallow container that has first been wiped down with water or rice vinegar. Add ¾ cup of the sushi vinegar to rice and incorporate by using a wooden paddle or rice spatula in a slicing motion. Add the rest of the sushi vinegar and incorporate until it is all evenly mixed into rice. Allow the sushi rice to cool until it is warm but not cold (cold rice is difficult to spread).

Soy-Mirin Reduction Combine soy sauce and mirin in a small pot on low heat. Cook for about 5 minutes, or until reduced by half and syrupy. Remove from the heat and allow to cool.

Pesto Place basil, garlic, soy sauce and a pinch of salt and pepper in a blender or food processor. Chop ingredients, then blend until fairly smooth. With the motor running, add oil in a slow steady stream until incorporated.

Prosciutto Rolls Wrap a sushi mat with plastic wrap to prevent rice from sticking to it. Spread about 1½ handfuls of sushi rice onto the mat in a rectangular shape. Place mango and cream cheese logs in a line down the centre of the rectangle. Lift the end of the sushi mat nearest you, along with the sushi rice, and carefully roll it over the mango and cheese filling, pressing down as you go. Repeat the process to make four rolls. Wrap a slice of prosciutto around each roll.

To Serve Cut each prosciutto roll into eight pieces, using a knife dipped in water to prevent rice from sticking to the blade. Arrange the pieces on a serving platter and drizzle with the soy-mirin reduction. Top each piece with a dab of pesto. Lastly, grind some black pepper over top.

Wine Gehringer Brothers Estate Winery Optimum Pinot Noir

The
Rising
Stars

BRITISH COLUMBIA'S NEW breed of chef is environmen-

tally conscious, savvy about wine, technically astute and

fully engaged in using the ingredients raised, caught or harvested in

our big backyard. Many have trained in the world's best restaurants

alongside famous chefs, but most came up through the ranks right

here. Now they lead some of our most respected kitchens,

and several have become award-winning restaurateurs in their own

right. Though some are still young, the maturity of their palates

and technique—amply displayed in the following pages—is proof

positive that the future of our cuisine is in strong hands. Each chef

understands the necessity of complexity without complication,

but often with nuances of the unexpected. And yes, you *can* do

this at home.

Qualicum Bay Scallops

with Wild Rice, Radish and Shiitake Mushroom Sauté,
Santa Rosa Plum Glaze

Plum Glaze

1 cup dry sherry

1 cup dry white wine

20 Santa Rosa plums,
very ripe, pitted

2 shallots, sliced

2 cloves garlic, sliced

4 sprigs oregano

4 sprigs thyme

**Wild Rice, Radish
and Shiitake Sauté**

5 Tbsp unsalted butter

2 Tbsp vegetable oil

3 shallots, thinly sliced

½-inch piece ginger root,
peeled, julienned

36 baby shiitake mushrooms,
stemmed, or 20 large shiitake,
stemmed and sliced

1 cup cooked and drained wild rice

30 sugar snap peas, cleaned,
strings removed and blanched

30 leaves baby kale,
2-inch diameter

6 Tbsp vegetable stock

3 Tbsp coarsely chopped
Italian flat-leaf parsley

6 French Breakfast radishes,
thinly sliced on the diagonal

6 sprigs pea shoots for garnish

Scallops

18 Qualicum Bay scallops,
tough outer muscle removed

2 to 3 Tbsp vegetable oil

Plump and beautifully textured, these scallops from Qualicum Bay on Vancouver Island will soak up the sweetness of their glaze. Though Santa Rosa plums are ideal, any juicy plum from the Okanagan, Similkameen or Kootenay valleys will do when in season. *Serves 6*

Plum Glaze Combine all of the ingredients in a small non-reactive pot on medium heat and bring to a simmer. Do not boil. Simmer slowly for 20 to 30 minutes, or until the sauce is viscous. Season to taste with salt. Strain through a fine-mesh sieve and discard solids.

Wild Rice, Radish and Shiitake Sauté Preheat the oven to 300°F. Melt butter and oil in a large frying pan on medium-high heat. Add shallots and sauté for 2 to 3 minutes, or until translucent. Add ginger and cook for 1 minute. Add mushrooms and cook, stirring, for 2 minutes, or until tender. Add wild rice and cook for 3 minutes to heat through. Turn down the heat to medium, then add snap peas, kale and stock. Cook for 4 minutes, or until kale is tender. Stir in parsley and radishes. Season to taste with salt and pepper. Keep warm in the oven while you cook the scallops.

Scallops Season scallops with salt and pepper. Heat oil in a heavy frying pan on medium-high heat. Add scallops and sear on one side for 1 to 2 minutes, or until caramelized. Flip over scallops and remove the pan from the heat (they will finish cooking in the pan off the heat).

To Serve While the scallops are cooking, gently reheat the plum glaze. Spoon the wild rice mixture onto warmed plates, drizzle with plum glaze and arrange three scallops on each serving. Garnish with pea shoots.

Wine Church & State Wines Viognier

Glorious Organics "Celebration" Greens
with Sapo Bravo Peach and Tarragon Vinaigrette

1 shallot, sliced

1 peach, peeled and pitted, from Sapo Bravo

3 Tbsp honey

5 Tbsp high-quality apple vinegar

1 tsp tarragon

2 Tbsp vegetable oil

6 cups Glorious Organics "celebration" greens or other mixed salad greens

Glorious Organics Co-operative delivers its "celebration" greens to several top Vancouver restaurants and to Vancouver farmers' markets from their land in the Fraser Valley. Peaches from Sapo Bravo, a farm outside Lytton, B.C., can be found at most farmers' markets, but any local peach will do. *Serves 6*

To make the dressing, place shallot, peach, honey, vinegar and tarragon in a blender. Blend until smooth. With the motor running, slowly add oil. Strain the dressing through a fine-mesh sieve and discard the solids.

To Serve Place salad greens in a large bowl, add dressing and toss gently. Arrange on individual chilled plates.

Wine Sandhill Pinot Gris King Family Vineyard or Glenterra Vineyards Pinot Gris

Grilled Ahi Tuna

with Spinach, Pickled Shiitake Mushrooms and Dashi

As long as it isn't overcooked, ahi tuna is a forgiving fish. This dish combines Asian flavours and French technique, a typical Vancouver approach. *Serves 4*

Ginger Oil Make the ginger oil first. Place ginger and oil in a small pot on medium-high heat and bring just to a boil. Turn off the heat, cover the pan and leave to infuse for 1 hour. Strain through a sieve, discard ginger and set ginger oil aside.

Shiitake Mushrooms Mix together mirin, vinegar and soy sauce in a pot on medium heat. Add shiitake mushrooms and ginger, bring to a boil, then remove from the heat and allow to cool.

Dashi Place water and kombu in a pot on medium heat. Bring to a boil and remove from the heat immediately. Remove and discard kombu. Stir in bonito flakes, cover and steep for 20 minutes. Strain through a fine-mesh sieve and discard solids. Stir in soy sauce and mirin.

Soy-Mirin Glaze Combine all of the ingredients in a small pot on medium-high heat and simmer for about 10 minutes, or until reduced by half. Strain through a fine-mesh sieve and discard solids.

Tuna Cut tuna into four equal portions, then season with salt and long pepper.

Heat a grill or a ridged grill pan on the stovetop on high. Brush the surface of the grill with grapeseed oil, and when it begins to smoke, add tuna and quickly sear on all sides. Remove from the heat and transfer the tuna to a plate to stop it from continuing to cook.

Heat another frying pan on medium heat, then add sesame oil and spinach. Season with salt and cook, stirring, for 4 to 5 minutes, or until spinach wilts. Remove from the heat.

To Serve Heat dashi and soy-mirin glaze in separate pots. Drain pickled shiitake mushrooms, then place them and spinach in warmed shallow bowls. Just before serving, thinly slice tuna and arrange on top of spinach and mushrooms, then drizzle with soy-mirin glaze. Pour dashi around the sides of the bowl to cover spinach. Garnish with a little ginger oil and purple micro shiso.

Wine Herder Winery & Vineyards Chardonnay

Ginger Oil
1-inch piece of ginger
½ cup grapeseed oil

Shiitake Mushrooms
½ cup mirin (Japanese sweet cooking rice wine)
½ cup Japanese rice vinegar
2 Tbsp soy sauce
4 oz baby shiitake mushrooms
1-inch piece ginger

Dashi
4 cups water
¼ sheet kombu (Japanese dried seaweed)
½ cup bonito flakes (Japanese dried smoked bonito)
2 Tbsp soy sauce
2 Tbsp mirin (Japanese sweet cooking rice wine)

Soy-Mirin Glaze
¼ cup soy sauce
⅔ cup mirin
1 orange, zest of
2 pods cardamom
1 tsp coriander seeds
1 tsp Szechuan peppercorns
1 star anise

Tuna
¾ lb ahi tuna, sashimi grade
Long pepper or Szechuan peppercorns
1 tsp grapeseed oil
1 Tbsp sesame oil
2 bunches spinach, stems off
Purple micro shiso for garnish

Seared Spring Salmon
with Artichokes, Swiss Chard and Herb Purée

Also known as chinook, king, tyee and hook bill, the mighty spring salmon is the largest and most prized of the six Pacific salmon species. *Serves 4*

Artichokes Artichokes may be prepared a day in advance. Make acidulated water by combining water and lemon juice in a bowl, then set aside. Remove and discard all the outer and inner leaves of artichokes. Use a small sharp paring knife to peel away the remaining bits of leaves around the hearts and to peel the stems. Use a small spoon to remove the fuzzy choke (the fibrous inside part). Discard everything but the cleaned hearts and tenderest part of the peeled stems. Cut each heart into quarters and submerge them in the acidulated water.

Heat oil in a pot on medium heat. Add shallots and cook for 2 to 3 minutes, or until softened. Add artichoke hearts, bay leaves and thyme. Stir in wine and stock. Season to taste with salt. Simmer for about 10 minutes, or until artichokes are soft. Remove from the heat and allow artichokes to cool in the liquid. Reserve. (If making ahead, leave artichokes in the liquid, cover and refrigerate. Will keep for a day.)

Herb Purée Remove and discard stems from basil, tarragon and parsley. Fill a large bowl with ice water. Bring a large pot of salted water to a boil on high heat. Add basil, tarragon, parsley and chives, then blanch for 30 seconds. Drain and immediately plunge into the ice water. Drain herbs and squeeze out the excess water from them. Place herbs in a blender on high speed with oil and stock, then process until smooth. Season with salt. Strain through a fine-mesh sieve and discard the solids.

Garnish Preheat the oven to 400°F. Roast pepper in a foil-lined baking pan for 15 to 20 minutes, rotating the pan every 2 to 3 minutes. Remove from the oven, cover and allow to rest until cool enough to handle. Remove and discard skin and seeds. Place in a container and cover with oil. Will keep in the refrigerator for several days. When you're ready to use it, cut pepper into ¼-inch dice.

Place shallots in a small pot on low heat and cover with oil. Cook on low heat for 15 minutes, or until tender. Remove from the heat and allow to cool.

Combine 2 Tbsp of the diced roasted red pepper and 2 Tbsp of the shallot confit with olives, preserved lemon, capers and roe.

Continued overleaf

Artichokes

4 cups water, room temperature
1 lemon, juice of
4 large artichokes
2 Tbsp olive oil
2 shallots, sliced into thin rings
2 bay leaves
2 sprigs thyme
½ cup dry white wine
1¼ cups vegetable stock

Herb Purée

1 bunch basil
1 bunch tarragon
1 bunch parsley
1 bunch chives
½ cup high-quality extra-virgin olive oil
½ cup vegetable stock

Garnish

1 red bell pepper
Olive oil as needed
2 shallots, in ⅛-inch dice
2 Tbsp diced (⅛ inch) Cerignola or other green olives
2 Tbsp diced (⅛ inch) preserved lemon (available in specialty food stores)
2 Tbsp small capers
2 Tbsp smoked steelhead roe or salmon roe

Swiss Chard

12 leaves Swiss chard

1 Tbsp unsalted butter

¾ cup + 2 Tbsp vegetable stock

Salmon

2 Tbsp grapeseed oil

4 fillets fresh wild spring salmon, each 5½ oz, skin on

2 Tbsp unsalted butter

Swiss Chard Cut off stems from chard leaves. Cut stems in julienne strips and leaves in a rough chiffonade (stack and roll leaves, then cut thinly across).

Melt butter in large pot on medium heat. Add chard stems and sauté, stirring, for 1 to 2 minutes, without browning. Add stock and deglaze the pan. Add salt to taste and simmer for about 10 minutes, or until most of the liquid has evaporated (stems should be tender). Add leaves and sauté together with stems for 4 to 5 minutes, or until leaves are tender. Keep warm.

Salmon Preheat the oven to 400°F. Heat oil in a large ovenproof frying pan on medium-high heat. Season salmon on both sides with salt to taste, then place skin-side down in the pan and sear for 2 minutes. Do not flip over fish. Roast in the oven for 3 to 4 minutes, or until medium done. Remove the pan from the oven and add butter, then baste fish with the melted butter for 2 to 3 minutes. Remove from the heat and allow salmon to rest for 2 minutes before serving.

To Serve Reheat artichokes in cooking liquid if already cooled, then drain just before serving. Place 1 Tbsp of herb purée in the bottom of each shallow warmed bowl. Arrange Swiss chard beside herb purée and top with artichoke hearts. Place salmon to overlap both the herb purée and artichokes, then top with a spoonful of the garnish.

Wine Averill Creek Vineyard Pinot Noir

Crispy Professor Albright Trout, Warm Dungeness Crab, Spot Prawn and Mushroom Salad
with Westbank Walnut Emulsion

Larry Albright, a retired professor from the Department of Biological Sciences at Simon Fraser University, raises these wholly sustainable rainbow trout on his freshwater fish farm in Langley. *Serves 6 to 8*

Walnut Emulsion Place egg yolks, salt, mustard and vinegar in a blender or food processor fitted with a metal chopping blade and run on low speed for 15 seconds. With the motor running on moderately high speed, slowly pour in vegetable oil in a thin stream. When the mixture begins to thicken, continue adding vegetable oil in a thin steady stream, alternating with water. Stop the motor and scrape the mixture down from the sides as needed. With the motor running, slowly pour in walnut oil in a thin stream. Season to taste with salt and pepper.

Crab, Prawn and Mushroom Salad Bring a pot of water to a boil on high heat, add spot prawns and blanch for 20 seconds. Drain, allow to cool and peel.

Heat oil in a heavy frying pan on medium-high heat. Add mushrooms and sauté for 1 minute. Add shallots, garlic and butter, then sauté, stirring constantly, for 30 seconds to 1 minute, or until shallots soften. Turn down the heat to medium-low, add wine and deglaze the pan. Continue simmering until the liquid is reduced by half. Add peeled prawns and crabmeat, then cook for 2 to 3 minutes, or until heated through. Stir in parsley and vinegar. Remove from the heat.

Trout Heat a large, seasoned cast-iron or a heavy non-stick frying pan on medium-high heat. Add oil. Season trout with salt and pepper. When oil is hot, add trout, skin-side down, and cook for about 2 minutes, or until skin is crisp. Add butter, then flip over fish and baste with butter for 30 seconds. Remove from the heat and season with a squeeze of lemon juice.

To Serve Smear walnut emulsion on each warmed plate and partially cover with warm crab, spot prawn and mushroom salad. Place a fillet of trout, skin-side up, on top of the salad.

Wine JoieFarm Wines Unoaked Chardonnay

Walnut Emulsion

2 egg yolks

Pinch of salt

1 Tbsp Dijon mustard

2 Tbsp white wine vinegar

2 cups vegetable oil

1 Tbsp water

¼ cup walnut oil

Crab, Prawn and Mushroom Salad

8 oz spot prawns

1 Tbsp grapeseed oil

1 lb mixed mushrooms (oyster, chanterelle, pine, morel, porcini, shiitake, portobello), in bite-size pieces

2 shallots, minced

4 cloves garlic, minced

2 Tbsp butter

¼ cup dry white wine

8 oz Dungeness crab leg meat

2 Tbsp chopped Italian flat-leaf parsley

3 tsp sherry vinegar

Trout

2 Tbsp grapeseed oil

6 to 8 fillets Professor Albright trout or rainbow trout

2 Tbsp butter

1 wedge lemon

Cured Baynes Sound Scallops

with Marinated Cucumber and Fennel, Tarragon Crème Fraîche

Tarragon Crème Fraîche
1 cup buttermilk
3 cups heavy whipping cream (36%)
½ cup chopped tarragon

Cured Scallops
½ orange, zest of
½ lemon, zest of
½ lime, zest of
½ cup salt
1 cup sugar
1 Tbsp finely ground black pepper
10 Baynes Sound scallops

Cucumber and Fennel
1 lemon, finely grated zest (use a microplane) and juice
1 tsp salt
1 Tbsp chopped tarragon
1 Tbsp sugar
1 bulb fennel, shaved on a mandoline
1 cucumber, shaved crosswise in rounds on a mandoline
2 Tbsp extra-virgin olive oil

Baynes Sound scallops, a local and sustainable product sourced off the east coast of Vancouver Island, are sweeter and meatier than scallops from the east coast of Canada. *Serves 6 to 8*

Tarragon Crème Fraîche Start making this at least 4 days before serving. Mix together buttermilk and cream in a bowl. Pour into a glass jar and cover the top with a double thickness of cheesecloth. Leave the jar in a warm spot in the kitchen for three days. (The crème fraîche will rise to the top and water will settle on the bottom.) Place the jar in the refrigerator for about 2 hours, or until the crème fraîche is firmly set.

Scoop out the crème fraîche and place on a double thickness of cheesecloth, then gather up the edges and tie the top closed. Hang overnight from a rack in the refrigerator over a bowl to catch the excess moisture.

The next day, discard the liquid in the bowl. Place the thickened crème fraîche in a bowl and fold in tarragon, then cover and refrigerate until needed. Will keep in the refrigerator for 1 week.

Cured Scallops Cure the scallops a day before serving. Combine zests of orange, lemon and lime with salt, sugar and pepper in a bowl. Add scallops and coat them well with this curing mixture. Cover the bowl and refrigerate for 10 hours.

Cucumber and Fennel Combine lemon zest and juice, salt, tarragon and sugar in a bowl. Add fennel and cucumber, then toss lightly. Drizzle with oil and allow to sit for 1 hour at room temperature before serving.

To Serve Rinse off the curing mixture from scallops with cold water and pat them dry. (Note that some of the citrus zest will adhere to scallops—leave it on.) Slice cured scallops crosswise into thin rounds and fan out on each chilled plate. Place a portion of marinated cucumber and fennel in the centre. Scoop up 2 Tbsp of the tarragon crème fraîche and shape into a quenelle; make six or eight, depending on how many you are serving, and place a quenelle on top of each salad.

Wine Howling Bluff Estate Winery Sauvignon Blanc

Smoked Cheddar Bison Burgers
with Roasted Garlic Mayonnaise

Mayonnaise
½ cup cloves garlic, peeled
1 tsp olive oil
1½ tsp lemon juice
¼ tsp kosher salt
1 cup mayonnaise

Jalapeño Ketchup
1 small jalapeño pepper
Vegetable oil
2 cups diced (1 inch) tomatoes
¼ cup brown sugar
¼ cup maple syrup
2 Tbsp cider vinegar
2 Tbsp malt vinegar
2 Tbsp soy sauce
1 stick cinnamon

Bison meat is leaner and significantly lower in cholesterol than beef, so your guests will forgive you should you get lavish with the roasted garlic mayonnaise. *Serves 8 (makes 24 mini burgers)*

Mayonnaise Preheat the oven to 350°F. Toss garlic with oil in a bowl, then spread out on a small rimmed baking sheet. Bake in the centre of the oven for about 15 minutes, or until golden brown on the outside and soft inside. Remove from the oven and allow to cool.

Place roasted garlic, lemon juice and salt in a blender, then purée. Set aside 1 Tbsp of the roasted garlic purée for the bison burgers.

Place mayonnaise in a bowl and whisk in ¼ cup of the roasted garlic purée. Cover and refrigerate. Will keep in the refrigerator for up to 2 weeks.

Jalapeño Ketchup Preheat the barbecue or oven broiler. Rub jalapeño with a little oil and place on a rimmed baking sheet. Place on the barbecue or under the broiler for 2 to 3 minutes, turning to char all sides. Remove from the oven, place in a bowl, cover and allow to cool. Remove and discard peel.

Place roasted jalapeño pepper and all of the remaining ingredients in a large pot on medium-low heat and simmer for about 1 hour, or until thick and dark red in colour. Remove and discard cinnamon. Purée in a blender or use a hand-held blender. Allow to cool, then refrigerate. Will keep for up to 2 weeks.

Bison Burgers Heat oil in a pot on medium-high heat. Add garlic, onion, celery and red pepper, then cook for 5 to 6 minutes, or until caramelization begins and vegetables are soft. Remove from the heat and allow to cool.

Place the vegetable mixture, ketchup, mustard, Worcestershire sauce, horseradish and eggs in a bowl and mix well. In a second bowl, combine bread crumbs, salt, pepper and Cajun spice. In a third bowl, thoroughly mix the wet vegetable mixture and the dry bread crumb mixture with ground bison meat. Make twenty-four meatballs and flatten them to fit the buns you are using.

Preheat a grill or ridged pan on the stovetop to medium-high. Grill burgers for about 5 minutes on each side, or until cooked through (165°F on a meat thermometer).

To Serve Cut mini-burger buns in half sideways. On the bottom half of each bun, spread jalapeño ketchup, then top with a cooked burger, a slice of cheese, 3 leaves of lettuce, some garlic mayonnaise and the top half of the bun.

Place three mini-burgers on each warmed plate or arrange all of them on a warmed platter. Garnish with mini dill pickles.

Wine Le Vieux Pin Époque or Apogée reds

Bison Burgers

1½ tsp oil

1 Tbsp roasted puréed garlic

½ cup diced (¼ inch) white onion

½ cup diced (¼ inch) celery

½ cup diced (¼ inch) red bell pepper

¼ cup ketchup

1 Tbsp + 1½ tsp Dijon mustard

1½ tsp Worcestershire sauce

1 Tbsp horseradish

3 eggs

2 cups fresh bread crumbs

1½ tsp salt

1½ tsp pepper

1 Tbsp + 1½ tsp Cajun spice

2½ lbs ground bison meat

24 mini-burger buns

¼ cup jalapeño ketchup

24 slices smoked cheddar cheese

72 leaves lettuce

¼ cup roasted garlic mayonnaise

Mini dill pickles for garnish

Chicken Orecchiette
with Double-smoked Bacon and Parmesan Sauce

Parmesan Sauce
½ stalk lemon grass, roughly chopped
1½ tsp chopped tarragon
1½ tsp thyme leaves
2 Tbsp unsalted butter
1 onion, chopped
2 Tbsp finely chopped garlic
1 cup arborio rice
1 cup dry white wine
2 Tbsp lemon juice
2 cups water
2 cups milk
4 cups whipping cream
5 oz Jersey Farm Parmesan cheese

Chicken Orecchiette
1¼ cups canola oil
8 half breasts chicken, boneless and skinless
8 quarts water
¼ cup kosher salt
5 cups orecchiette pasta
8 oz double-smoked bacon
¼ cup olive oil
2 Tbsp minced garlic
1 cup dry white wine
8 cups Parmesan sauce
Grated Parmesan cheese for garnish

A distant cousin of the restorative carbonara, this thick and creamy pasta is layered with smoky flavour. The "little ear" orecchiette are ideal for their sauce retention, but they can be replaced with any indented noodle such as farfalle or fusilli. *Serves 8*

Parmesan Sauce May be made 2 days ahead. Make a bouquet garni by placing lemon grass, tarragon and thyme in a piece of cheesecloth and tying it up.

Melt butter in a large pot on medium heat. Add onion and garlic, then sauté, stirring, for about 5 minutes, until translucent, without browning. Add rice, stirring until the grains are coated with butter. Add the bouquet garni. Stir in wine and lemon juice, then simmer for about 10 minutes, or until reduced by half. Stir in water, milk and cream. Bring to a boil, stirring often, then turn down the heat to low and simmer for about 20 minutes, or until rice starts to fall apart. Remove and discard the bouquet garni, squeezing its liquid into the pan. Stir in Parmesan cheese until it melts. Remove from the heat and allow to cool slightly.

Fill a bowl with ice water. Purée the cheese mixture in a blender, then pour into a storage container and place in the ice water to cool. Store, covered, in the refrigerator. Will keep in the refrigerator for 3 to 4 days. Makes about 12 cups. (You will need 8 cups of sauce for the pasta, so freeze the rest. Will keep in the freezer for 2 months.)

Chicken Orecchiette Preheat a grill, barbecue or a ridged stove-top pan to medium. Mix ½ cup of the canola oil with salt and pepper to taste in a small bowl. Lightly coat chicken with this seasoned oil and grill on each side for 7 to 8 minutes, or until juices run clear yellow. Remove from the grill and allow to cool. Pull the chicken meat into strips.

Bring water to a boil in a stockpot on high heat, together with kosher salt and half of the remaining canola oil. Add orecchiette pasta and cook, stirring often, for about 8 minutes, or until al dente. Drain and toss with the remaining canola oil. Spread out pasta on a rimmed baking sheet to cool.

Sauté bacon in a large pot on medium-high heat until nearly crisp. Remove the bacon from the pan, allow to cool and chop roughly. Pour out and discard bacon fat, then add olive oil and turn up the heat to medium-high. Add pulled chicken, bacon and garlic, then cook, stirring, until heated through. Add wine and deglaze the pan. Turn down the heat to medium-low, then stir in the Parmesan sauce. Bring to a simmer, stir in pasta and cook until pasta is hot and the sauce is thick and creamy. Season with salt and pepper to taste.

To Serve Ladle pasta into heated bowls and sprinkle with a generous amount of grated Parmesan cheese.

Wine Black Widow Winery Pinot Gris

Minestrone Verde
with Extra-Virgin Olive Oil

At Cibo, this soup comes and goes from the menu and morphs again and again to celebrate the best of what is in season. Feel free to make it using alternative ingredients. *Serves 4 to 6*

Bring a large pot of salted water to a boil on high heat. Add spinach and blanch for 2 to 3 minutes, or until tender. Use tongs to transfer spinach (keeping the water in the pot) to a plate and allow to cool, then chop roughly.

Bring the same pot of salted water to a boil on high heat. Add chard leaves and blanch for 4 to 5 minutes, or until tender. Use tongs to transfer chard (keeping the water in the pot) to a plate and allow to cool, then chop roughly.

Fill a bowl with ice water. Bring the same pot of salted water to a boil on high heat. Add fava beans and blanch for 15 seconds, then drain and plunge into the ice water. Allow to cool, then drain. Peel and discard the outside skins.

Heat olive oil in a heavy-bottomed pot on medium-low heat. Add onions, leeks, garlic and salt, then sauté, stirring occasionally, for about 30 minutes, or until totally soft and translucent. Add stock and bring to a boil, then turn down the heat to low and bring to a simmer. Add fava beans and peas, then cook for about 2 minutes, or until tender. Add spinach, chard and parsley, then cook for another few minutes, until heated through. Season to taste with salt and pepper.

To Serve Stir salami piccante (optional) into the soup. Ladle soup into warmed bowls, then garnish with freshly grated Parmesan cheese and a generous drizzle of extra-virgin olive oil.

Wine Sandhill Estate Vineyard Rosé

4 bunches large-leaf spinach, stems off

2 bunches rainbow chard, stalks off

1 cup shelled fava beans

2 Tbsp olive oil

2 large red onions, ¼-inch dice

2 large leeks, white and light green parts only, ¼-inch dice

4 cloves garlic, minced

Pinch of salt

4 cups chicken stock

1 cup shelled English peas

3 Tbsp chopped Italian flat-leaf parsley

3 Tbsp matchstick-size pieces salami piccante or pepperoni (optional)

Freshly grated Parmesan cheese for garnish

Extra-virgin olive oil for garnish

Dungeness Crab Tagliarini
with Chili, Garlic and Parsley

Tagliarini
4¼ cups Tipo 00 flour
or all-purpose flour
Pinch of salt
12 organic egg yolks
Semolina flour for dusting

Crab Sauce
6 Tbsp extra-virgin olive oil
plus extra for garnish
3 cloves garlic, finely chopped
2 Tbsp fennel seeds, crushed
1 large red chili, seeded,
finely chopped
12 oz fresh Dungeness crabmeat
1 lemon, cut into wedges
1 large bunch Italian flat-leaf
parsley, roughly chopped

The base of this simple pasta is similar to that Roman classic, *aglio e olio* (garlic and oil). The Dungeness crab, trapped off the province's coasts, thrives on the tickle of chili heat. Tagliarini is the narrowest of flat ribbon pastas. Instead of making it, you may substitute store-bought tagliatelli or fettuccine. *Serves 4 to 6*

Tagliarini Mix flour and salt in a large bowl. Make a well in the centre and add egg yolks. Use a fork to lightly beat eggs until smooth, then mix flour into beaten eggs little by little, until the mixture becomes sticky. Flour both of your hands, then knead the mixture until it is smooth and elastic. Wrap in plastic wrap and leave to rest for 30 minutes.

Roll out the dough on a lightly floured surface to a thickness of ½ inch. With the pasta machine at its widest setting, roll out the pasta dough, turning the handle with one hand and supporting the dough with the other as it comes through.

Change the pasta machine to its next setting (tighter) and roll the dough through again, dusting it with a little flour if needed. Repeat this process until you get to setting number 4 on the machine (you should now have a long, smooth, shiny length of dough).

Fold the dough sheet so that it is the width of the pasta machine. Start at the widest setting, number 1, and progress to the thinnest, number 6. Feed the dough through the machine, this time widthwise instead of lengthwise, until you get to a thickness of about ⅛ inch.

Cut the sheet into individual lengths of about 10 inches. Using the tagliarini (narrowest) cutter on the pasta machine, feed the dough through while supporting the pasta as it comes out. Dust with a little semolina and store on a tray lined with parchment paper until needed.

Crab Sauce Heat oil in a large heavy pot on medium heat. Add garlic and fennel seeds, then sauté for 2 to 3 minutes, or until garlic is golden. Add chili and crabmeat, stirring lightly to incorporate well. As soon as crabmeat is hot, remove the pot from the heat. Season with salt, pepper and lemon juice to taste. Keep warm (but not for long).

To Finish Tagliarini Bring a large pot of salted water to a boil on high heat. Add pasta and cook for 5 to 8 minutes, or until cooked through but not al dente, then drain. Stir the crab sauce into the pasta and add the parsley.

To Serve Ladle pasta onto warmed plates and garnish with a generous drizzle of extra-virgin olive oil.

Wine Tantalus Vineyards Old Vines Riesling

Moroccan Spiced Lamb Chop

with Cucumber, Olive and Sheep's Milk
Feta Salad, Yogurt-Garlic Dressing

With its myriad flavours gathered from around the Mediterranean, this summer dish balances an exotically spiced marinade with the accompanying coolness of yogurt, cucumber and feta. *Serves 8*

Pickled Red Onions Make this dish the day before serving. Combine sugar and vinegar in a pot on high heat and bring to a boil. Place red onions in a non-reactive bowl and then pour the hot sugar mixture over them. Allow onions to cool in the liquid completely, then cover and refrigerate. The pickled onions will be ready to use the next day. Will keep in the refrigerator for up to 4 weeks.

Confit Garlic Preheat the oven to 325°F. Place oil and garlic in an ovenproof dish, cover with aluminum foil and bake in the oven for 1 hour, or until garlic is soft. Remove from the oven and allow garlic to cool in the oil before using. Store garlic in the oil in a covered container in the refrigerator. Will keep in the refrigerator for up to 3 weeks.

Oregano Dressing Combine all of the ingredients in a blender or food processor and blend until emulsified. Refrigerate until needed. Will keep in the refrigerator for up to 3 weeks.

Yogurt-Garlic Dressing Place all of the ingredients in a bowl and mix until thoroughly blended. Refrigerate until needed. Will keep in the refrigerator for 2 days.

Continued overleaf

Pickled Red Onions
¾ cup sugar
1½ cups red wine vinegar
2 red onions, peeled, finely sliced

Confit Garlic
1 cup extra-virgin olive oil
1 cup peeled garlic cloves

Oregano Dressing
1 Tbsp Dijon mustard
⅓ cup canola oil
⅔ cup extra-virgin olive oil
1 tsp freshly ground black pepper
2 tsp salt
⅓ cup oregano leaves
2 Tbsp lemon juice
⅓ cup pickling liquid
from red onions
¼ cup confit garlic, drained

Yogurt-Garlic Dressing
1 cup yogurt
½ tsp salt
1 clove garlic, finely grated
2 Tbsp finely chopped
Italian flat-leaf parsley
2 Tbsp finely chopped chives

Salad

1 English cucumber, seeded, in ¼-inch dice

1 red bell pepper, seeded, cut into small diamonds

1 yellow bell pepper, seeded, cut into small diamonds

1 orange bell pepper, seeded, cut into small diamonds

½ cup Kalamata olives, halved and pitted

½ cup drained pickled red onion

1 cup crumbled sheep's milk feta cheese

16 cherry tomatoes, quartered

1 recipe oregano dressing

Spiced Lamb Chop

1 tsp black peppercorns

½ tsp coriander seeds

½ tsp fennel seeds

2 pieces star anise

8 double-bone lamb chops, each 6 to 7 oz, frenched

2 Tbsp extra-virgin olive oil

1 clove garlic, finely grated

Salad Just before serving, combine all of the ingredients—except for the oregano dressing—in a bowl. Add enough oregano dressing to coat the vegetables and toss gently.

Spiced Lamb Chop Toast peppercorns, coriander seeds, fennel seeds and star anise in a small frying pan on low heat for 3 to 4 minutes, or until aromatic. Remove from the heat and allow to cool completely, then grind in a spice grinder or a clean coffee grinder.

Rub lamb chops with oil, garlic and ground spices, coating all sides of the meat but keeping the frenched bones clean. Allow to marinate at room temperature for 1 hour before grilling.

Preheat a grill or a ridged pan on the stovetop to medium-high. Grill lamb for 5 to 8 minutes on each side, or until medium-rare. Remove from the grill and allow to rest for 5 minutes before serving.

To Serve Place a lamb chop on each plate, accompanied by cucumber, olive and feta salad. Garnish with pickled red onions. Pass a bowl of yogurt-garlic dressing on the side.

Wine Osoyoos Larose Estate Winery Le Grand Vin (a blend of the five Bordeaux varietals)

Savoury Mushroom Tart
with Aged White Cheddar, Oloroso Sherry and Balsamic Glaze

You can use store-bought balsamic glaze or use a ten-year-old traditional balsamic vinegar, which is thick enough as is. Or simmer ½ cup balsamic vinegar on low heat until it is reduced to a light syrup. A small green salad makes a good accompaniment to this dish. *Serves 8*

Pastry Pulse together flour and butter in a food processor fitted with a steel blade, or until the mixture resembles coarse crumbs. Stir in salt. With the motor running, slowly drizzle in water just until the dough holds together when pinched between your fingers (you may not need all the water.)

Place the dough on a lightly floured surface, knead gently and gather into a ball. Flatten, wrap in plastic wrap and refrigerate for a minimum of 1 hour.

Roll out the dough on a lightly floured surface to a thickness of ⅛ inch. Use a fork to pierce the dough all over. Use a 3½- or 4-inch diameter cookie cutter to cut out eight circles and use them to line eight 2½-inch diameter tart pans. Refrigerate for 30 minutes.

Preheat the oven to 350°F. Line the cold tart shells with aluminum foil, placed directly on the surface of the pastry. Bake in the oven for 10 minutes, then remove the foil and return the tart shells to the oven for 5 to 7 minutes, or until they become golden (watch closely as every oven is different).

Mushroom and Cheddar Filling Heat oil in a large frying pan on medium-high heat. Add mushrooms and cook for about 10 minutes, or until caramelized and juices have evaporated. Season with salt. Add sherry and butter, then continue cooking until butter is melted. Remove from the heat.

To Assemble Carefully remove tart shells from the pans. Line each tart shell with enough cheddar cheese to cover the bottom, spoon hot mushroom filling over the cheese and top with two slices of cheese. (The mushroom filling is hot enough to melt the cheese.)

To Serve Place each tart on a warmed plate and garnish with a drizzle of balsamic glaze.

Wine Poplar Grove Winery Benchmark Merlot or Cabernet Franc

Pastry
2 cups all-purpose flour

1⅓ cups unsalted butter

Pinch of salt

⅔ cup or less, cold water

Mushroom and Cheddar Filling
¼ cup canola oil

4 lbs mixed mushrooms (crimini, baby oyster, shimeji), chopped

½ cup oloroso sherry

½ cup unsalted butter

8 oz five-year-old aged cheddar cheese, thinly sliced

Balsamic glaze for garnish

Berkshire Pork Duo
Tenderloin and Crispy Belly with Sauerkraut, Horseradish Coleslaw and Mustard Pork Jus

Pork belly, being a fattier cut, requires a few hours of cooking to develop the best flavour and will remain moist in spite of the long cooking time. The lean tenderloin, on the other hand, cooks very quickly. *Serves 4*

Confit Pork Belly Start making this recipe the morning of the day before serving. In the morning, combine thyme, bay leaf, rosemary, salt, shallots, garlic and pepper in a bowl. Rub the spice mixture all over pork. Wrap well with plastic wrap, then refrigerate and allow to marinate for at least 5 hours.

In the afternoon, preheat the oven to 350°F. Rinse off the spice rub from pork belly, pat dry and place in an ovenproof casserole dish. Melt duck fat in a pot on low heat and slowly pour it over pork. Place in the oven and when the fat starts to barely simmer, turn down the heat to 250°F, cover the casserole dish with aluminum foil and cook pork for about 3 hours, or until tender.

Remove from the oven and allow pork to cool at room temperature in the fat. Remove pork belly from fat, wrap in plastic and chill in the refrigerator for 2 hours. Set aside 1 Tbsp of the duck fat for the horseradish sauerkraut. (Strain the rest of the fat through a sieve, pour into containers and freeze for future use. Will keep in the freezer for up to 3 months.)

Mustard Pork Jus Preheat the oven to 500°F. Place pork trimmings and bones in a single layer on a rimmed baking sheet. Brown in the oven, turning often, for about 30 minutes.

Transfer bones and scraps to a large stockpot. Reserve the roasting pan and pan juices. Cover the bones and scraps with cold water by 1 inch. Bring the contents of the stockpot to a boil on high heat, skimming off and discarding any scum that rises to the surface. Turn down the heat to low, bring the stock to a simmer and keep it there.

Meanwhile, place the reserved roasting pan on the stovetop on high heat and add onion, celery, carrot, garlic, leek, bouquet garni and spice sachet. Cook, stirring, for about 5 minutes, or until vegetables are lightly browned. Add the vegetable mixture to the stock in the stockpot and simmer for 1½ to 2 hours, until all the flavour is extracted from the bones. Remove from the heat, strain through a fine-mesh sieve into a bowl and discard solids. Allow to cool, then refrigerate the pork jus until needed.

Continued overleaf

Confit Pork Belly
2 sprigs thyme
1 bay leaf
1 sprig rosemary
1 lb kosher salt
2 shallots, minced
1 clove garlic, minced
1 Tbsp freshly ground black pepper
2 lbs pork belly, whole
5 cups duck fat

Mustard Pork Jus
1 lb pork trimmings and bones, in 3- to 4-inch pieces
1 onion, in 1-inch dice
1 rib celery, in 1-inch dice
1 carrot, in 1-inch dice
½ head garlic, cut crosswise, unpeeled
½ leek, in 1-inch dice
1 *bouquet garni:* 1 sprig parsley, 1 sprig thyme, 1 sprig sage and 1 bay leaf in a cheesecloth tied with butcher's twine
1 *spice sachet:* 4 white peppercorns, 4 coriander seeds and 1 whole clove in a cheesecloth tied with butcher's twine
1 Tbsp butter
1 Tbsp flour
2 Tbsp whole grain mustard

Horseradish Sauerkraut

4 cups good-quality sauerkraut

1 Tbsp duck fat

½ onion, finely sliced

8-oz piece smoked slab bacon

½ carrot

1 *bouquet garni:*
1 sprig parsley, 1 sprig thyme
and 1 bay leaf, wrapped
in an outer piece of leek (white)
in a cheesecloth tied with
butcher's twine

1 *spice sachet:*
2 whole cloves, ½ tsp juniper,
½ tsp white peppercorns
and ½ tsp coriander seeds
in a cheesecloth tied with
butcher's twine

1 cup Alsatian Riesling wine

8 cups white pork stock
or chicken stock

Horseradish Coleslaw

1 Tbsp sea salt

1 tsp sherry vinegar

1 head green cabbage,
in ¼-inch thick slices

2 carrots, julienned

2 Tbsp mayonnaise

2 Tbsp whole grain mustard

1 Tbsp freshly grated horseradish

Splash of apple cider

Horseradish Sauerkraut Rinse sauerkraut lightly and drain well. Melt duck fat in a large pot on medium heat. Add onion to the duck fat and cook, stirring, for about 10 minutes, or until tender and translucent. Add sauerkraut, bacon, carrot, bouquet garni and spice sachet. Turn up the heat to high, stir in wine and cook for about 5 minutes, or until the wine is absorbed. Add stock, turn down the heat to low and simmer slowly for 1 hour, or until sauerkraut is tender and most of the stock has been absorbed. Remove from the heat. Remove and discard bacon, bouquet garni and spice sachet. Allow to cool, then refrigerate until needed.

Horseradish Coleslaw Combine salt, vinegar, cabbage and carrots in a bowl, then allow to rest for 20 minutes. Drain and discard the liquid. Squeeze cabbage and carrots until very dry and discard liquid. Place cabbage and carrots in a bowl and add mayonnaise, mustard, horseradish, apple cider and freshly ground black pepper; mix until well combined. Taste and adjust seasoning if necessary. Refrigerate until needed.

Garnish Place potatoes in a pot with cold water to cover and bring to a boil on high heat. Turn down the heat to medium-low and simmer for 15 to 20 minutes, or until tender. Remove from the heat.

Place turnips in another pot with cold water to cover and bring to a boil on high heat. Turn down the heat to medium-low and simmer 10 to 12 minutes, or until tender. Remove from the heat.

Drain potatoes and turnips, cover and set aside.

Pork Tenderloin When you are ready to serve the pork duo, preheat the oven to 400°F (use the same oven for tenderloins and to finish confit pork belly, see below).

Tie each of the tenderloins with butcher's twine to hold its shape. Season well with kosher salt and black pepper. Heat oil in an oven-proof pan on medium-high heat and brown tenderloins on all sides, for about 5 minutes total. Add thyme and garlic, then roast in the oven for 10 to 15 minutes, or until done (135°F on a meat thermometer). Remove from the oven, transfer to a cutting board and cover loosely with foil. Allow to rest for 10 minutes before carving.

To Finish Mustard Pork Jus While the tenderloins are roasting, place butter and flour in a large pot on low heat. Cook, stirring, until well combined. Gradually whisk in the strained pork jus and bring to a simmer. Turn up the heat to medium-low and reduce slowly for about 30 minutes, or until the pork jus reaches a rich, saucelike consistency. Stir in mustard and keep warm on the lowest heat; do not allow the mixture to boil.

To Finish Confit Pork Belly Cut the confit pork belly into 2-inch cubes. Place a large, ovenproof, non-stick frying pan on medium-high heat. Add pork belly, skin-side down, and sear until crisp. Continue to sauté for 1 to 2 minutes, then place in the oven for 8 to 10 minutes, or until heated through. Remove from the oven and keep warm.

To Finish Garnish Melt butter in a pot on medium heat. Add potatoes and turnips, then cook, basting with butter, for 2 to 3 minutes, or until heated through. Season to taste with salt and pepper, then sprinkle with parsley.

To Serve Heat horseradish sauerkraut in a small frying pan on medium heat. Carve pork tenderloins and confit pork belly into slices ½-inch thick.

Place potatoes and turnips down the centre of each warmed plate. Place warm sauerkraut on one side and cold horseradish coleslaw on the other side. Arrange 3 slices of pork tenderloin on top of the sauerkraut and 3 slices of the crispy pork belly on top of the coleslaw. Garnish each serving of pork belly with ½ tsp of mustard and drizzle mustard pork jus around the plate.

Wine Mission Hill Family Estate Winery Perpetua Chardonnay

Garnish
1 lb fingerling potatoes
1 lb baby turnips
2 Tbsp butter
3 sprigs parsley, leaves only
2 tsp whole grain mustard
for garnish

Pork Tenderloin
2 pork tenderloins, about 1 lb each
1 Tbsp vegetable oil
1 sprig thyme
1 clove garlic, crushed

Spring Pea Soup

with Hand-peeled Shrimp and Tarragon Crème Fraîche

Shelling a bowl full of peas is a lot of work, but this soup makes the effort worthwhile. *Serves 6 to 8*

Melt butter in a large pot on medium heat. Add onions, leeks and celery, then cook, stirring, for about 8 minutes, or until vegetables are soft and translucent. Add stock and bring to a boil. Add star anise, thyme, tarragon and peppercorns. Turn down the heat to low and simmer for 30 minutes. Gently stir in peas, remove from the heat and allow the soup to sit for about 2 minutes. Take out a few of the peas and reserve for garnish. Remove and discard star anise, thyme, tarragon and peppercorns.

Fill a bowl with ice. Purée the soup well in a blender, pass through a fine-mesh sieve and discard the solids. Transfer the soup to a bowl and place it on the ice to chill, stirring frequently. Stir whipping cream into the chilled soup, then taste and season with salt, if necessary.

Gently toss together shrimp, lemon juice and chives in a small bowl. In another small bowl, mix together crème fraîche and tarragon.

To Serve Divide the soup among chilled bowls. Garnish with a few peas and the shrimp mixture. Place ½ tsp of the tarragon crème fraîche on top of the shrimp and dot it with salmon roe. Finish with a drizzle of extra-virgin olive oil and a few grinds of freshly cracked white peppercorns.

Wine Summerhill Pyramid Winery Cipes Brut Sparkling Wine or Blue Mountain Vineyard & Cellars Brut Sparkling Wine

½ cup unsalted butter

½ cup diced (⅛ inch) white onions

½ cup diced (⅛ inch) leeks

¼ cup finely chopped celery

4 cups vegetable stock

3 pieces star anise

3 sprigs thyme

3 sprigs tarragon

10 white peppercorns

2 lbs fresh English peas, shelled

2 cups whipping cream

Kosher salt to taste

4 oz hand-peeled fresh shrimp

1 tsp fresh lemon juice

1 tsp finely chopped chives

1 Tbsp crème fraîche, store-bought

1 tsp chopped tarragon

2 tsp salmon roe

2 Tbsp extra-virgin olive oil

Freshly cracked white peppercorns

White Chocolate and Passion Fruit Mousse
with Sesame Tuiles

Sesame Tuiles
¼ cup unsalted butter
2 Tbsp liquid honey
½ cup icing sugar
½ cup all-purpose flour
1 egg white
1 Tbsp mixed black and white sesame seeds

Mousse
2 cups whipping cream
12 oz white chocolate, finely chopped
⅓ cup passion fruit purée (available at specialty food stores)
⅔ cup egg whites (5 to 6 eggs)
¼ cup sugar

Serve these delicate, tasty sesame tuiles with the white chocolate passion fruit mousse or on their own with a cup of tea. *Serves 8 or more*

Sesame Tuiles Cream together butter and honey in the bowl of a stand mixer fitted with a paddle or in a bowl and using a hand-held mixer, until light and fluffy. Add sugar, flour and egg white, then mix on low speed until incorporated. Increase speed to high and mix for 2 minutes. Refrigerate the batter for 1 hour before using it.

Preheat the oven to 325°F. Line baking sheets with parchment paper or silicone baking liners. Spread the batter thinly (⅛ inch) into desired shapes, using a stencil or freehand. Leave 3 inches between the tuiles. Sprinkle with sesame seeds. Bake in the oven for 10 to 12 minutes, until light golden brown. Leave tuiles in the pan and set the pan on a rack to allow them to cool, then carefully remove tuiles, using a metal spatula. Store in an airtight container; will keep for up to 3 days.

Mousse Whip cream until stiff and refrigerate until needed.

Melt 4 oz of the white chocolate in a bowl placed over a pot of hot but not simmering water (a bain-marie). Since white chocolate burns at a lower temperature than milk chocolate or dark chocolate, the temperature of the water should not exceed 110°F. Stir passion fruit purée into the melted chocolate, remove from the heat and set aside.

Melt the remaining 8 oz of white chocolate in a clean bain-marie, then set aside to cool slightly.

Place egg whites in the bowl of a stand mixer fitted with a whisk or use a hand-held mixer and whip them until soft peaks form. Gradually add sugar and continue whipping until the peaks are stiff and glossy.

Vigorously whisk a third of the egg whites into the slightly cooled 8 oz of melted chocolate until well blended. Fold in the remaining egg whites, followed by the whipped cream, until the mousse is smooth. Swirl in the passion fruit and chocolate mixture. Do not overmix.

To Serve Place mousse in parfait glasses or similar glass dessert dishes that hold about ⅓ to ½ cup and refrigerate for at least 1 hour, or until ready to serve. (Will keep in the refrigerator for 1 day.) Arrange sesame tuiles on a serving plate on the side.

Wine Tinhorn Creek Vineyards Kerner Icewine

Carnaroli Risotto
on Heirloom Tomato and Basil Salad

Carnaroli rice is native to the Novara and Vercelli regions of northern Italy. The grains are slightly larger than the more common arborio rice, which means they absorb more liquid, resulting in a slightly creamier risotto. *Serves 6*

Tomato and Basil Salad Slice tomatoes ¼-inch thick and divide among six plates. Season with salt and pepper, then set aside.

Carnaroli Risotto Heat water in a medium pot on medium heat and keep it at a gentle simmer, turning down the heat if necessary.

Heat oil in a large heavy-bottomed pot on medium-high heat. Add onion and garlic, then sauté, stirring, for about 5 minutes, or until onion is translucent. Season well with salt and pepper. Stir in rice and cook for another 4 minutes, or until the grains are well coated with oil. Add wine and 1 cup of the simmering water, stirring constantly until the rice absorbs the liquid. Gradually add the remaining water, about ½ cup at a time, so rice is always covered in liquid. Keep stirring. (It should take about 18 minutes for the rice to be perfectly cooked. Taste it at various intervals near the end. You may need a little more or a little less water, depending on the age of the rice.) When all the liquid is absorbed and rice is al dente, stir in butter and Parmesan. Stir vigorously to emulsify everything together. Season if necessary.

To Serve Divide risotto evenly on top of plated tomatoes, leaving at least one-third of the colourful tomatoes exposed. Place a few basil leaves around each plate and garnish with a drizzle of balsamic vinegar (optional).

Wine Desert Hills Estate Winery Gamay

Tomato and Basil Salad

6 large heirloom tomatoes (different colours if possible)

½ cup basil leaves

3 Tbsp traditional balsamic vinegar from Modena, Italy, or Venturi-Schulze (optional)

Carnaroli Risotto

4 cups water

2 Tbsp extra-virgin olive oil

½ medium onion, minced

1 clove garlic, minced

½ cup carnaroli rice

¼ cup dry white wine

2 Tbsp butter

¼ cup grated Parmesan cheese

Dry-aged Rib-eye Steak
with Morels, Nugget Potatoes and Gentleman's Butter

The prime beef used for this recipe was dry-aged for 40 days. To find steaks that have been aged past the standard three weeks, try to develop a good relationship with a local butcher. *Serves 6*

Gentleman's Butter Make this the day before serving. Mix together all of the ingredients in a small bowl. Spread a piece of plastic wrap, 12 inches long, on a work surface. Place the butter mixture along one of the long sides, 2 inches from the edge, and roll into a log. Twist the ends tightly to close. Refrigerate for a day before using.

Before serving, slice the gentleman's butter into twelve rounds, 1-inch thick, and remove the plastic wrap. Keep cold.

Morels and Potatoes Melt butter in a large frying pan on medium-high heat. When the butter foam subsides, add morels and thyme, then cook for 5 minutes, or until mushrooms begin to soften. Stir in onion and garlic, then cook for about 5 minutes, or until onion starts to brown. Add potatoes and cook for about 5 minutes, or until heated through. Season to taste with salt and pepper. Keep hot until steaks are cooked.

Rib-Eye Steak Heat oil in two large frying pans (to accommodate steaks without crowding them) on high heat. Season steaks with salt and pepper on both sides. When the pan is hot, add steaks, garlic and thyme. Cook steaks for about 2 minutes on each side for medium-rare, then remove from the heat. Discard garlic and thyme stems.

To Serve Place each steak on a warmed dinner plate, then top with two pats of gentleman's butter and allow to rest for 2 to 3 minutes before serving. Arrange morels and potatoes on the side.

Wine Morning Bay Vineyard & Estate Winery Merlot

Gentleman's Butter
1 cup butter, room temperature
1 Tbsp diced (⅛ inch) shallot
1 Tbsp rendered bone marrow or bacon fat
1 Tbsp chopped parsley
1 tsp sliced tarragon
2 Tbsp smooth Dijon mustard
1 tsp sherry vinegar
Pinch of salt
1 tsp freshly ground extra-bold Tellicherry pepper
1 lemon, zest of
1 tsp brandy

Morels and Potatoes
3 Tbsp butter
6 cups fresh morels
2 sprigs thyme, leaves only
1 cup minced onion
2 cloves garlic, minced
4 cups nugget potatoes, cooked and quartered

Rib-Eye Steak
4 Tbsp canola oil
6 prime beef, 40-day dry-aged rib-eye steaks, each 8 to 12 oz, 1½-inches thick
4 cloves garlic, skin on but cracked
4 sprigs thyme

Melon Almond Gazpacho

with Dungeness Crab Salad and Basil Oil

Basil Oil

1 cup canola oil

2 cups basil leaves,
stems removed

Pinch of salt

Gazpacho

1 tsp olive oil

1 onion, sliced

½ cup raw almonds

2 slices white bread

1 medium honeydew melon,
peeled and seeded

2 English cucumbers,
peeled and seeded

¾ cup verjus

6 Tbsp sherry vinegar

½ cup extra-virgin olive oil

8 cherry tomatoes,
halved, for garnish

The summer flavours of this refreshing and uncomplicated soup are amplified by that of the fresh local Dungeness crab. Look for the verjus at gourmet specialty shops. *Serves 6*

Basil Oil Freeze canola oil for at least 2 hours before starting this recipe. The basil oil must be made at least 2½ hours before serving.

Fill a bowl with ice water. Bring a pot of salted water to a boil on high heat, blanch basil leaves for 5 seconds, drain and plunge into ice water. When cool, drain and squeeze basil to remove as much moisture as possible. Place in a blender with the ice-cold canola oil and salt, then purée on high speed for 1 minute (do not overblend or the basil will turn colour). Strain the basil oil through a coffee filter. Will keep in the refrigerator for 1 week or in the freezer for 6 months.

Gazpacho Heat olive oil in a frying pan on medium-low heat. Add onion and sauté, stirring, for about 10 minutes, or until translucent (turn down the heat if necessary to prevent browning). Remove from the heat and allow to cool.

Place almonds in a dry pot on medium heat. Gently toast almonds, stirring often, for 6 to 8 minutes. Turn down the heat to medium-low or low, add ¾ cup water and simmer for 20 minutes to extract the almond flavour. Remove from the heat and transfer the pot's contents to a bowl. Use a hand-held blender to process almonds and their cooking water as smoothly as possible, then strain through a fine-mesh sieve, discarding the solids. Return the almond purée to the pot on medium-low heat and simmer until reduced by about half.

Soak bread in 1¼ cups water. Once bread is completely soaked, squeeze it gently and discard water.

Cut melon and cucumber roughly into 1-inch cubes. In a blender on high speed, process onion, almond purée, bread, melon, cucumber, verjus, vinegar and extra-virgin oil until smooth. Season to taste with salt. Strain through a fine-mesh sieve, pressing with a ladle to extract all possible liquid. Discard the solids. Chill the gazpacho in the refrigerator for 3 to 4 hours (the flavour improves as it chills).

Crab Salad Fill a bowl with ice water. Bring a large pot of salted water to a boil on high heat. Drop in crab and cook for 8 minutes, then plunge into the bowl of ice water. Drain, remove all the meat from crab and place in a bowl. Gently toss crabmeat with oil and lemon juice. Season with salt and pepper to taste.

Use a mandoline to slice cucumber lengthwise into six pieces. Divide crab salad into six portions and roll a slice of cucumber around each portion.

To Serve Place a crab salad roll in each chilled soup bowl, then carefully pour gazpacho around it and drizzle with basil oil. Garnish with halved cherry tomatoes and assorted fresh herbs.

Wine Nk'Mip Cellars Pinot Blanc

Crab Salad

1 live Dungeness crab (1 lb)
or ½ lb fresh crabmeat

1 Tbsp olive oil

½ lemon, juice of

1 English cucumber

Assorted herbs or greens
(basil, cilantro, micro greens,
edible flowers) for garnish

Organic Confit Pork Belly

with Apricot Purée, Red Quinoa,
Shiitake Mushrooms, Plums and Chocolate Mint

The organic pork comes from Qualicum Beach's Sloping Hill Farm on Vancouver Island. It is prized by B.C. chefs for its high percentage of intramuscular fat, darker colour, exquisite marbling and superior taste. *Serves 6*

Pork Belly Start making this 2 days before serving. Chop half of the garlic in a food processor. Add bay leaves, thyme, juniper berries, peppercorns, Guinea pepper and sugar. Pulse for 30 seconds and slowly add rock salt until well incorporated. Do not overblend as the salt should be coarse for curing.

Rub salt mixture all over pork belly, place in a non-reactive pan, cover and cure for 12 hours or overnight in the refrigerator.

Preheat the oven to 225°F. Wash the salt mixture off pork and pat dry with paper towels. Place pork in a roasting pan. Melt duck fat in a pot on low heat and pour over pork. Add the remaining garlic cloves. Roast pork in the oven for 4 hours, or until fork-tender. Remove from the oven and allow meat to cool in the fat for 2 hours. Remove meat from the fat and refrigerate until chilled. Reserve 1 Tbsp of duck fat to use later to finish the pork. (Melt duck fat, strain through a fine-mesh sieve, pour into clean jars and freeze for your next batch of confit or use some of it to cook potatoes. Will keep in the freezer for up to 3 months.)

Quinoa Place quinoa and water in a pot on medium heat and bring to a boil. Turn down the heat to low and simmer gently for 10 to 15 minutes, or until the white germ separates from the seed. Cover, remove from the heat and let stand for 5 minutes. Remove lid, drain and allow to cool.

Heat butter in a small frying pan on medium heat. Add plums and sauté for 1 minute.

Place lardons and mushrooms in another frying pan on medium-high heat, then sauté for about 5 minutes, or until lardons are brown. Stir in cooked quinoa, then season with salt and pepper. Fold in cooked plums and chocolate mint. Keep warm. (May be made a day ahead and reheated before serving.)

Continued overleaf

Pork Belly

2 heads garlic, separated into cloves, peeled

4 bay leaves

1 Tbsp thyme leaves

1 Tbsp juniper berries

1 Tbsp black peppercorns

1 tsp Guinea pepper (also known as Grains of Paradise)

½ cup sugar

2 cups rock salt

¼ slab of organic pork belly, about 2 lbs

12 cups of rendered duck fat or peanut oil or lard

Quinoa

1 cup red quinoa

8 cups water

1 tsp butter

4 plums (any variety of red plum), halved and pitted

7 oz bacon lardons

8 shiitake mushrooms, sliced, discard stems

4 sprigs chocolate mint or peppermint or spicy globe basil

Apricot Purée
1 to 2 tsp sugar, to taste
10 apricots
1 vanilla bean

Chocolate Sauce
1 cup demi-glace
1¾ oz dark chocolate, chopped
1 Tbsp sherry vinegar

Sorrel
1 bunch sorrel or
micro greens
1 tsp olive oil

Apricot Purée Bring a pot of water and sugar to taste to a boil on high heat. Add apricots and poach for 10 minutes, then remove using a slotted spoon. Reserve the cooking liquid and the pot.

Peel apricots, then remove and discard the pits. Purée poached apricots with some of the cooking liquid in a blender until smooth. Cut vanilla bean lengthwise down the centre and scrape out the seeds. Add vanilla seeds to puréed apricots and mix well. Discard vanilla pod (or rinse, dry, wrap and refrigerate to use again as a flavouring agent).

Return the apricot purée to the remaining cooking liquid in the pot on low heat and cook for about 10 minutes, or until reduced by a third, to concentrate the apricot flavour. Keep warm. (May be made a day ahead and reheated before serving.)

Chocolate Sauce Place demi-glace in a small pot on medium heat and simmer for 5 to 8 minutes, or until reduced by about half. Add dark chocolate, stirring until it melts, then add vinegar. Season with salt and pepper to taste. Keep warm.

Sorrel Place sorrel in a bowl and toss with oil.

To Serve Cut pork into six pieces. Heat the 1 Tbsp of reserved duck fat in a frying pan on medium heat. Add pork pieces, skin-side down, and cook for about 4 minutes, or until skin is crisp, then quickly sear the flesh sides for 1 to 2 minutes on each side. Remove from the heat. Dress each warmed plate with sorrel and apricot purée. Place a piece of crispy pork belly on top and drizzle with chocolate sauce.

Wine Fairview Cellars Madcap Red (predominantly Merlot with some Cabernet)

Bruschetta Sampler

Bruschetta

18 slices ciabatta bread, ½-inch thick

4 to 6 Tbsp olive oil

1 to 1½ tsp Maldon sea salt

3 cloves garlic, peeled

Tomato Topping

6 organic heirloom tomatoes

3 shallots, finely diced

2 sprigs basil, thinly sliced

1 tsp lemon juice

3 Tbsp extra-virgin olive oil, plus extra for garnish

Sea salt to taste

Cracked black pepper to taste

6 Tbsp grated pecorino cheese

Garlic in Oil

8 cloves garlic, peeled

1 cup extra-virgin olive oil

1 sprig thyme

½ tsp sea salt

Bruschetta is grilled bread, rubbed with garlic and drizzled with olive oil. A coarse, crusty bread such as ciabatta from a good Italian bakery is a good base for a variety of tasty toppings. *Makes 18 slices*

Bruschetta   Preheat the oven to 325°F. Arrange ciabatta slices in a single layer on a baking sheet. Drizzle with oil and season with cracked Maldon sea salt. Toast slices in the oven on each side for 3 to 4 minutes, or until golden brown but not dried out. Remove from the oven and rub each slice on one side with a garlic clove.

Tomato Topping   Core tomatoes, cut into 1-inch cubes and place in a bowl. Add shallots, basil, lemon juice and oil. Season to taste with sea salt and cracked black pepper. Divide tomato mixture evenly as a topping among six slices of the bruschetta. Garnish with pecorino cheese and a drizzle of extra-virgin olive oil.

Garlic in Oil   Preheat the oven to 350°F. Bring a small pot of salted water on high heat to a boil. Add garlic, blanch for 30 seconds, drain and dry on a paper towel. Place garlic, oil, thyme and sea salt in a small ovenproof pan and cover with foil. Bake in the oven for 30 minutes. Remove from the oven carefully (the oil will be very hot) and place the pan on a rack to cool.

You will use all the garlic cloves for the octopus and cannellini bean topping, but you will not use the oil the garlic was cooked in. The garlic-infused oil will keep in the refrigerator for 1 week; use it for salad dressings or to cook with.

Octopus and Cannellini Bean Topping Place octopus, wine corks, vinegar, water and salt in a large pot on medium-high heat and bring to a simmer. Turn down the heat, if necessary, to keep it at a simmer. Cook until the legs of the octopus pull away from the body, which could take 1 hour or more. When a sharp-bladed knife enters octopus easily, it is ready. Remove from the heat. Clean off and discard the skin, then pat octopus dry with paper towels.

Preheat a grill or a stovetop ridged grill pan on high. Brush the grill surface with a little oil. Season octopus with salt and grill for 3 to 4 minutes on each side, or until slightly crisp. Remove from the grill and slice thinly on the bias. Place octopus slices in a bowl and toss with lemon juice and 3 Tbsp of extra-virgin olive oil.

Remove garlic cloves from their oil and add to octopus. Add beans, sun-dried tomato, red onion, lemon and lime zest, parsley and the remaining 2 Tbsp of extra-virgin olive oil, then toss together gently. Season to taste with salt and use as a topping for six slices of the bruschetta.

Lamb Sausage Topping Preheat the oven to 375°F. Heat olive oil a large frying pan on medium heat. Add onions and cook, stirring occasionally, for 25 to 30 minutes, or until caramelized. Stir in lamb sausage meat and sauté for 10 to 15 minutes, or until fully cooked. Add mushrooms and cook for 1 minute. Spoon the mixture on the remaining six slices of the bruschetta and sprinkle with goat cheese. Crack 1 quail egg on top of each serving. Place in the oven for 3 minutes. Remove from the oven and garnish with frisée and extra-virgin olive oil.

To Serve Arrange the different bruschettas on a warmed serving platter.

Wine Recline Ridge Vineyards & Winery Siegerrebe

Octopus and Cannellini Bean Topping

2 lb B.C. octopus

2 wine corks

¼ cup red wine vinegar

8 cups water

1 tsp coarse salt

2 Tbsp lemon juice

5 Tbsp extra-virgin olive oil

1 recipe garlic in oil

1 cup drained and rinsed canned cannellini beans

1 sun-dried tomato, sliced

½ red onion, thinly sliced

1 lemon, zest of

1 lime, zest of

3 sprigs Italian flat-leaf parsley, chopped

Lamb Sausage Topping

2 Tbsp olive oil

2 white onions, thinly sliced

4 lamb merguez sausages, casings removed

8 oz chanterelle mushrooms, cut in half if very large

3 oz Okanagan goat cheese, crumbled

6 quail eggs

½ cup frisée lettuce (pale green variety), torn, for garnish

1 Tbsp extra-virgin olive oil for garnish

B.C. Honey Mussels
with Thyme and Gruyère Frites

Frites

Vegetable oil for deep-frying

1 russet potato, peeled,
cut like french fries

2 sprigs thyme, leaves only,
chopped

2 Tbsp grated Gruyère cheese

Honey Mussels

1 lb B.C. Honey Mussels

2 oz bacon lardons,
in ¼-inch cubes

2 cloves garlic, chopped

1 shallot, thinly sliced

2 Tbsp Pernod

⅓ cup heavy whipping
cream (36%)

5 Tbsp chicken stock

1 sprig basil, chopped

1 sprig parsley, chopped

The Honey Mussel is a wholly sustainable bivalve farmed on British Columbia's coasts. High in protein but low in cholesterol and calories, they are plump, juicy and deliciously sweet. This dish is a variation on the traditional *moules frites* (mussels with fries) of southern France. *Serves 1*

Frites Place oil in a deep fryer to the marked line or half-fill a tall-sided heavy pot on the stovetop and heat to 300°F. Add potato and blanch for 4 minutes. Remove fries using a slotted spoon, drain on paper towels, allow to cool and refrigerate for 1 hour. Keep the oil in the deep fryer or pot, as you will be deep-frying the frites again.

Honey Mussels Wash mussels well under cold running water, then remove and discard beards. Tap the shells of any mussels that are open; if they do not close, discard them.

Heat a frying pan on medium-high heat, add bacon and cook for 3 to 4 minutes, or until crisp. Add garlic and shallot, then cook for about 3 minutes, or until shallot is translucent. Add mussels and toss gently. Add Pernod and deglaze the pan. Stir in cream, then stir in stock and simmer for about 8 minutes, or until reduced by half. Discard any mussels that have not opened during cooking.

To Serve Heat oil in a deep fryer or a tall-sided heavy pot on the stovetop to 400°F. Finish cooking the frites just before serving by deep-frying for 3 to 4 minutes, or until golden brown and crisp. Drain on paper towels, place in a warmed serving bowl and gently toss with thyme, Gruyère and salt to taste.

Place mussels in another warmed serving bowl and garnish with basil and parsley. Season to taste with sea salt.

Wine Quinta Ferreira Estate Winery Unoaked Chardonnay

Vodka and Beet–cured Hamachi
with Horseradish Cream

Hamachi

3 large red beets, 12 to 15 oz total weight

1 cup kosher salt

½ cup sugar

½ cup vodka

1 fillet hamachi, about 1 lb, trimmed

Olive oil to brush on hamachi when serving

Horseradish Cream

1-inch piece of horseradish, finely grated

1 cup heavy whipping cream (36%)

Chive Oil

¼ cup chopped chives

¼ cup olive oil

Garnishes

½ cup beet juice (reserved from the curing liquid)

8 baby red beets

8 baby yellow beets

Olive oil as needed

Sherry vinegar to taste

2 oz caviar

4 red radishes, thinly sliced

Baby watercress

This dish is delicious served with fresh, crispy, pumpernickel toast. *Serves 8*

Hamachi Peel beets and chop roughly. Juice beets, using either a vegetable juicer or by puréeing them in a blender with ¼ cup water. Strain the juice through a fine-mesh sieve and discard solids. Set aside ½ cup of the beet juice for a garnish. Combine the remaining beet juice with salt, sugar and vodka in a flat dish. Add hamachi and coat with the curing liquid, then cover and marinate in the refrigerator for 40 minutes.

Remove the hamachi from the curing liquid, rinse and pat dry. Discard the curing liquid. Slice the fillet against the grain into ¼-inch thick pieces and reserve, covered, in the refrigerator.

Horseradish Cream Combine horseradish and cream in a small pot on medium-high heat, then bring to a simmer for 1½ minutes. Remove from the heat, cover and allow to rest at room temperature for 20 minutes. Strain through a fine-mesh sieve and discard the horseradish. Chill the infused cream in the refrigerator. Once chilled, season the cream to taste with salt and pepper. When ready to serve, whip cream to stiff peaks.

Chive Oil Fill a bowl with ice. Place chives and oil in a blender and purée to make a smooth paste. Transfer the paste to a small frying pan on high heat and simmer for 1 to 2 minutes, until the bubbles begin to subside. Strain through a fine-mesh sieve lined with a coffee filter into a small bowl and chill the chive oil immediately over the ice. Discard chives.

Garnishes Heat beet juice in a small pot on medium-high heat and simmer for 3 to 4 minutes, until reduced by two-thirds. Reserve in the refrigerator.

The remaining ingredients are for optional garnishes. Place red and yellow beets in separate pots, cover each with cold water and stir in 1 tsp salt. Bring both pots to a boil on high heat, then turn down the heat to low and simmer beets for 8 to 10 minutes, until tender. Drain beets and, while they are still slightly warm, peel away the skin, using your fingers. Refrigerate, keeping the coloured beets separate. When ready to serve, cut beets in half and season each batch of beets with oil, vinegar, salt and pepper to taste.

To Serve Lay slices of hamachi in the centre of each chilled plate and brush lightly with olive oil. Garnish each plate with a spoonful of horseradish cream. Drizzle each plate with a bit of the reduced beet juice and chive oil. Optional garnishes per serving include two or three pieces each of yellow and red baby beets, 1½ tsp of caviar, a few radish slices and a bit of baby watercress.

Wine Road 13 Vineyards Old Vines Chenin Blanc

Late Summer Vegetable Lasagna

A totally raw, vegetarian lasagna can taste really good, thanks to the bounty of late summer vegetables. *Serves 6*

Zucchini Noodles Slice zucchini thinly lengthwise, using a knife or a mandoline. Individual lasagnas will each require 4 to 8 slices of zucchini, depending on the size of zucchini; for six servings, prepare 24 to 48 slices.

In a flat, non-reactive pan 9 × 13 inches, lay out slices of zucchini in a layer to cover the bottom. Drizzle with 1 Tbsp vinegar and 1 Tbsp oil, then sprinkle with salt and pepper. Repeat until you have used up all the zucchini. Cover and leave at room temperature for a few hours. (For extra flavour, place the marinated zucchini in a dehydrator or grill, though then the dish will no longer be raw.) Refrigerate until needed.

Spiced Walnuts Place carrots, red pepper and tomatoes in a food processor and pulse. Add walnuts and pulse again until everything is all minced together. Transfer to a bowl.

Place chili powder, cumin seeds, fennel seeds and sea salt in a spice mill or clean coffee grinder, then grind into powder. Stir the spice powder, vinegar and oil into the walnut mixture. Refrigerate until needed.

Marinara Sauce Soak sun-dried tomatoes in water to cover for 30 to 40 minutes, or until soft. Drain and discard soaking water. Place sun-dried tomatoes, spring water, dates, garlic, tomatoes, vinegar, salt, paprika (optional), black pepper and cayenne pepper (optional) in a blender and process at high speed. If your blender is struggling, you may need to add a touch more water. Stir in oregano, then refrigerate until needed.

Continued overleaf

Zucchini Noodles

4 to 5 medium zucchini

1 Tbsp apple cider vinegar for each layer

1 Tbsp extra-virgin olive oil for each layer

Spiced Walnuts

2 cups chopped carrots

1 cup chopped red bell pepper

1 cup chopped tomatoes

3 cups walnuts

2 tsp chili powder

2 tsp cumin seeds

2 tsp fennel seeds

2 tsp Celtic sea salt or fleur de sel

2 Tbsp apple cider vinegar

3 Tbsp olive oil

Marinara Sauce

2 cups sun-dried tomatoes

2 cups bottled spring water

5 large Medjool dates, pitted

2 medium cloves garlic, peeled

1 cup chopped vine-ripened tomatoes

6 Tbsp apple cider vinegar

½ tsp salt

Pinch of smoked paprika (optional)

¼ tsp cracked black pepper

Pinch of cayenne pepper (optional)

2 Tbsp roughly chopped oregano leaves

Parsley Salsa

1 cup chopped parsley

1 cup chopped red bell pepper

½ cup olive oil

½ tsp Celtic sea salt or fleur de sel

Filling

1 Tbsp finely chopped oregano

2 Tbsp finely chopped parsley

3 to 4 ripe tomatoes, cut into a total of 18 slices

6 calendulas or other edible flowers (optional)

Parsley Salsa Place all of the ingredients in a food processor and pulse until well mixed and slightly chunky.

To Serve Remove all of the lasagna ingredients from the refrigerator and bring to room temperature.

Lay one large or two small overlapping zucchini strips on each plate. Sprinkle with oregano and parsley. Spread about 3 Tbsp of the spiced walnut mixture evenly along the centre of the zucchini, leaving a little space on each side. Arrange another layer of zucchini on top, then spoon the marinara sauce along the centre, leaving a little space on each side. Next, add a layer of three slices of tomato. Repeat the layering process, minus tomato slices, until all the zucchini has been used. Place a dollop of parsley salsa on top. Season with freshly ground black pepper and garnish with a calendula (optional).

Wine JoieFarm Wines Rosé

Candied Bull Kelp Salad

This dish is cutting edge—nutrition meets flavour explosion—and could be called "Juxtaposition" or "The Real Surf and Turf." It is very simple to prepare and delicious. The spirulina powder is sold in health food stores, and the sun-dried bull kelp is sold at specialty grocers. *Serves 8*

Candied Bull Kelp Place oil and spirulina in a bowl and mix with a fork. Drizzle in honey, whisking continuously. In another bowl, mix together basil and bull kelp, then add to the spirulina mixture. Stir together well, then pack into a glass jar. Use immediately or refrigerate. Will keep for up to a month.

Salad Peel and cut cucumber into 8 thin lengthwise slices. Cut cherry tomatoes in half.

To Serve Make two small bird's nests, one of each kind of sprout, on each chilled plate. Balance a cucumber slice on top of the nests. Place another pair of sprout nests on top of the cucumber, then arrange some candied bull kelp on top. Garnish with cherry tomatoes, cut-side up.

Wine Noble Ridge Vineyard & Winery Pinot Grigio

Candied Bull Kelp

1 cup organic extra-virgin olive oil

3 Tbsp spirulina powder

3 Tbsp Babe's wildflower honey

1 cup basil leaves, torn by hand

1 package (60 g) sun-dried bull kelp, crumbled

Salad

1 local English cucumber

16 ripe home-grown cherry tomatoes

7 oz alfalfa sprouts

7 oz sunflower sprouts

B.C. Albacore Tuna Ceviche
with Avocado Purée, Pickled Red Onions and Chili Lime Chips

Pickled Red Onions
2 cups red wine vinegar

1 cup berry sugar

1 red onion, sliced on a mandoline

Chili Lime Chips
Canola oil for deep-frying

20 frozen won ton wrappers, thawed

Chili powder to taste

1 tsp lime powder or 2 tsp grated fresh or dried lime zest

Avocado Purée
4 semi-ripe avocados

4 limes, juice of

¼ tsp kosher salt

Tuna Ceviche
1 lb B.C. albacore tuna loin

4 limes

½ tsp Mexican chili powder

½ tsp sambal oelek

1⅔ cups extra-virgin olive oil

3 tsp chopped cilantro, plus extra for garnish

2 green onions, julienned, for garnish

Chili powder for garnish

This ceviche is an excellent dish to serve as an appetizer or to share with friends in a dinner of assorted small plates. *Serves 8*

Pickled Red Onions Place vinegar in a pot on medium-high heat and bring to a boil. Stir in sugar until dissolved, then add red onion. Remove from the heat and allow to stand for half an hour, then refrigerate until needed.

Chili Lime Chips Place oil in a deep fryer to the marked line or half-fill a tall-sided heavy pot on the stovetop and heat to 320°F. Cut won ton wrappers diagonally into quarters, making triangular shapes. Deep-fry won ton pieces for 20 to 30 seconds, or until crispy and golden. Use a slotted spoon to remove them from the oil. Season with chili powder, salt to taste and lime powder.

Avocado Purée Peel and remove stones from avocados, then place the flesh in a blender. Add lime juice and salt, then purée until smooth. (This makes more than is needed; use leftover purée as a dip, on a sandwich or in a salad.)

Tuna Ceviche Cut tuna loin into ¼-inch cubes and place in a stainless steel bowl on ice. Cover and refrigerate until needed.

To make citrus marinade, cut limes in half and juice through a fine-mesh sieve into a small bowl and discard solids. Stir in chili powder, sambal oelek and oil.

To Serve Pour citrus marinade over tuna, tossing gently to coat well. Add 3 tsp cilantro and toss gently. Season to taste with kosher salt.

Spoon 1 Tbsp of the avocado purée onto each chilled plate and smear it with an offset palette knife. Place ¼ cup of the tuna into a 2-inch ring mould beside the avocado purée on each plate, pressing down gently so tuna will hold its shape, then remove the mould. Garnish tuna with cilantro, green onion and a pinch of chili powder. Place a small mound of well-drained pickled red onion on the side.

Divide won ton chips among individual side bowls or arrange some on each plate.

Wine Sumac Ridge Estate Winery Meritage White

Westham Island Farm Strawberries

with Venturi-Schulze Balsamic Zabaglione, Agassiz Hazelnut Oil

Peppered
Balsamic Syrup

⅓ cup sugar

2 cups balsamic vinegar

1 Tbsp cracked black pepper

Strawberries

1 lb Westham Island strawberries

3 Tbsp sugar

Balsamic Zabaglione

6 egg yolks

⅓ cup berry sugar

2 Tbsp Venturi-Schulze
balsamic vinegar

¾ cup Marsala wine

Agassiz hazelnut oil
for garnish

Local strawberries are worth the wait for their lusciousness and can be celebrated with this elegant yet simple preparation.
Serves 6

Peppered Balsamic Syrup Dissolve sugar in vinegar in a pot on low heat. Stir in black pepper and simmer until syrupy. Remove from the heat and allow to cool.

Strawberries Quarter or halve strawberries to keep pieces uniform in size. Place in a bowl and toss gently with sugar.

Balsamic Zabaglione Half-fill a pot with water on high heat and bring to a boil, then turn down the heat to medium and keep at a simmer, turning down heat if necessary. Place egg yolks, sugar and vinegar in a stainless steel bowl over the simmering water (a bain-marie), whisking constantly until yolks triple in volume and are light and fluffy. Stir in wine and remove the bowl from the heat.

To Serve Preheat the oven broiler, with the rack 4 to 6 inches below the element. Set ovenproof serving plates on a large rimmed baking sheet. Place strawberries in 3-inch heat-resistant ring moulds on each plate and spoon the zabaglione mixture over them. Place the baking sheet under the broiler and caramelize for 1 to 2 minutes, or until tops are golden brown. Remove from the broiler.

Remove the hot ring moulds (be careful not to burn yourself) and drizzle each serving with hazelnut oil. Drizzle some peppered balsamic syrup around the edge of each plate.

Wine Venturi-Schulze Vineyards Brandenburg No. 3 or Vista d'Oro Vineyard Fortified Walnut Wine

Leek and Prosciutto Terrine
with Warm Leek and Endive Salad, Maple-smoked Bacon and Hazelnut Dressing

BliS Elixer Vinegar is extra-old fine solera sherry vinegar aged a second time in rare, eighteen-year-old, maple-cured, single-bourbon casks. If it is not available, use aged balsamic vinegar. *Serves 4*

Terrine Soak leeks in a bowl of warm water to remove any sand or dirt. Place leeks, hazelnut oil, bay leaf and thyme in a pot large enough to hold leeks in a single layer. Cook, covered, on medium-low heat, for 30 to 40 minutes, or until leeks are tender but not brown, turning down the heat if necessary. Drain and allow to cool.

On a 12-inch piece of parchment paper, lay out prosciutto slices, overlapping them slightly, to form a rectangle. Lay cooked leeks on top of the prosciutto and roll up, using the paper to help make a snug roll. Wrap in plastic wrap. Chill in the refrigerator for about 2 hours before using.

Sauce Gribiche Whisk oil and mustard together in a bowl until emulsified, then fold in all of the remaining ingredients.

Hazelnut Vinaigrette Whisk vinegar, mustard and oil together in a bowl. Stir in hazelnuts.

Bacon and Hazelnut Dressing Whisk together sauce gribiche, vinegar and hazelnut vinaigrette in a bowl. Just before serving, add the bacon.

Leek and Endive Salad Toss lettuce, radicchio and endives in a bowl with enough bacon and hazelnut dressing to coat the greens lightly.

To Serve Cut the prosciutto and leek parcel into four portions and remove the plastic wrap. Heat vegetable oil in a frying pan on medium heat, then sear the four parcels for 1 to 2 minutes on each side, just until warm.

Arrange the leek and endive salad on individual plates, then garnish with croutons. Top with a slice of warm leek and prosciutto terrine. Drizzle with bacon and hazelnut dressing.

Wine Auxerrois from Little Straw Vineyards Old Vines or Lang Vineyards

Terrine
4 large leeks, white and pale green parts only

6 Tbsp + 1½ tsp hazelnut oil

1 bay leaf

4 sprigs thyme

7 oz prosciutto di Parma, thinly sliced

2 tsp vegetable oil

Sauce Gribiche
⅓ cup canola oil

½ tsp Dijon mustard

1 egg, hard-boiled, chopped

1 tsp tarragon vinegar

1 Tbsp + 1 tsp chopped gherkins

1 Tbsp + 1 tsp chopped capers

1 tsp chopped parsley

1 tsp chopped chives

1 tsp chopped chervil

½ tsp julienned tarragon

Pinch of salt and pepper

Hazelnut Vinaigrette
1 Tbsp cider vinegar

½ tsp Dijon mustard

½ cup hazelnut oil

3 Tbsp chopped toasted hazelnuts

Bacon and Hazelnut Dressing
1 Tbsp + 1 tsp sauce gribiche

2 tsp BliS Elixer Vinegar

¼ cup + 2 Tbsp hazelnut vinaigrette

¼ cup maple-smoked bacon lardons, cooked until crisp

Leek and Endive Salad
1 cup (not packed) frisée lettuce

2 leaves red radicchio, julienned

2 yellow endives, julienned

3 Tbsp diced (¼ inch) brioche croutons

Sesame-crusted Frog Legs
with Chili Barbecue Sauce and Wakame Salad

Cucumber Pickle

⅓ English cucumber, thinly sliced

⅓ cup Japanese rice vinegar

2 Tbsp sugar

Wakame Salad

2 cups (not packed) wakame salad (from an Asian food market)

1 small carrot, julienned

½ daikon, julienned

¼ large Fuji or Granny Smith apple, julienned

¼ cup drained cucumber pickle

Chili Barbecue Sauce

6 Tbsp mirin (Japanese sweet cooking rice wine)

2 Tbsp + 2 tsp soy sauce

½ tsp Tabasco sauce

⅞ cup canola oil

½ tsp sesame oil

2 tsp ketchup

1 Tbsp + 2 tsp grated ginger

2 Tbsp tomato paste

1½ tsp sambal oelek

Frog Legs

24 frog legs

1 Tbsp vegetable oil

1 tsp toasted black or white sesame seeds

1 recipe chili barbecue sauce, warm

1 tsp micro herbs for garnish

4 cherry tomatoes, cut into quarters

The sesame-flavoured, Asian-inspired chili barbecue sauce in this recipe is very versatile. Try using it with various kinds of meat, with or without the sesame oil. The wakame salad is sold at Asian food markets. *Serves 4*

Cucumber Pickle Place cucumber slices in a heatproof bowl. Mix vinegar and sugar together in a pot on high heat, bring to a boil and pour over cucumber. Allow to cool, then refrigerate.

Wakame Salad Place wakame salad in a large bowl. Add carrot, daikon, apple and cucumber pickle. Toss together gently and set aside.

Chili Barbecue Sauce Combine all of the ingredients in a pot on medium-high heat and bring to a boil. Remove from the heat. Makes 1 cup.

Frog Legs Bone the frog legs in chicken drumette style (remove the thigh bones). Heat oil in a large frying pan on medium-high heat. Sprinkle frog legs with sesame seeds and fry for about 5 minutes, or until golden and cooked. Transfer frog legs to a bowl and toss gently with warm chili barbecue sauce.

To Serve Divide wakame salad among serving plates and arrange frog legs on top. Garnish with micro herbs and cherry tomatoes.

Wine Laughing Stock Vineyards Chardonnay

The
Culinary
Vanguard

HERE IS OUR culinary vanguard, the pioneering chefs

who trained a new generation and sparked the ascension

of Vancouver as an internationally celebrated food city. It is they

who first reached out to local suppliers to lay down the founda-

tions of Vancouver's culinary new world. Having come from diverse

backgrounds and having been schooled in different traditions, they

provided a wide perspective while convincing us of the quality

and diversity of our local provender.

The efforts of these chefs, our mentors and icons, have laid a

solid foundation upon which our newest stars—many of whom

toiled under their expert tutelage—continue to build upon today in

top-tier restaurants of their own. Together, they hold in common

a deep appreciation of the providential bounty of British Columbia

and a determination to celebrate it by sharing it with the world.

But first, they wish to share it with you.

Vila Gracinda Chocolate and Quebec Maple Syrup Cone

with Whiskey, Sorrento Nut and Vanilla Milkshake

This is a whimsical dessert duo to please the child in all of us—an ice cream cone and a milkshake—with a difference! You can serve them together or separately. We make our own chocolate cones from Vila Gracinda chocolate, but you can use ready-made chocolate or waffle cones. *Makes 4 filled cones and 4 milkshakes*

Chantilly Whisk together cream and sugar until firm peaks form. Cover and refrigerate until needed.

Maple Ganache Place milk and cream in a stainless steel pot on medium heat and bring just to the boiling point (you will see bubbles around the edge and steam rising from the centre). Remove from the heat.

Whisk together egg yolks and sugar in a small bowl. Very slowly, whisking constantly, add the hot milk mixture to the egg mixture. Next, pour the mixture back into the pot and place on low heat. Cook, stirring constantly, for about 5 minutes, until the mixture thickens enough to coat the back of a spoon.

Place grated chocolate in a bowl and pour the hot mixture over it. Mix everything together with a hand-held blender. Cover and refrigerate until needed.

Maple Salted Butter Fill a bowl with ice water. Place glucose and maple syrup in a pot on medium-high heat and bring to a boil for 2 minutes. Turn down the heat to medium and stir in cream, ¼ cup at a time, then boil the mixture for 5 to 10 minutes, until it reaches 220°F on a candy thermometer. Remove from the heat, pour the maple syrup mixture into a bowl and place on the ice water until it goes down to 86°F or room temperature.

Cream the butter in a blender for 2 minutes, then gradually add the cooled maple syrup mixture until emulsified (it should have the consistency of mayonnaise). Keep at room temperature until needed.

Continued overleaf

4 ready-made Michel Cuizel
dark chocolate cones
or waffle cones

Chantilly

½ cup whipping cream

2 Tbsp maple sugar

Maple Ganache

½ cup milk

½ cup whipping cream

2 egg yolks (or to measure ¼ cup)

3 Tbsp maple sugar

¼ cup grated Vila Gracinda
chocolate or other
high-quality dark chocolate

Chocolate pearls
for garnish (optional)

Maple Salted Butter

1 Tbsp + 2 tsp glucose
or corn syrup

¼ cup + 1 tsp maple syrup

¾ cup whipping cream

1 Tbsp + 1 tsp butter,
room temperature

Milkshake

1¼ cups vanilla ice cream

½ cup whipping cream

½ cup milk

½ cup Sortilège Maple Syrup and Whisky Liqueur or other whisky

1 Tbsp of Sorrento Nut Paste (walnut paste)

Yuzu juice or lemon juice (enough to coat the rim of each glass)

Maple sugar (enough to coat the rim of each glass)

Milkshake Place ice cream, cream, milk, Sortilège and nut paste in a blender, then process until everything is well combined. Add a little more milk if the mixture is too thick.

To Serve For the ice cream cones, place the maple salted butter, ganache and chantilly into three different piping bags. Into each cone, pipe the maple salted butter (saving a bit for garnish, optional), then the ganache, then the chantilly. Garnish the chantilly with a dab of maple salted butter (optional) and chocolate pearls (optional).

For the milkshake, place yuzu juice and sugar on separate plates. Dip the rim of each serving glass in yuzu juice, then in sugar, then pour in the milkshake.

Wine The maple syrup wines from Lang Vineyards, or Vidal Icewine from either Prospect Winery The Lost Bars or Inniskillin Okanagan

Prosciutto-wrapped Albacore Tuna
with Creamy Polenta and Tomato Olive Vinaigrette

The tomato vinaigrette may be made up to 2 days ahead of serving. Do not, however, add the fresh herbs until you are ready to serve, as the acid in the vinegar will turn them brown. Adding fresh watercress as a garnish (optional) lightens up the dish as well. *Serves 4*

Tuna Wrap a slice of prosciutto around each piece of tuna. (Do not add salt or pepper, as the prosciutto provides the seasoning.) Cover and refrigerate until needed.

Vinaigrette Fill a bowl with ice water. Bring a pot of water to a boil on high heat. Add tomatoes and blanch for 20 to 30 seconds. Drain, then plunge tomatoes into the ice water. Drain, pat dry and remove the skin, which should rub off easily. Cut tomatoes into quarters, then remove and discard seeds. Roughly dice the tomatoes (the French term for this is concassé).

Place tomatoes in a bowl. Add olives, capers, shallot, vinegar and oil, then toss lightly. Cover and refrigerate until needed.

Polenta Heat oil in a heavy-bottomed pot on medium-high heat. Add shallots and garlic, then cook, stirring, for about 5 minutes, until softened and translucent. Slowly stir in milk and stock. Once the liquid is simmering, slowly whisk in cornmeal. Once all cornmeal is added, turn down the heat to low and cook for 30 minutes, stirring occasionally.

Just before serving, stir in butter until incorporated, then stir in Parmesan. Season to taste with salt and pepper. Keep warm.

To Finish Tuna Bring prosciutto-wrapped tuna to room temperature. Heat oil in a frying pan on high heat. Add tuna and sear for about 1½ minutes on each side (tuna should be served rare to medium-rare).

To Serve Slice each piece of prosciutto-wrapped tuna diagonally into three pieces. To the tomato vinaigrette, add parsley, chives and watercress (optional), then toss lightly.

Divide polenta among warmed plates, then arrange three slices of wrapped tuna on top of each serving. Garnish each plate with a few spoonfuls of tomato vinaigrette.

Wine Domaine de Chaberton Estates Winery Canoe Cove Chardonnay

Tuna

4 slices prosciutto

4 pieces albacore tuna, each 4½ oz

1 Tbsp grapeseed oil

Vinaigrette

4 vine-ripened tomatoes

5 Tbsp pitted, sliced Niçoise olives

1 Tbsp capers, rinsed, chopped

1 shallot, minced

2 Tbsp aged balsamic vinegar

3 Tbsp + 1 tsp extra-virgin olive oil

2 Tbsp finely chopped parsley

1 Tbsp chopped chives

½ cup watercress, stems removed (optional)

Polenta

1 Tbsp grapeseed oil

3 shallots, chopped

1 clove garlic, chopped

6 cups milk

6 cups vegetable stock

2½ cups cornmeal

1 cup unsalted butter, room temperature

¾ cup grated Parmesan cheese (5 oz)

Fanny Bay Oyster Soup

3 Tbsp butter

2 shallots, chopped

1 quart (2 dozen) freshly shucked
beach oysters and their juice

3 cups dry white wine

2 cups whipping cream

½ tsp lemon zest

2 Tbsp finely chopped parsley

2 Tbsp good olive oil

Fanny Bay on Vancouver Island has become famous all across
North America for the delicious beach oysters harvested around
there, but you can use any large oysters in season. Serve this soup
with slices of warm crusty bread or, better still, freshly made garlic
croutons. *Serves 6*

Melt butter in a small stockpot on medium heat. Add shallots, cover
and cook for about 5 minutes, or until soft. Add shucked oysters
and their juice, then gently stir in wine and cream. Add lemon zest,
then season soup with salt and pepper to taste. Turn up the heat to
medium-high and bring to a boil, then turn down the heat to low,
cover and simmer for 8 to 10 minutes, or until oysters are cooked.
Remove from the heat, allow to cool slightly, then transfer to a
blender or food processor and purée until smooth. Strain the soup
through a fine-mesh sieve and discard the solids.

To Serve Place the soup in a pot on medium heat to reheat it, then
stir in parsley. Ladle soup into warmed bowls and drizzle with olive
oil. If you like, sprinkle with garlic croutons.

Wine Larch Hills Winery Ortega

Oven-braised Venison Ragout

with Juniper Berries and Fresh Herbs—A Christmas Recipe

1½ lbs venison stew meat, in 1-inch cubes

1 cup flour

½ cup vegetable oil

1 onion, chopped

1 carrot, in ¼-inch dice

½ cup diced (¼ inch) celery root

½ cup diced (¼ inch) fennel bulb

1 cup sliced shiitake mushrooms or chanterelles

4 cloves garlic, sliced

½ cup tomato paste

½ bottle (375 mL) dry red wine

4 cups beef or chicken stock, heated

¼ cup whole juniper berries

1 tsp chopped rosemary

1 tsp chopped thyme

1 bay leaf

Pinch of allspice

Pinch of paprika

Pinch of Chinese five-spice powder

2 Tbsp honey

¼ cup single malt Scotch or a good blended Scotch whiskey

2 tangerines, juice of

12 oz sausage meat, in twelve 1-oz balls

¼ cup chopped parsley for garnish

Since venison is a lean meat, the addition of meatballs is a good way to add juiciness and another texture to the dish. Instead of venison, you can use bison, beef, lamb or pork. *Serves 6*

Season venison with salt and freshly ground black pepper, then toss in flour, coating all sides. Heat oil in a large frying pan on medium-high heat. Add venison and sear until all sides are browned and sealed, then transfer to a large lidded casserole dish. Keep the frying pan and its juices.

Preheat the oven to 375°F. Place the frying pan back on the burner on medium-high heat. Add onion, carrot, celery root, fennel bulb, mushrooms and garlic, then cover and cook for 5 to 10 minutes, or until vegetables soften. Stir in tomato paste, wine and heated stock. Add juniper berries, rosemary, thyme, bay leaf, allspice, paprika, Chinese five-spice and honey. Season to taste with salt and pepper. Stir mixture well, then pour over the venison in the casserole dish. Cover the casserole and bake in the oven for 1½ hours.

Remove the casserole from the oven. Gently stir whiskey and tangerine juice into the ragout, then dot the top with meatballs. Re-cover the casserole and return to the oven to cook for 20 minutes.

To Serve Ladle the ragout into warmed soup plates and garnish with parsley.

Wine Hillside Estate Winery Mosaic red blend or Robin Ridge Winery Merlot

Cured B.C. Sardines
with Pickled Vegetable and Jellyfish Salad

Fresh sardines are excellent prepared in numerous ways. This cured version is set off perfectly by the crunch in the salad provided by the jellyfish. You can find the prepared jellyfish in the refrigerated section of Asian grocers. *Serves 6*

Cured Sardines Start making this a day before serving. Fillet sardines, rinse in cold water and pat dry. Lay fish, skin-side down, in a single layer in a non-reactive container. Combine sugar, salt and dill seeds in a bowl, then sprinkle this dry brine mixture over fish. Cover and cure in the refrigerator for 5 hours.

Remove fish from the dry brine and soak in cold water for 2 hours, changing the water every 20 to 30 minutes.

To make the pickling liquid, combine water, vinegar, maple syrup, shallots, carrot, bay leaves, allspice and peppercorns in a pot on high heat and bring to a boil. Remove from the heat and allow to cool.

Place the cured sardines in a single layer in a non-reactive container and pour the cooled pickling mixture over them. Cover and refrigerate overnight or for up to 3 days.

Salad Remove sardines from the pickling liquid, pat dry and reserve. Remove and discard bay leaves, allspice and peppercorns from the pickling liquid.

Remove shallots and carrot from the pickling liquid and toss them with jellyfish, radishes and green onions in a bowl. Adjust the seasoning of the salad with a bit of the remaining pickling liquid.

To Serve Arrange the pickled vegetable and jellyfish salad on each chilled plate and place a cured sardine on the side, along with a slice of rye bread and some crème fraîche.

Wine Glenugie Winery Christina Sparkling Pinot Noir

Cured Sardines

6 whole B.C. sardines, each 6½ oz

½ cup sugar

½ cup kosher salt

2 tsp dill seeds, ground

2 cups water

1 cup Japanese seasoned rice vinegar

¼ cup maple syrup

½ cup very thinly sliced shallots

¼ cup thinly sliced carrot rounds

3 bay leaves

3 allspice berries

10 peppercorns

Salad

1 recipe cured sardines

½ cup prepared jellyfish (discard sauce sold with the jellyfish)

½ cup sliced radishes

¼ cup sliced green onions

6 slices rye bread

½ cup crème fraîche

Roast B.C. Bison Tenderloin
with Bison Goulash

Bison is becoming an increasingly popular meat choice for many reasons: it is naturally raised, rich, tender, sweetly flavourful, lean and low fat. Serve this dish with Pemberton mashed potatoes and North Arm Farm root vegetables. *Serves 6 to 8*

Bison Goulash Start this recipe the day before serving. Heat oil in a heavy pot on medium-high heat. Add meat and brown. Add onions, carrots, celery and garlic, then cook, stirring, for about 10 minutes, or until translucent. Add paprika and cook, stirring, for 1 minute. Add stock and stir well, then turn down the heat to medium-low, cover, and simmer for 1 to 2 hours, or until meat is tender and the sauce is reduced. Remove from the heat and cool quickly, then cover and refrigerate the goulash to mature overnight.

Bison Tenderloin Start this recipe the day before serving. Place bison on a rack set on a rimmed baking sheet and leave, uncovered, in the refrigerator overnight. The meat will dehydrate slightly and intensify the flavour. Remove meat from the refrigerator 1 hour before cooking.

Preheat the oven to 275°F. Season meat with salt and pepper to taste. Fill the bottom of a roasting pan with water. Set meat on a rack and place it in the roasting pan (the drippings from the meat will fall into the water, which helps with clean up). Roast meat in the oven for about 15 minutes, or until medium-rare (145°F to 150°F on a meat thermometer). Remove from the oven and allow to rest for 10 minutes before carving.

To Serve While the bison tenderloin is resting, reheat the goulash in a pot on medium heat for about for 5 minutes, or until heated through. Carve bison tenderloin into thin slices and arrange on heated plates with mashed potatoes, roasted root vegetables and the goulash as sauce.

Wine Domaine de Chaberton Estate Winery Canoe Cove Shiraz or Jackson-Triggs Okanagan Estates SunRock Syrah

Bison Goulash

2 Tbsp extra-virgin olive oil

1 lb stewing bison meat, in ½-inch cubes, or ground bison

1 cup diced (½ inch) onions

½ cup diced (½ inch) carrot

½ cup diced (½ inch) celery

1 Tbsp minced garlic

1 Tbsp smoked paprika

1 to 2 cups beef, veal or chicken stock (the more stock you use and reduce, the richer the goulash)

Bison Tenderloin

18 oz whole bison tenderloin or six 3-oz steaks

Barbecued Peking Duck Soup and Homemade Won Tons

with Lime, Chili, Ginger and Green Onion

Peking Duck Soup

2 Chinese barbecued
ducks (store-bought)

1 Tbsp canola oil

1 onion, in ⅛-inch dice

½ carrot, in ¼-inch dice

2 ribs celery, in ¼-inch dice

2 Tbsp dark soy sauce

2 Tbsp oyster sauce

1 Tbsp roughly chopped ginger

½ stalk lemon grass

1 Tbsp coriander seeds

1 Tbsp black peppercorns

1 orange, zest of

20 cups water

Won Tons

Reserved duck meat,
in ¼-inch dice

1 lb barbecued pork
(store-bought), in ¼-inch dice

1 tsp minced ginger

1 bunch green onions,
finely chopped

1 small bunch cilantro,
finely chopped

1 tsp sesame oil

1 tsp soy sauce

1 tsp mirin (Japanese
sweet cooking rice wine)

1 tsp Japanese rice vinegar

1 package frozen
won ton skins, thawed

Lime, Chili, Ginger
and Green Onion

1 Tbsp minced ginger

1 Tbsp minced green onion

1 Tbsp minced garlic

1 Tbsp minced Thai chili

2 limes, cut into
wedges, for garnish

Both the duck broth and the won tons in this recipe freeze well and would be worth making ahead and storing in the freezer for future use. *Serves 4*

Peking Duck Soup This dish is best made the day before serving. Remove the breast and leg meat from the ducks and reserve in the refrigerator. You will use the carcasses to make the soup.

Heat oil in a large stockpot on medium heat. Add onion and sauté for at least 10 minutes, or until lightly caramelized. Turn up the heat to high and add all of the remaining ingredients, including the duck carcasses (but not the duck meat), and bring to a boil. Turn down the heat to low and simmer for 2 hours. Remove from the heat and strain through a fine-mesh sieve; discard solids. Allow to cool and refrigerate overnight.

The next day, skim off the fat from the soup. You will need 3 cups of duck soup for this recipe. The soup will keep in the refrigerator for 1 week, or in the freezer for up to 4 months.

Won Tons To make the filling, combine all of the ingredients— except for the won ton skins—and mix well. Place 1 Tbsp of the filling in the centre of each won ton skin and brush the edges with a finger dipped in cold water. Bring the four corners up together and pinch to seal shut. Repeat the process until all won ton skins are used. Makes two dozen or more pieces. Use right away or freeze until needed. Will keep in the freezer for up to 3 months.

Lime, Chili, Ginger and Green Onion Combine ginger and green onion in a small bowl. In another small bowl, combine garlic and chili.

To Serve Heat 3 cups of the duck soup in a pot on medium heat. While the soup is heating up, bring a pot of water to a boil on high heat and cover with a Chinese bamboo steamer. Add the won tons, cover and steam over the boiling water for about 5 minutes (if won tons are frozen, steam for 8 minutes).

Place steamed won tons in warmed bowls, then pour hot duck soup around them. Place garnishes of lime wedges, ginger-green onion mixture and garlic-chili mixture in small bowls to pass around.

Wine Sumac Ridge Estate Winery Meritage White

Potato-crusted Lois Lake Steelhead
with Celery Root Purée and Cabernet Reduction

Potato Crust
2 Yukon Gold potatoes
1 Tbsp melted butter

Celery Root Purée
2 cups chopped celery root
½ cup whipping cream
1 Tbsp butter

Cabernet Reduction
½ cup Mission Hill Cabernet Sauvignon or any good B.C. dry red wine
⅓ cup demi-glace

Steelhead
4 fillets Lois Lake steelhead, each 6 oz
1 Tbsp olive oil
4 to 5 sprigs thyme
1 large lemon, zest in large strips
1 Tbsp butter

Lois Lake, north of Powell River on the British Columbia mainland, is the source of this sustainable, delicious steelhead. If it is not available, you may substitute wild salmon. *Serves 4*

Potato Crust This can be made ahead of time. Preheat the oven to 350°F. Peel potatoes and slice them as thinly as possible. On a non-stick baking sheet, arrange potato slices three wide and three long, overlapping them. Make at least six or seven of these potato cakes. (The starch in the potatoes will make the slices stick together.)

Brush the top of each potato cake very lightly with melted butter. Season with salt and pepper to taste. Bake in the oven for 10 to 15 minutes, or until crispy. Remove from the baking sheet and place on parchment paper until needed.

Celery Root Purée Place celery root in a pot of salted water on high heat and bring to a boil. Turn down the heat to medium-low and cook for about 15 minutes, or until celery root is tender. Drain and place in a bowl, then stir in cream and butter. Season to taste with salt and pepper. Pass through a fine-mesh sieve into a bowl and cover with plastic wrap. Keep warm until ready to serve.

Cabernet Reduction Place wine in a small pot and bring to a boil on medium-high heat, then turn down the heat to low and simmer for about 5 minutes, or until reduced by two-thirds or a light syrup forms. Stir in demi-glace, turn up the heat to medium-high and bring to a boil. Remove from the heat, then season to taste with salt and pepper. Keep warm.

Steelhead For ultimate flavour, the best method is to sauté then roast the fish. Preheat the oven to 350°F. Season fish on both sides with salt and pepper. Heat oil in a stainless steel frying pan or a very good non-stick frying pan on high heat until it begins to lightly smoke. Add fish, skin-side down, and sauté for 30 seconds. Remove from the heat, flip over the fish, then roast in the oven for at least 2 minutes. Remove from the oven, add thyme, lemon zest and butter, then return to the oven for 1 minute. Remove from the oven and drizzle the pan juices over fish. Transfer fish to a clean warmed plate. Discard thyme and lemon.

To Serve Spoon warm celery root purée in the centre of each warmed plate. Place a fillet of fish on the purée and top it with a potato cake. Spoon the wine reduction around the plate.

Wine Church & State Wines Winery Church Mouse Cabernet Blanc

Wild Halibut Carpaccio
with Prawn Vinaigrette and Tomatoes

Fish fumet is a concentrated, very flavourful fish stock made with the roasted bones of a white, non-oily fish such as halibut. If it's not available, use a concentrated chicken stock. *Serves 4*

Vinaigrette Place wine, lemon juice and fish fumet in a small pot on medium-high heat and bring to a boil. Turn down the heat to low and simmer until reduced by half. Salt and pepper prawns, then add them to the pot. Cover and remove from the heat.

Halibut Carpaccio Preheat the oven to 425°F. Season halibut with salt and pepper, then place four slices on each of four heatproof serving plates. Bake in the oven for 1 minute, then take out.

Garnishes Fill a bowl with ice water. Bring a pot of water to a boil on high heat. Add tomatoes and blanch for 20 to 30 seconds. Drain, then plunge tomatoes into the ice water. Drain, pat dry and remove the skin, which should rub off easily. Cut tomatoes into quarters, then remove and discard seeds. Cut into ¼-inch dice, then season to taste with salt and pepper.

To Serve Spoon prawn vinaigrette and tomatoes over halibut. Garnish with tomatoes and basil, then drizzle with oil. Place 1 tsp of the caviar in the centre of each serving.

Wine Quails' Gate Estate Winery Chenin Blanc

Vinaigrette
3 Tbsp + 1 tsp dry white wine

2 Tbsp lemon juice

2 tsp fish fumet

4 spot prawns, peeled, finely chopped

Halibut Carpaccio
16 thin slices fresh halibut, each ⅓-inch thick

Garnishes
2 Roma tomatoes

1 leaf basil, torn into small pieces

2 Tbsp olive oil

4 tsp Quebec sturgeon caviar

Boneless Cornish Hens
with Bread Stuffing and Escargot Ragout

If you don't want to remove the bones from the Cornish hens, ask your butcher, who will do a neat job for a fee. Or you may just cut out the backbone with kitchen scissors and leave the remaining bones in, which will make cutting the birds in half more difficult, but not impossible. *Serves 4*

Smoked Bacon Vinaigrette Cook bacon in a small frying pan on low heat until crisp. Remove from the heat, then drain and discard fat. Stir in balsamic and sherry vinegars, then whisk in oil. Season to taste with salt and pepper.

Cornish Hens Place bread cubes in a bowl and pour warm milk over them.

Heat a frying pan on medium heat. Add oil, prosciutto, porcini, shallot and truffle, then cook for about 5 minutes, or until mushrooms are soft. Remove from the heat and add milk-soaked bread, thyme and nutmeg. Season to taste with salt and pepper. Stir in Parmesan cheese and semolina, then allow the mixture to cool. Stir in beaten eggs and blend well.

Preheat the oven to 400°F. Lay Cornish hens skin-side down on a work surface. Season the flesh with salt and pepper. Divide stuffing between the hens, then reform them into the shape of a hen. Close with skewers and string to retain their shape while roasting.

Place hens in a pan and roast in the oven for 35 to 40 minutes, or until thigh juices run clear and skin is a golden brown. Remove from the oven.

Escargot Ragout Heat oil in a pot on medium-high heat. Add morels and shallot, then cook for 5 to 8 minutes, or until shallots are translucent and mushrooms are soft. Turn down the heat to medium, then stir in escargots and cook for about 10 minutes, or until the mixture is hot. Stir in green onions and remove from the heat.

To Serve Carefully cut Cornish hens in half and place each half, cut-side down, on a warmed plate. Spoon ragout around each hen and drizzle the hens with smoked bacon vinaigrette. Garnish with parsley and chives.

Wine CedarCreek Estate Winery Platinum Merlot

Smoked Bacon Vinaigrette

3 slices smoked bacon, chopped

1 Tbsp balsamic vinegar

1½ tsp sherry vinegar

2 Tbsp olive oil

Cornish Hens

6 slices stale white bread, in ¼-inch cubes

3 Tbsp milk, warmed

2 Tbsp olive oil

1 Tbsp minced prosciutto

2 Tbsp chopped fresh porcini or portobello mushrooms

1 shallot, chopped

1½ tsp finely chopped black truffle

1 tsp thyme leaves

Pinch of nutmeg

1 Tbsp grated Parmesan cheese

1 Tbsp + 1 tsp semolina flour

2 eggs, beaten

2 Cornish hens, each 1 lb, boneless

Escargot Ragout

1 Tbsp + 2 tsp olive oil

2 oz morels, halved if very large

1 shallot, chopped

2 dozen escargots, well rinsed

4 green onions, thinly sliced

2 tsp finely chopped parsley for garnish

2 tsp finely chopped chives for garnish

Pineapple and Crab Cannelloni
with Edamame and Daikon Salad, Yuzu-Soy Dressing

Cannelloni

1 golden pineapple

1 mango

¾ cup fresh Dungeness crabmeat

1 Tbsp Japanese mayonnaise

1 tsp finely minced cilantro

½ lime, juice of

½ tsp minced jalapeño pepper (no seeds, no ribs) or more to taste

2 tsp fish roe for garnish (optional)

Salad

12 pods edamame (baby soybeans)

2 pieces peeled daikon, each 2 inches long, or 1 piece of English cucumber, 2 inches long, seeded

2 tsp yuzu juice

2 tsp Japanese rice vinegar

1 tsp soy sauce

1 Tbsp grapeseed oil

Micro cilantro sprouts for garnish

For an easier and equally attractive presentation, instead of forming the pineapple and filling into cannelloni, cut thin slices of pineapple into 2½-inch squares. Stack two or three pineapple squares, with the filling between the layers of pineapple, on each chilled serving plate. Place some edamame and daikon salad beside each stack and garnish with cilantro sprouts. *Serves 8 as an amuse bouche, 4 as an appetizer*

Cannelloni Peel pineapple. Slice it from top to bottom, just off centre, and remove a half-moon-shaped piece. Use a mandoline on the cut side of the pineapple to make three paper-thin lengthwise slices, then place them on a paper towel–lined tray to remove excess moisture. (The remaining pineapple will not be used in this recipe.)

To make the filling, peel mango, slice half of it away from the pit and cut into ¼-inch dice. (The remaining mango will not be used in this recipe.) Gently squeeze any excess moisture out of crabmeat and place it in a bowl. Add mango, mayonnaise, cilantro, lime juice and jalapeño pepper to taste, then toss gently. Season to taste with salt and pepper.

To make the cannelloni, cut an 18-inch length of plastic wrap and place it on a work surface. Place the 3 pineapple slices on it lengthwise, slightly overlapping. Place the crab mixture evenly down the length of the pineapple in a 1-inch high mound. Use the plastic wrap to aid in rolling: pull the edge closest to you and gently enfold crab filling inside pineapple. Use the plastic wrap to tighten the cannelloni as you roll it into a tube shape. Twist the ends of the plastic wrap and tie them up. Refrigerate for up to 4 hours before serving.

Salad Fill a bowl with ice water. Bring a pot of water to a boil on high heat. Add edamame and blanch for 2 minutes. Drain and plunge into the ice water. Remove and discard pods and outer membrane from edamame, then cut soybeans into fine julienne.

Cut daikon into fine julienne pieces (a mandoline works well). Combine edamame and daikon in a non-reactive bowl. Add yuzu juice, vinegar and soy sauce to the salad, tossing lightly. Add oil and toss to coat salad evenly. Season to taste with salt and pepper.

To Serve For an amuse bouche, cut cannelloni into eight pieces.
Cut through the plastic wrap with a sharp knife and discard the
wrap as you plate each portion. Place each portion of cannelloni in
a Chinese ceramic soup spoon and top with a little of the edamame
and daikon salad. Garnish with a touch of cilantro sprouts.

For an appetizer, cut cannelloni into four pieces. Put a piece of
cannelloni on each serving plate, place edamame and daikon salad
on the side of the plate, then garnish with cilantro sprouts and fish
roe (optional).

Wine See Ya Later Ranch Semillon

Pan-seared Ling Cod

with Truffle Chanterelle Purée, Sauté of Sugar Pumpkin
and Baby Zucchini with Bacon Emulsion

Truffle Chanterelle Purée
2 tsp olive oil
1 shallot, ¼-inch dice
1 cup chanterelle mushrooms
½ cup chicken stock
1 tsp truffle oil (or ¼ of a fresh truffle, grated on a micro rasp)

Bacon Emulsion
4 strips double-smoked bacon, chopped
2 shallots, minced
1 clove garlic, lightly crushed
1 cup chicken stock
1 tsp coriander seeds
1 pod cardamom
2 sprigs thyme
½ cup skim milk

Ling Cod
2 cups diced (¼ inch) sugar pumpkin or a winter squash
8 fillets ling cod, 6 oz each, skin on
1 Tbsp kosher salt
2 tsp grapeseed oil
1 Tbsp + 1 tsp butter
2 sprigs thyme
1 clove garlic, crushed
4 baby yellow pattypan squash, each cut into 8 segments
8 baby green zucchini, cut into wafer-thin coins

Prepare this dish in early autumn when chanterelles, baby zucchini and sugar pumpkins are for sale in farmers' markets. Depending on the season, instead of ling cod, you may use fresh halibut, sablefish, arctic char, scallops or spring salmon. *Serves 8*

Truffle Chanterelle Purée Heat olive oil in a small frying pan on medium heat. Add shallot and cook for 2 to 3 minutes, or until translucent. Add chanterelles and cook for about 5 minutes, or until they begin to soften. Add stock and simmer for 7 to 10 minutes, until reduced by half. Remove from the heat and process in a high-speed blender. Add salt and pepper to taste. Just before serving, stir in truffle oil.

Bacon Emulsion Place bacon, shallots and garlic in a pot on medium-high heat and cook, stirring, for 3 to 4 minutes, or until shallots are translucent. Add stock and turn down the heat to medium; simmer slowly for about 30 minutes, or until reduced by half. Turn off the heat, then stir in coriander seeds, cardamom, thyme and milk. Cover and allow to steep for at least 1 hour. Strain through a fine-mesh strainer into a clean pot and discard solids.

Ling Cod To prepare pumpkin, fill a large bowl with ice water. Bring a large pot of water to a boil on high heat. Add pumpkin and blanch for about 3 minutes, or until just tender. Drain and plunge into the ice water to cool, then drain and reserve.

To prepare ling cod, score skin with a sharp knife to prevent curling while cooking. Place fish in a single layer in a non-reactive dish and sprinkle lightly with salt, then allow to stand for 7 to 8 minutes. Rinse off salt from fish in cold water and pat dry with paper towels. Reserve fish, covered, in the refrigerator, until needed.

To finish ling cod, preheat the oven to 350°F. Season fish with salt and pepper. Heat oil in a large ovenproof frying pan on medium-high heat until it begins to smoke. Add fish, skin-side down, and cook for 2 to 3 minutes. Do not disturb fish until a golden colour appears about ¼ inch around fillet. Place in the oven and roast for 4 minutes. Flip over fish, then add 1 Tbsp of the butter, thyme and garlic to pan, then baste fish. Return to the oven for 2 minutes. Take out of the oven and allow to rest for 5 minutes.

While fish is in the oven, melt the remaining 1 tsp of the butter in a frying pan on medium heat. Add squash and zucchini, then sauté for 4 to 5 minutes, or until nearly tender. Add pumpkin and cook for 2 to 3 minutes, or until heated through. Season to taste with salt and pepper.

To Serve Reheat both the bacon emulsion and the truffle chanterelle purée in separate pots. Stir truffle oil into the reheated chanterelle purée and place a dollop on each warmed plate, using the back of a spoon to draw a swirl through the purée.

Place a ring mould on each plate, spoon some of the vegetable mixture into it and press gently to set the shape. Remove the moulds. Place a fillet of ling cod on top of vegetables. Use a hand-held blender or a whisk to froth the bacon emulsion and pour a small pool onto each plate.

Wine Ridge Estate Winery Sparkling Pinnacle Pinot Noir (aged on the lees for four years)

Torched Mackerel
with Citrus Sauce

Mackerel is a dark-fleshed, very flavourful fish with a high oil content. It's both healthy and delicious. *Serves 4*

Mackerel Lay fish on its back and gently run your finger along the flesh, feeling for any missed bones. Use tweezers to remove any stray bones.

Place ¼ inch of kosher salt in the bottom of a non-reactive container and arrange mackerel fillets on it in a single layer. Add more salt to completely cover fish. Cure mackerel for 1½ hours in the refrigerator. Rinse salt off mackerel with cold water and pat dry with paper towels.

Place fish in a non-reactive container and completely cover with vinegar. Marinate for 1 hour in the refrigerator. Pour off and discard vinegar. Pat fish dry, cover and refrigerate until needed.

Citrus Sauce First, make simple syrup by combining ¼ cup of water and sugar in a small pot on medium-high heat and bring to a boil. Add the remaining water and kumquats, then bring to a gentle boil. Turn down the heat to low and simmer for 5 minutes. Stir in soy sauce, mirin and sake, then turn up the heat to medium-high and bring to a boil. Remove from the heat and allow to cool, then stir in lime zest. Purée in a blender, then refrigerate until needed.

To Finish Mackerel Place mackerel on a cutting surface and square off each piece by removing the belly flap, tail and flesh from behind the head. Cut widthwise into ¼-inch strips but keep the strips together as a unit in their rectangles.

Preheat the broiler with the oven rack at its highest position or use a kitchen blowtorch. Line a rimmed baking sheet with foil. Carefully lift each rectangle of sliced fish and arrange them in a single layer on the baking sheet.

If using the broiler, place the pan under the heat for 15 to 20 seconds, watching constantly until fish is caramelized on top. (If using a kitchen blowtorch, flame the mackerel for 20 to 30 seconds, moving the flame up and down the fish.) The fish will spatter and caramelize, creating a wonderful flavour. The mackerel will be medium-rare, the outer surface warm but the inside still cool.

To Serve Carefully transfer each rectangle of sliced fish to a warmed serving plate, then drizzle each serving with 2 Tbsp of the citrus sauce. Garnish with an assortment of Japanese pickles, umeboshi, cucumber and daikon.

Wine Oliver Twist Estate Winery Kerner

Mackerel
4 mackerel fillets, each 4 oz, boneless, skinless

1¼ lbs kosher salt

3 cups Japanese rice vinegar

Citrus Sauce
½ cup water

¼ cup sugar

¼ cup sliced kumquats

¼ cup soy sauce

¼ cup mirin (Japanese sweet cooking rice wine)

¼ cup sake

1 lime, zest only

Japanese pickles, umeboshi (pickled plum), cucumber and daikon for garnish

Hamachi, Foie Gras and Barbecued Eel
with Soy-Mirin Glaze

8 oz hamachi, sushi grade, cut into 4 portions

8 oz piece foie gras, sliced into 4 medallions, chilled

5 oz barbecued eel, cut into 4 pieces

¼ cup soy sauce

¾ cup mirin (Japanese sweet cooking rice wine)

1 tsp finely julienned green onions, in cold water

1 tsp toasted sesame seeds for garnish

1 tsp tobiko (flying fish roe) for garnish

Sushi-grade hamachi, barbecued eel, tobiko and other ingredients will require a visit to a Japanese food store, where you are likely to discover many other delectable items. *Serves 4*

Cut each hamachi portion into pieces ½-inch thick. Keep chilled in the refrigerator.

Preheat the oven to 350°F. Lightly score one side of foie gras medallions, ⅛-inch deep, then season with salt and pepper. Heat a heavy frying pan on medium-high heat until the pan begins to smoke. Add foie gras and sear for about 1½ minutes, or until caramelized. Flip over and remove from the heat, leaving the foie gras in the pan to finish cooking.

Place barbecued eel on a parchment paper–lined baking sheet and bake in the oven for 2 to 4 minutes, or until heated through. Remove from the oven.

To make the soy-mirin glaze, combine soy sauce and mirin in a small pot on medium heat and simmer for 7 to 10 minutes, or until syrupy.

To Serve Arrange sliced raw hamachi in the centre of each plate and top with seared foie gras, then with eel. Pour soy-mirin glaze over all. Garnish with green onions, sesame seeds and tobiko.

Wine JoieFarm Wines Riesling

Pine Mushrooms en Papillote

The pine mushroom, or matsutake, is harvested in British Columbia's mature forests in the autumn. It is prized in culinary circles for its spicy aroma, and many of them are exported to Japan. *Serves 4*

Daikon To make dashi (stock), place kombu and cold water in a pot on high heat and bring to a boil. As soon as the water boils, remove the pot from the heat. Remove and discard kombu. Stir in bonito flakes, then allow to cool. Strain through a fine-mesh sieve and discard solids.

Place dashi, daikon and soy sauce in a pot on medium heat, then simmer for about 15 minutes, or until daikon is soft.

Pine Mushrooms en Papillote Preheat the oven to 400°F. Cut four pieces of parchment paper, each 8 × 12 inches, and lay them on a work surface. In the centre of each piece of paper, place a quarter of the pine mushrooms, a slice of smoked sablefish, a slice of cooked daikon, a slice of lime, 1 Tbsp + 2 tsp of the sake, 1 tsp of the oil, a quarter of the spring onions and a pinch of kosher salt. Fold each sheet of parchment paper over itself, then seal the edges tightly by creasing with your fingers as you fold the package into a half-moon shape.

Place the sealed packages on a rimmed baking sheet and bake in the oven for about 12 minutes, until the packages begin to puff up and the paper turns slightly brown.

To Serve Place each parchment package on a warmed plate. At the table, cut open the package with scissors (watch out for the hot steam) and enjoy the aromas.

Wine Foxtrot Vineyards Pinot Noir

Daikon

3 sheets kombu (dried seaweed)

2 cups cold water

1 Tbsp bonito flakes
(Japanese dried smoked bonito)

4 rounds daikon,
each ¾-inch thick

1 Tbsp + 2 tsp dark soy sauce

Pine Mushrooms en Papillote

2 large pine mushrooms,
thinly sliced

4 slices smoked sablefish,
each 2 oz

4 thin slices lime

7 Tbsp good-quality sake

1 Tbsp + 1 tsp extra-virgin olive oil

2 spring onions or
green onions, thinly sliced

Kosher salt

Red Wine–braised Oxtail

with Sugar Pumpkin Gnocchi, Shallots and Pancetta

Braised Oxtail

8 oz pork caul

1 bottle (750 mL)
full-bodied red wine

1 oxtail (ask butcher to
cut into 6 equal pieces)

1 carrot, finely sliced

1 onion, finely sliced

2 cloves garlic,
peeled and crushed

1 rib celery, finely sliced

1 tsp crushed
black peppercorns

1 sprig thyme

1 bay leaf

3 Tbsp vegetable oil

8 cups chicken stock

2 Tbsp creamed horseradish

An old standby for soup and stews, oxtail is given a sophisticated treatment here, served boneless, in spheres, with pumpkin gnocchi. *Serves 4*

Braised Oxtail This recipe must be started 6 days before serving. Place pork caul in water in a covered bowl in the refrigerator for 5 days, changing the water daily.

Warm the wine to just over room temperature in a non-reactive pot on medium heat. Remove from the heat, then add oxtail, carrot, onion, garlic, celery, peppercorns, thyme and bay leaf. Cover and marinate in the refrigerator for 24 hours.

Remove oxtail from the marinade and pat dry. Drain vegetables and reserve. Reserve the marinade.

Preheat the oven to 285°F. Heat 1½ Tbsp of the oil in a frying pan on medium heat. Add oxtail and brown all over.

At the same time, in a large ovenproof pot, slowly cook the reserved vegetables with 1 Tbsp of the oil on medium heat for about 10 minutes, or until soft. Add the reserved marinade and simmer for 10 minutes, or until reduced by four-fifths. Add oxtail and cover with stock, then bring to a boil and remove from the heat.

Cut out a parchment paper circle, with a small hole in the centre, to fit just inside the pot. Place the paper circle right on top of the liquid and bake in the oven for 4 hours, or until meat begins to fall off the bone.

Remove from the oven, strain the cooking liquid through a fine-mesh sieve and reserve the solids. Separate vegetables from meat; keep carrots but discard the remaining vegetables.

Place the cooking liquid in a pot on medium-high heat and simmer for about 20 minutes, or until reduced by about four-fifths to a sauce consistency. Strain the sauce through a fine-mesh sieve into a bowl.

Remove the meat from the bones, shred and combine with the reserved carrots. Stir in horseradish and a few tablespoons of the sauce, then season with salt and pepper.

Form the oxtail mixture into four pieces the size of golf balls, place on a tray and refrigerate for 1 hour or longer. Wrap each meatball with pork caul and refrigerate for 1 hour or longer.

Heat the remaining ½ Tbsp of the oil in a frying pan on medium heat. Add meatballs and sear gently until browned. Transfer meatballs to a small pot and add the remaining sauce.

Pumpkin Gnocchi Preheat the oven to 350°F. Cut pumpkin in half, then remove and discard seeds. Season with nutmeg, salt and pepper, then drizzle with extra-virgin olive oil.

Place pumpkin, cut-side up, on a rimmed baking sheet and bake in the oven for 1 to 1½ hours, or until tender.

Scrape out pumpkin flesh, pass through a food mill into a large bowl and allow to cool to room temperature. Mix in egg and egg yolk, then begin to work in flour a little at a time, adding only enough to form a dough. (The amount of flour used will depend on how wet the pumpkin is. If it appears very wet after it has come out of the oven, dry it a bit in a pan on the stovetop.)

When the dough begins to come together, knead for 1 minute. Roll into logs 1 inch in diameter, then cut the logs into ¾-inch-long cylinders and pinch the ends to create a pillow-like shape.

Bring a pot of salted water to a boil on medium heat. Add gnocchi, poach for about 1 minute, then drain. Add olive oil and toss gently.

Shallots and Pancetta Preheat the oven to 400°F. Heat oil in an ovenproof frying pan on medium-high heat. Add shallots and pancetta and cook for about 5 minutes, or until shallots are caramelized. Drain and discard any excess fat. Season with salt and pepper, stir in stock and bake in the oven for about 15 minutes, or until shallots are soft and liquid is reduced by four-fifths.

Remove from the oven and place on the stovetop on medium heat. Add vinegar and deglaze the pan. Stir in butter, spooning over shallots to glaze them.

To Serve Heat up oxtail meatballs in the sauce. Bring a pot of water to a boil, add gnocchi and simmer for 20 seconds, then drain and season with salt and pepper. Arrange meatballs on warmed plates, top with gnocchi and spoon the shallot and pancetta mixture over each serving.

Wine Mission Hill Family Estate Winery Quatrain (with Syrah in the Bordeaux blend)

Pumpkin Gnocchi

2 lbs sugar pumpkin

Pinch of grated nutmeg

3 Tbsp + 1 tsp extra-virgin olive oil

1 egg

1 egg yolk

1 cup or less Tipo oo flour or all-purpose flour

1 Tbsp olive oil

Shallots and Pancetta

2 tsp olive oil

12 shallots, peeled

3½ oz pancetta, in ¾-inch pieces

½ cup chicken stock

2 Tbsp sherry vinegar

2 tsp unsalted butter

Terrine of Goat Cheese
with Apple and Port Wine Gelée

6 leaves gold gelatin

3 egg yolks

¼ cup apple cider

10½ oz Salt Spring Island
goat cheese

¾ cup unsweetened
applesauce

2 Tbsp ruby port

2 Tbsp blackberry purée
or black currant juice

1 cup pea shoots for garnish

2 to 3 Tbsp oil and vinegar
dressing, your favourite

This tangy cheese terrine may be served at the beginning of a meal or as a small cheese course at the end. *Serves 8*

Line the bottom of a loaf pan 8 × 3 or 4 inches with plastic wrap, keeping it as smooth as possible. Following the package directions, bloom 2 leaves of the gelatin in cold water.

In a bowl set over a pot of simmering water on low heat (a bain-marie), whip together egg yolks and apple cider, incorporating as much air as possible, until it reaches 160°F on a candy thermometer. Remove the bowl from the bain-marie but keep the pot on the heat.

Take out bloomed gelatin from the water and gently squeeze out excess water, then stir into the egg yolk mixture until it dissolves. Stir in cheese and return the bowl to the bain-marie. When the cheese mixture is warm enough to pour, fill the terrine mould, smooth the surface and refrigerate for about 1 hour, or until set.

Bloom 3 leaves of the remaining gelatin in cold water. Remove from the water and gently squeeze out excess water. Heat applesauce in a pot on medium heat to 140°F on a candy thermometer, then stir in the bloomed gelatin until it dissolves. Pour this mixture over cheese in the terrine mould. Refrigerate for 1 hour to set.

Bloom the remaining leaf of gelatin in cold water. Remove from the water and gently squeeze out excess water. Combine port and blackberry purée in a pot on medium heat until it reaches 140°F on a candy thermometer, then stir in gelatin until it dissolves. Pour gelatin in a very thin layer on the top of the terrine, then refrigerate for 15 minutes to set.

To Serve Place pea shoots in a bowl and toss lightly with oil and vinegar dressing. Remove the terrine from the mould and carefully peel away the plastic wrap. Use a warmed knife to cut the terrine into eight wedges, and place a piece on each chilled plate. Arrange a 2 Tbsp mound of pea shoot salad on the side.

Wine Granite Creek Estate Wines Ehrenfelser

Parisienne Chocolate Mousse and Vanilla-poached Pear

with Pear Gelée

Chocolate Mousse

4½ oz milk chocolate (Valrhona Jivara Lactée)

3 oz dark chocolate (Valrhona Manjari)

¼ cup + 1 Tbsp unsalted butter, in 1-inch cubes

5 egg yolks

¼ cup sugar

1½ cup heavy whipping cream (36%)

Poached Pear

3 cups sugar

2 cups water

2 cups Riesling

½ lemon, juice of

2 vanilla beans, split open, seeds scraped and saved

10 small Anjou or Bosc pears, peeled, cored

6 leaves gold gelatin

Chocolate and pear are a tasty combination. Search for the smallest ripe pears for an elegant presentation. *Serves 10*

Chocolate Mousse Start this recipe the day before serving. Roughly chop milk and dark chocolates. In a bowl set over a pot of simmering water on low heat (a bain-marie), melt milk chocolate and dark chocolate, then heat to 112°F on a candy thermometer. Stir in butter, then remove the bowl from the bain-marie. Keep the pot on the heat.

Beat together egg yolks and sugar in another bowl placed over the bain-marie, whisking until sugar melts and the mixture increases in volume and reaches 160°F on a candy thermometer. Remove the bowl from the bain-marie. Fold the egg mixture into the chocolate mixture.

Line ten 2-inch diameter ramekins or dariole moulds with plastic wrap. Pour cream into a bowl and whip to soft peaks, then fold it into the egg and chocolate mixture. Pour into the moulds and refrigerate overnight to set.

Poached Pear To poach pears, combine sugar, water, wine, lemon juice and vanilla beans and seeds in a large pot on medium heat and bring to a boil. Add pears and set a plate on top to keep them submerged. Turn down the heat to medium-low or low and poach pears for 25 minutes at a slow simmer. Remove from the heat. Allow pears to cool in the poaching liquid.

To make pear gelée, bloom gelatin according to the package directions. Remove gelatin from the water and gently squeeze out excess water. Strain 1½ cups of the poaching liquid through a fine-mesh sieve into a pot. Heat on medium until the liquid reaches the boiling point, remove from the heat, then stir in gelatin until it dissolves.

Lightly oil a cake pan 9 × 12 inches and pour in a thin layer of pear gelée. Keep on a very level surface and allow 10 minutes to set at room temperature, then refrigerate. Once set, the pear gelée may be cut into rectangles of desired size.

Garnishes Preheat the oven to 300°F. Lay spring roll wrappers on a cutting board, brush liberally with some of the melted butter and sprinkle with sugar. Cut into rectangles about 1 × 4 inches, then roll each rectangle into a 1-inch diameter tube and brush with the remaining melted butter. Place the tubes on a parchment-lined baking sheet and bake in the oven for about 10 minutes, or until golden.

To Serve Unmould a chocolate mousse onto each chilled plate and leave at room temperature for 30 minutes. In the meantime, heat pears in their poaching liquid in a pot on medium heat until just warm, then drain well and discard liquid. Place a pear beside each chocolate mousse, then top each mousse with a rectangle of pear gelée. Garnish with a crisp spring roll tube. To gild the lily, you may spoon a little ice cream (optional) inside the tube at the last moment.

Wine Thornhaven Estates Winery Diosa Late Harvest Chardonnay

Garnishes

3 spring roll wrappers, thawed
1 Tbsp melted butter
3 Tbsp + 1 tsp sugar
Ice cream (optional)

Salade de Homard Printanière

The lobster, asparagus, potatoes and quail eggs can all be pre-pared in the morning and refrigerated, covered, until serving time, making this an ideal dish for entertaining. *Serves 4*

Place 8 cups of water in a large stockpot and stir in 2 Tbsp salt. Bring the water to a rolling boil on high heat, add a steaming basket, and put in lobsters. Cover the stockpot and steam lobsters for 6 minutes, then remove them from the pot and allow to cool. Remove meat from the shell, taking care to remove meat from the tail as neatly as possible. Remove claws whole and keep separate for garnish. Refrigerate lobster meat and claws until needed, then thinly slice meat from lobster tail.

Fill a pot with salted water and bring to a boil on high heat. Add potatoes and cook for about 15 minutes, or until soft. Drain and refrigerate. When cool, slice thinly.

Break off and discard tough bottoms of asparagus. Fill a bowl with ice water. Bring a pot of salted water to a boil on high heat, then add asparagus and cook for about 4 minutes. Drain and place in ice water to cool and retain colour. Drain, then cut into ¾-inch lengths.

Place sliced lobster tail meat, potatoes, asparagus, onion, radishes and basil in a large bowl. Make a dressing by mixing together lemon juice, oil, vinegar and mustard in a small bowl. Pour just enough of the dressing over the lobster salad to moisten the ingredients and toss gently.

To Serve Cut cucumber thinly lengthwise into four slices and place one on the bottom of each chilled plate. Arrange lobster salad in the centre. Cut quail eggs in half and set on top. Drizzle the remaining dressing over all. Crack lobster claws and place one on each plate.

Wine Burrowing Owl Estate Winery Chardonnay or Blue Mountain Vineyard & Cellars Chardonnay

2 lobsters,
each 1¼ lbs

4 large red-skinned
potatoes, skins on

6 stalks asparagus

1 Tbsp finely chopped onion

2 Tbsp very thinly sliced radishes

4 leaves basil, torn

¼ cup fresh lemon juice

¼ cup olive oil

2 Tbsp white wine vinegar

1 Tbsp Dijon mustard

½ English cucumber,
peeled, seeded

4 quail eggs,
hardboiled, peeled

Joues de Veau Braisées, Brunoise aux Potirons, Pappardelle et Sauce Pinot Noir

8 pieces veal cheeks,
each 3 oz

1 Tbsp vegetable oil

1 cup veal stock

1 cup Pinot Noir

1 sprig thyme

2 cloves

1 bay leaf

1 clove garlic

7 to 8 oz butternut squash
(about half a small squash),
peeled, in ½-inch cubes

14 oz pappardelle pasta

3 Tbsp butter

Freshly grated Parmesan cheese

Truffle oil (optional)

The fat content in veal cheeks makes them very succulent. You may prepare them as much as two days in advance of dinner and keep refrigerated. *Serves 4*

Clean veal cheeks by removing some, but not all, of the fat. Heat vegetable oil in a pot on medium-high heat. Add veal cheeks and sear until well browned all over. Pour stock and wine over meat, then add water as needed to cover. Stir in thyme, cloves, bay leaf and garlic. Cover and turn down the heat to medium, then cook for 2 hours, or until veal is tender. Turn down the heat more if necessary to keep liquid at a simmer rather than a boil.

Use a slotted spoon to remove the meat and reserve. Keep the pan on the heat and simmer until the liquid is reduced by half. Add squash and cook for about 10 minutes, or until tender.

Bring a large pot with plenty of salted water to a boil on high heat. Add pappardelle and cook for about 8 minutes, or until al dente. Drain, then return to the pot. Add veal cheeks, the reduced cooking liquid, squash and butter, mixing gently together without breaking the cheeks. Season to taste with salt and pepper.

To Serve Arrange pappardelle in warmed pasta bowls, with two veal cheeks for each serving. Sprinkle with Parmesan cheese and drizzle with truffle oil (optional).

Wine CedarCreek Estate Winery Platinum Pinot Noir

Chanterelle Open-faced Ravioli
with Crisp Berkshire Bacon

Look for chanterelles that are shaped like regular button mushrooms and that are not too large. Brush off the dirt and pine needles. If the mushrooms are wet and dirty, briefly submerge them in water to remove all the dirt. Remove from water, check for cleanliness and dry on trays covered with paper towels, well ahead of cooking time. Cooked green beans with toasted hazelnuts make a tasty accompaniment to this dish. *Serves 6*

Pasta Dough Make this the morning of or the night before serving. Stir together flour and salt in a bowl, then add 1 egg yolk at a time, mixing each in well, until the dough forms. Knead a little until the dough is almost smooth, but do not overknead. Brush oil all over the dough, wrap in plastic wrap and refrigerate for 12 hours to rest.

Cut dough into four equal pieces and roll out each into a rectangle that will fit in your pasta machine. Roll each piece through the pasta machine until it is smooth and thin. Cut pasta into sheets 4½ × 2 inches. Lay the sheets on floured parchment paper and reserve, well wrapped to prevent drying out, until needed.

Chanterelle Stuffing Place stock in a small pot on medium heat and bring to a boil, then turn down the heat to low and simmer until reduced by half. Remove from the heat.

Place a large pot on medium heat. Add bacon, shallots and half of the butter, then cook for about 5 minutes, or until shallots are soft. Add chanterelles and turn up the heat to medium-high, adding the remaining butter as needed, and cook until chanterelles are soft and golden. Stir in thyme, then season with salt and pepper to taste. Add whisky and deglaze the pan, allowing the alcohol to burn off. Add vinegar and simmer for a few minutes, or until reduced by half. Stir in reduced stock and cream, then simmer for 5 minutes, or until reduced by half. Just before serving, stir in chives.

To Serve Bring a large pot of heavily salted water to a boil on high heat. Add pasta sheets and cook for 3 to 4 minutes, or until al dente. Remove from the water and drain for a few seconds on paper towels.

Place a pasta sheet on each warmed plate and brush lightly with melted butter. Add a layer of the chanterelle stuffing, then top with a second sheet of pasta. Lay a crisp slice of bacon on top of each serving.

Wine Alderlea Vineyards Fusion (a cross of Cabernet Sauvignon and Maréchal Foch)

Pasta Dough

1¼ cups + 1 Tbsp all-purpose flour

1½ tsp kosher salt

7 egg yolks

2 Tbsp olive oil

2 to 3 Tbsp butter, melted

Chanterelle Stuffing

1 cup dark chicken stock (made using roasted bones)

4 Tbsp finely chopped double-smoked bacon

¼ cup diced (¼ inch) shallots

¼ cup butter

3 lbs fresh chanterelles, trimmed

1 tsp chopped thyme

¼ cup rye whisky or brandy

1 Tbsp Banyuls vinegar or sherry vinegar

½ cup whipping cream

1 Tbsp chopped chives

2 Tbsp melted butter to brush on cooked pasta

12 thin slices Berkshire bacon, baked in the oven until crisp

Terrine of Smoked Trout Bellies
with Pickled Root Vegetables and Thyme Crème Fraîche

Crème Fraîche
½ cup whipping cream
¼ cup buttermilk
1 lemon, juice of
1 sprig thyme

Trout Terrine
1 lb trout bellies
¼ cup + 1 Tbsp kosher salt
¼ cup + 1 Tbsp brown sugar
2 tsp fennel seeds, finely ground
2 tsp whole caraway seeds
1 lemon, zest of
2 Tbsp finely sliced chervil

This tasty terrine featuring smoked trout, the pickled root vegetables and the thyme crème fraîche can all be prepared ahead of time, making the host's life easier. *Serves 4 to 6*

Crème Fraîche Start this recipe 2 or more days ahead. Combine all of the ingredients in a bowl, cover and set in a warm place for 24 hours. Remove and discard thyme, then refrigerate for an additional 24 to 48 hours. Once thickened, you may use crème fraîche as you would whipping cream. Will keep in the refrigerator for 1 week.

Trout Terrine Start making this the day before serving. Place trout in a single layer in a non-reactive container. To make the curing mixture, combine salt, brown sugar, ground fennel, caraway and lemon zest in a bowl. Sprinkle over trout, cover and refrigerate for 3 to 4 hours.

Rinse off curing mixture from the trout under cold water and pat dry.

To smoke the trout bellies, soak 2 oz of smoking chips in water for 1 hour, then remove them from the water and place in the bottom of a heavy pan. Add 2 oz of dry smoking chips and mix together. Ignite the chips in several places and allow to burn for 1 minute. Extinguish the flames. Place the fish in a container made of heavy foil, perforated, and cover it with foil. Place the container on the hot chips and let sit for 10 minutes, then remove the fish from the heat.

Use plastic wrap to line a loaf pan 8 × 2½ inches (the terrine will fill up only to a depth of about 1½ inches at the bottom). Layer trout in the mould, sprinkling chervil between each layer. Cover trout with plastic wrap, place a weight on top and refrigerate overnight.

Pickled Vegetables Make this the day before serving. Cut yellow beet, red beet, carrot and pearl onions into shapes of your choice. Fill four bowls with ice water. Bring four pots of salted water to the boil—one for each vegetable separately—then simmer until tender (time will vary for each vegetable). Drain and plunge into separate bowls of ice water to cool. Place vegetables in a non-reactive container.

To make pickling juice, combine sugar, vinegar, coriander seeds, peppercorns, saffron, bay leaf and water in a non-reactive pot on high heat and cook, stirring, for about 5 minutes, until sugar dissolves. Pour the pickling juice over the cooked vegetables and allow to cool, then marinate overnight in the refrigerator.

To Serve Unmould terrine and use a sharp knife to cut into slices ¹/₂-inch thick. Place a slice of smoked trout terrine on each chilled plate and arrange pickled vegetables on the side. Garnish with a dollop of thyme crème fraîche.

Wine Calona Vineyards Sovereign Opal

Pickled Vegetables

1 yellow beet

1 red beet

1 carrot

12 pearl onions, peeled

1 cup sugar

½ cup + 1 Tbsp champagne vinegar

1 tsp coriander seeds

1 tsp peppercorns

Pinch of saffron

1 bay leaf

3 cups water

Duck Confit Ravioli
with Cipollini Onion and Chestnut Chutney

Pasta Dough
1¾ cups all-purpose flour
6 free-range egg yolks
1 free-range egg
½ tsp sea salt
2 tsp extra-virgin olive oil, plus 1 Tbsp + 1 tsp for coating cooked ravioli
Flour for dusting
3 Tbsp chilled water

Duck Confit Stuffing
1 lb confit duck legs (about 2 pieces)
3 Tbsp extra-virgin olive oil
2 Tbsp diced (¼ inch) celery root
2 Tbsp diced (¼ inch) leek, white part only
2 Tbsp diced (¼ inch) carrot
2 tsp sea salt
½ tsp freshly ground black pepper
2 tsp finely sliced chives

The height of comfort food with an elegant touch: pasta and duck confit. For ease of preparation, make the pasta and the filling the day before serving and assemble later. *Serves 4*

Pasta Dough Start this recipe the day before serving. Place flour on a clean work surface and make a well in the centre. Whisk together egg yolks, egg, salt and the 2 tsp of oil in a small bowl. Pour this liquid mixture into the well and use your index finger to stir slowly in a circular motion, working in a little flour at a time. When the dough begins to cling together, knead until it forms a smooth ball with a slightly springy texture. Wrap with plastic wrap and rest in the refrigerator for a minimum of 30 minutes, but preferably overnight.

Duck Confit Stuffing Clean all meat from the duck legs and reserve. Discard the bones, fat and skin. Cut meat into pea-sized pieces and refrigerate until needed.

Heat oil in a non-stick frying pan on medium-high heat. Add celery root, leek, carrot, salt and pepper; stir constantly to avoid browning and cook for about 5 minutes, or until vegetables are translucent. Remove from the heat, then add the reserved duck confit meat and chives, mixing well. Place the stuffing in a bowl and allow to cool to room temperature. Cover and refrigerate for 1 to 2 hours.

To Assemble Divide pasta dough into four equal portions. Use a pasta machine to roll out each piece of pasta until very thin (setting number 6 on most machines). Dust pasta sheets well with flour and place them on a parchment paper–lined rimmed baking sheet. Cover with a sheet of parchment paper, then alternate layers of pasta sheets and parchment paper, keeping a damp tea towel on top, until all the sheets are used up.

Place a pasta sheet on a ravioli tray and use a small floured ball of scrap dough to indent each individual well. Spoon chilled duck confit mixture into the indentations, being careful not to overfill them. Brush another sheet of pasta with cold water and place on top of the filled ravioli tray, lining up the edges of the sheets and covering the filling. Pat down the top sheet by hand, then dust it lightly with flour and run a rolling pin over it all to separate the ravioli. Invert the finished ravioli onto a well-floured or parchment paper–lined tray in a single layer. Refrigerate until needed.

Chutney Preheat the oven to 375°F. Place chestnuts on a rimmed baking sheet and roast in the oven for 12 to 15 minutes, or until nicely coloured. Remove from the oven, allow to cool and cut into quarters.

Place grapes, raisins and grappa in a non-reactive bowl, then toss to coat thoroughly.

Place sugar in a heavy-bottomed frying pan on medium heat and carefully heat until sugar turns a nutty brown colour. Do not stir. As the sugar begins to caramelize, shake and swirl the pan gently to prevent the sugar from burning in any one spot. Add butter carefully, as it will sizzle and pop, then swirl the pan to blend butter and sugar. Add onions, thyme and tarragon, then cook for 5 to 10 minutes, or until onions are a deep brown. Add stock and deglaze the pan. Add chestnuts, then season with salt and pepper.

Turn down the heat to medium-low heat and cook for about 15 minutes, or until the liquid reaches the consistency of sauce. Add the grape mixture, then very carefully ignite the grappa in the pan and allow the alcohol to burn off. Mix thoroughly. If the liquid is still too thin for a sauce, simmer for a few minutes to reduce it until it is almost syrupy. Taste and adjust the seasoning, then remove and discard thyme and tarragon. Pour into a warmed sauce bowl and keep warm.

To Serve Place 16 cups of salted water in a small stockpot on high heat and bring to a boil. Drop in the ravioli, bring the water back to a boil and cook for 8 to 10 minutes, or until al dente. Use a slotted spoon to carefully transfer ravioli to a warmed serving bowl, then toss them gently with oil to coat. Place the onion and chestnut chutney in a warmed bowl to pass around.

Wine Burrowing Owl Estate Winery Cabernet Franc

Chutney

6 fresh chestnuts, peeled

½ cup green grapes, halved

3 Tbsp organic golden raisins

¼ cup grappa

1 Tbsp sugar

2 Tbsp unsalted butter

6 organic cipollini onions, peeled, quartered

1 sprig thyme

1 sprig tarragon

¾ cup + 2 Tbsp chicken or vegetable stock

1 tsp sea salt

¼ tsp freshly ground black pepper

Lavender-crusted Shortcake and Summer "Thyme" Macerated Fruit and Berries
with Vanilla Cream

Vanilla Cream
2 cups heavy whipping cream (36%), cold

1 tsp vanilla extract

1 vanilla bean, split lengthwise, seeds scraped and saved

¼ cup + 1 Tbsp granulated sugar

Shortcake
5¼ cups all-purpose flour

2 Tbsp baking powder

½ cup sugar

1½ tsp salt

⅞ cup unsalted butter, cold, in ½-inch cubes

2 cups heavy whipping cream (36%), cold

¼ cup milk or cream

3 Tbsp lavender-infused sugar

Macerated Fruit
2 lbs field-ripened mixed berries and orchard fruits

½ cup + 3 Tbsp sugar

¼ cup fresh lemon juice

2 Tbsp stemmed and chiffonaded lemon thyme leaves

1 Tbsp + 2 tsp wildflower honey

A constantly changing variety of berries and orchard fruits in season can be used for this dessert: strawberries, raspberries, blueberries, peaches, apricots and cherries. Instead of the lemon thyme, you may use spearmint, peppermint, lemon mint, cinnamon basil or lemon basil. You can buy lavender-infused sugar or make your own by placing ½ cup sugar and 1 tsp organic lavender together in a small jar for 2 to 3 days. *Serves 12*

Vanilla Cream Combine cream, vanilla extract and scraped seeds in a stand mixer fitted with a whisk attachment. Whisk on medium speed, until cream begins to thicken and increase in volume. Slowly add the sugar, then increase the speed to medium-high. Continue to whip until medium peaks form. Transfer the vanilla cream to a clean covered container and refrigerate until needed.

Shortcake Preheat the oven to 400°F. Sift together flour, baking powder, sugar and salt into a bowl. Sprinkle butter cubes over the flour mixture. Cut butter into the flour mixture, using a pastry blender or two knives, until pea-sized lumps form. Make a well in the centre and pour in heavy whipping cream. Use a wooden spoon to mix the dough until it just starts to come together in a shaggy mass. Do not overmix.

Place dough on a floured work surface and gently roll out to a thickness of 1 inch. Use a 4-inch floured cutter to cut out twelve rounds. Place these shortcakes on a parchment paper–lined baking sheet. Brush the tops with milk and sprinkle very liberally with lavender sugar. Bake in the oven for 12 to 15 minutes, or until the tops are golden brown. Remove from the oven and place on a rack to cool to room temperature.

Macerated Fruit Leave berries whole. Peel, core and cut orchard fruits into same size as berries. Combine fruit, sugar and lemon juice in a bowl, mixing carefully to ensure all fruit is well covered with sugar. Crush berries lightly while mixing to release some juice to create a sauce. Macerate the fruit, mixing occasionally, for 2 to 3 hours at room temperature, or overnight in the refrigerator. If overnight, bring to room temperature before serving.

Add lemon thyme no earlier than 10 to 15 minutes before serving or it may turn the mixture black.

To Serve Split shortcakes in half horizontally, then place each bottom half on a plate. Spoon on some berries and orchard fruits with their juice, then add a dollop of vanilla cream. Cover with the top half of the shortcake, then spoon on some more berries and orchard fruits and another dollop of vanilla cream. Drizzle with honey.

Wine Stoneboat Vineyards Verglas (botrytized from old vines Oraniensteiner and Pinot Blanc)

Pear Almond Tart
with Black Currant Jam

Shortbread
⅓ cup sugar
¾ cup butter
Pinch of salt
1½ cup + 2 Tbsp all purpose flour
1 egg, beaten, only half
of which may be needed

Black Currant Jam
½ cup black currant purée
½ cup + 2 Tbsp sugar

Almond Cream
¾ cup + 1 Tbsp (7 oz)
unsalted butter
1½ cups + 2 Tbsp icing sugar
1½ cups blanched ground almonds
2 Tbsp cornstarch
2 large eggs, beaten
2 to 3 Tbsp slivered
almonds for garnish
Cinnamon for dusting

Kalamansi-poached Pears
2⅔ cups sugar
12 cups water
1 piece star anise
2 vanilla beans, slit lengthwise
½ cup kalamansi purée
5 Bartlett pears

If you cannot find black currant purée, use huckleberries or organic blueberries. Combine 1 cup berries with ½ cup + 2 Tbsp sugar in a pot on medium-high heat. Bring to a boil, stir and remove from the heat. Strain through a fine-mesh sieve, discarding solids.

Kalamansi is a small citrus fruit similar to lime mixed with tangerine. The purée is sold at Filipino grocers. If you can't find it, use lime juice. *Serves 8*

Shortbread Cream together sugar, butter and salt in a bowl. Add flour without overmixing the dough. Add only enough egg, mixing gently, to hold the dough together. Gather the dough into a ball and flatten, then wrap in plastic wrap and refrigerate for a minimum of 1 hour.

Black Currant Jam Combine black currant purée and sugar in a pot on medium-high heat. Bring to a boil, stir and remove from the heat. Strain through a fine-mesh sieve, discard solids and allow to cool before using.

Almond Cream Have all of the ingredients at room temperature. Use a stand mixer with a paddle attachment to cream together butter and sugar. Remove the bowl from the mixer.

Combine ground almonds and cornstarch in another bowl. Alternately add almond mixture and beaten eggs to the butter mixture, stirring just until combined.

Kalamansi-poached Pears To make the poaching liquid, pour sugar into a heavy pot on medium heat and do not stir. As the sugar begins to caramelize, shake and swirl the pan gently to prevent the sugar from burning in any one spot. Once the sugar has melted into a rich caramel brown, deglaze the pan slowly and carefully with water, as the mixture will splatter. Stir until sugar is totally dissolved. Add star anise, vanilla beans and kalamansi purée.

Peel and core pears, add to the poaching liquid, then simmer until tender. Remove from the heat and place a plate over the pears to keep them submerged in the poaching liquid as they cool.

To Assemble Preheat the oven to 325°F. On a lightly floured surface, roll out shortbread dough into a circle 11½ inches in diameter and ⅛-inch thick. Use it to line a 9-inch tart pan (with removable bottom). Cut off excess dough and crimp around the edge.

Pipe or spread black currant jam on the bottom of the tart. Next, pipe or spread a layer of almond cream to within three-quarters of the top. Cut poached pears in half, then slice each half vertically into about eight pieces. Keeping the slices together, arrange pears on top of almond cream to cover. Sprinkle the top with slivered almonds and a dusting of cinnamon. Bake in the oven for 45 to 60 minutes, or until the centre of the tart is set. Remove from the oven.

To Serve Serve the tart at room temperature. Cut into eight wedges and place each on a warmed serving plate.

Wine Inniskillin Okanagan Vineyards Winery Riesling Icewine or Jackson-Triggs Okanagan Estate Proprietor's Reserve Riesling Icewine

Double Chocolate Chip Cookies

½ cup unsalted butter

¼ cup + 2 Tbsp golden yellow sugar

⅓ cup + 1 Tbsp granulated sugar

2 Tbsp best brown sugar

¼ cup corn syrup

1 egg

1½ tsp vanilla extract

1⅓ cups + 1 Tbsp cake flour

Pinch of salt

1½ tsp baking soda

2 Tbsp cocoa powder

1 oz dark chocolate, melted

1⅔ cups chocolate chips

Everyone needs another recipe for the beloved chocolate chip cookie. This one is special. *Makes about 3 dozen*

Preheat the oven to 325°F. Place butter with golden yellow, granulated and brown sugars, and corn syrup in a bowl and cream together. Gradually mix in egg and vanilla.

Sift together flour, salt, baking soda and cocoa powder into a bowl. Fold this dry mixture into the butter mixture. Stir in melted chocolate and chocolate chips.

Scoop the dough into thirty-six mounds, without flattening, on parchment paper–lined baking sheets, leaving 3 inches of space between them (the cookies spread while baking). Bake in the oven for 12 to 15 minutes, or until just set when lightly touched. Remove cookies from the baking sheets and cool on racks.

Wine Elephant Island Orchard Wines Cherry Stellaport

Tojo's Sablefish

The marinade adds all the flavour necessary for the buttery, delicious roasted sablefish. *Serves 8*

Begin making this 2 days before serving. Cut sablefish into eight pieces, about 3 oz each, and place in a ziplock bag. Mix together soy sauce, mirin, sugar and ginger in a bowl, then pour over fish. Close the bag and marinate in the refrigerator for 2 days.

Preheat the oven to 450°F. Shake off the marinade from fish, pat dry with paper towels and place on a rimmed baking sheet. Roast in the oven for 10 to 12 minutes, or until done (the flesh flakes easily).

While fish is cooking, heat oil in a large pot on medium-high heat. Add spinach and garlic, then cook for about 5 minutes, or until spinach wilts. Season with salt and pepper to taste.

To Serve Divide cooked spinach among warmed plates and top each serving with a piece of roasted sablefish.

Wine Quails' Gate Estate Winery Stewart Family Reserve Chardonnay

1½ lbs Canadian sablefish

½ cup + 2 Tbsp dark soy sauce

7 Tbsp mirin (Japanese sweet cooking rice wine)

2 Tbsp sugar

4 tsp freshly ground ginger

2 tsp vegetable oil

2 bunches spinach, stems discarded

2 tsp grated garlic

Ohba Scallops

Serve these little golden bundles of flavour with a selection of small plates to share at the table. The surimi is white fish sticks, sold at Japanese food stores. *Serves 6*

Place scallops, surimi, shallot and tobiko in a small bowl. In another bowl, combine yuzu kosho and mayonnaise, then add to the scallop mixture, mixing well, and allow to sit for 20 minutes.

Place oil in a deep fryer to the marked line or half-fill a tall-sided heavy pot on the stovetop and heat to 350°F. Coat the underside of each ohba leaf with flour, then lay them flat, flour-side up, on a work surface. Divide the scallop mixture evenly among the leaves, then roll them up from the base to the tip of the leaf, enclosing the filling. Dip the exposed seafood on the sides in panko, but do not coat the ohba leaves themselves. Deep-fry the rolls for about 1½ minutes, or until golden. Drain on paper towels.

To Serve Arrange the rolls on a warmed serving platter.

Wine St Hubertus Chasselas

1½ oz scallops (2 large), in ½-inch cubes

2¼ oz surimi, in ¼-cubes

1 Tbsp finely minced shallot

2 Tbsp tobiko (flying fish roe)

⅓ tsp yuzu kosho (Japanese yuzu and chili paste)

½ tsp mayonnaise

Vegetable oil for deep-frying

12 leaves ohba (shiso)

¼ cup flour

1 cup fine panko (Japanese bread crumbs)

The Chefs

LISA AHIER, SOBO After graduating with honours from the Culinary Institute of America, Lisa Ahier and her business partner and husband, Artie, moved to Texas to open the lodge at the Fossil Rim Wildlife Center and later managed the luxury Cibolo Creek Ranch. After arriving in the town of Tofino on Vancouver Island's west coast, the pair launched SoBo (short for "Sophisticated Bohemian") in 2002. Originally cooking from a purple catering truck and being recognized by *enRoute* magazine as one of the top ten best new restaurants in Canada, the Ahiers moved the restaurant into a building in Tofino two years ago. Lisa is a free-spirited chef who gambols through local ingredients with obvious affection.

ANGUS AN, GASTROPOD CATERING AND PRIVATE DINING Angus An emigrated from Taiwan to Canada at the age of eleven. After receiving a fine arts degree from the University of British Columbia, he moved to New York to apprentice at Jean-Georges Vongerichten's JoJo while studying at the French Culinary Institute. After graduating first in his class, he spent several years with chef Norman Laprise at Montreal's acclaimed Toqué, then moved on to the U.K. to work at The Fat Duck, Le Manoir aux Quat' Saisons and Nahm (the world's only Michelin-starred Thai restaurant). He returned to Canada in 2006 with his wife, Kate, to open his own restaurant, Gastropod, which promptly won *Vancouver* magazine's Best New Fine Dining award.

JEREMIE BASTIEN, BONETA Jeremie Bastien was born into the restaurant trade. His father, chef Richard Bastien, owns three of Quebec's best-known restaurants: Café des Beaux Arts and Leméac in Montreal, and Le Mitoyen in Laval. By age sixteen, Jeremie had worked his way through nearly every station on the line. Once out of culinary school, he travelled to France to work for David Zuddas at the Michelin-starred L'Auberge de la Charme and later to San Francisco to cook at Boulevard. A call from Lumière brought him to Vancouver. After three years working there with chef Rob Feenie, the twenty-six-year old took his first executive chef position at Gastown's popular and award-winning Boneta.

MATT BATEY, THE TERRACE RESTAURANT AT MISSION HILL FAMILY
ESTATE WINERY Mentored by Michael Allemeier, Matt was The Terrace's
chef from 2007 until 2009, when he was promoted to oversee all of
Mission Hill's food program as winery chef. He was instrumental in
securing several important distinctions for Terrace, including a 2008
Travel + Leisure magazine rating as "one of the five best winery restaurants in the world." Matt begins with the winery's extensive portfolio
of varietals and blends, then marries local and seasonal ingredients to
them. Prior to joining Mission Hill, he worked at the Wedgewood Hotel
and La Belle Auberge in Vancouver, Catch in Calgary and the Empress
Hotel in Victoria. He is also a winner of numerous team and individual
international competitions.

ROBERT BELCHAM, FUEL RESTAURANT After training at Victoria's
Camosun College, Robert made his start at Rebar, one of Canada's most
celebrated vegetarian restaurants, then moved to Vancouver Island's
Aerie Resort and became its executive sous chef. He spent a year as chef
de partie at Thomas Keller's famous Californian restaurant, The French
Laundry. In 2002, he returned to Canada and joined the team at
C Restaurant, rising to the position of chef de cuisine under executive
chef Rob Clark. He opened Fuel with another C alumnus, sommelier
Tom Doughty, in 2007, and it claimed the Best New Fine Dining award
at the *Vancouver* magazine restaurant awards. His second restaurant, the
casual Italian-themed Campagnolo, opened in 2008, also to raves.

NED BELL, CABANA BAR AND GRILLE Born in B.C.'s Okanagan Valley
wine country, Ned grew up with a passion for cooking. He began his
career under the tutelage of Le Crocodile's Michel Jacob and gradu-
ated to the sous chef position at Lumière in 1995. In 1997, Bell moved
east to become the executive chef at Niagara-on-the-Lake's Peninsula
Ridge Estates Winery, later heading to Toronto to helm the kitchens at
Accolade and Sen5es. During that time, Bell became a regular fixture on
Food Network Canada's *Cook Like a Chef* program. He returned home to
Kelowna in 2007 to open his first restaurant, the wildly popular
Cabana Bar and Grille.

JOHN BISHOP, BISHOP'S It took a Brit to tell us that our local ingredients were among the finest in the world. And that's exactly what John did, beginning in 1973 as head chef at Il Giardino. In 1985, John opened Bishop's and began trumpeting the merits of local organic produce, sustainable fish, and beef and poultry from local farms. John was a founding director of the Chefs' Table Society, was inducted into the B.C. Restaurant Hall of Fame and won the *Vancouver* magazine Lifetime Achievement Award for Excellence in the Culinary Arts. He has written four cookbooks and has brilliantly trained many chefs, not just in rigorous technique but also to serve what is fresh and local.

JULIAN BOND, PACIFIC INSTITUTE OF CULINARY ARTS Julian brings a wealth of experience to his calling: training our next generation of chefs. In 1999, the former executive chef of Star Anise and Oritalia was named "Young Chef of the Millennium" by the *Globe and Mail*, while *Maclean's* tapped him as one of the "Top 100 Canadians under 30." From 2000 to 2005, he was program director of the Dubrulle School of Culinary Arts, and then was the corporate executive chef with Cactus Club Cafes. In 2007, he became program director and chef instructor at the Pacific Institute of Culinary Arts. Julian (a director of the Chefs' Table Society) and his students, in close conjunction with co-editor Joan Cross, tested the recipes in this book.

THIERRY BUSSET, CINCIN No less than Gordon Ramsay recently called Thierry "one of the best pastry chefs in the world." Frenchman Busset learned his craft in some of the world's best Michelin-starred restaurants, including London's Le Gavroche, France's L'Auberge du Père Bise and Marco Pierre White's The Restaurant at the Hyde Park Hotel, where he worked for almost a decade. He was a member of the opening team at South Granville's West Restaurant in 2000 and has since moved on to its sister restaurant, the Mediterranean-themed CinCin, where he is known as the "angel of the kitchen" for his all-white apparel and heavenly desserts.

JAMES CAMPBELL, TOMATO FRESH FOOD CAFÉ After apprenticing at Toronto's Beaujolais and Remy's in Vancouver, Campbell honed his knives in Vancouver at the Delta Pacific Resort and the William Tell Restaurant before starting as sous chef at Tomato Fresh Food Café in 2000. Since becoming executive chef in 2003, he has worked with local suppliers and buys the freshest regional ingredients direct from the source to create menus that steer global influences forward with local, seasonal flavours.

ANDREA CARLSON, BISHOP'S A graduate of the Art Institute of Vancouver's culinary program, Andrea trained at Star Anise before joining C Restaurant as executive sous chef in 1998. After travels across eastern Europe and Turkey, she started a bakery on remote Savary Island before moving to Vancouver Island's Sooke Harbour House, where she worked with Edward Tuson and Sinclair Philip. She rejoined C as pastry chef in 2003 and then moved on to chef de cuisine at its sister restaurant, Raincity Grill, where she helped to popularize the locavore movement by launching a "100-Mile Menu." She became executive chef at Bishop's restaurant in 2008 and is considered one of Vancouver's most exciting regional cooks.

BERNARD CASAVANT, SONORA ROOM AT BURROWING OWL ESTATE WINERY Bernard completed the Culinary Arts Program at Malaspina College and in 1986 was one of the first chefs in Canada to earn his Certified Chef de Cuisine ticket. Later, he became the first westerner to represent Canada at the Bocuse d'Or competition. He has worked in many leading kitchens, including the Fairmont Chateau Whistler, where he was executive chef. He then opened his own venture, Chef Bernard's Café, also in Whistler. He is now the proprietor and chef of The Sonora Room in Osoyoos, the heart of our red wine country. Bernard was inducted into the B.C. Restaurant Hall of Fame, in part for his dedication in giving back to young chefs and our culinary community.

MARC-ANDRÉ CHOQUETTE, VOYA RESTAURANT AT THE LODEN HOTEL
Marc-André was born and raised in Laval, Quebec, and began his
career as an apprentice sous chef at Richard Bastien's Le Mitoyen. After
receiving his trade diploma from Montreal's Institut de Tourisme et
d'Hôtellerie du Québec, he finished both the Interprovincial Standards
Red Seal Program and the International Sommelier Guild Wine Funda-
mentals. He received further training in France, the U.S. and Australia,
then settled on the West Coast, working at Vancouver Island's Sooke
Harbour House and in Vancouver at West, Feenie's and Lumière. Now
executive chef at Voya, he is considered one of Canada's top chefs, highly
regarded for his masterful blendings of French and Asian cuisines, and
equally for mentoring younger cooks.

ROBERT CLARK, C RESTAURANT Clark is Mr. Sustainability. The early,
gently vocal champion of a sustainable coastal fishery, he has introduced
colourful, flavourful local seafood plates at C Restaurant while ensuring
that they are eco-conscious. He often fishes with fishermen (then makes
them dinner), and he pioneered the Spot Prawn Festival. Rob was also
the first to sign on with the Vancouver Aquarium's Ocean Wise Program
and made sure his peers were right behind him. Now, he oversees the
kitchens at C and its sister restaurants, Nu and Raincity Grill, while
keeping the lines open with local fishermen, farmers and foragers. He
brings a vigour to his role as a director of the Chefs' Table Society, quietly
educating, never remonstrating.

ROB CORDONIER, SONORA ROOM AT BURROWING OWL ESTATE
WINERY Rob grew up in Kamloops with a huge backyard vegetable
garden (complete with chicken coop) and an affection for hunting and
fishing. The lessons of his parents—putting a meal on the table through
growing and catching—made an indelible impact on his approach to
cooking. Once finished his cook certification program at the University
College of the Cariboo, he took a job at the Fairmont Chateau Whistler
and worked part-time at chef Bernard Casavant's popular café across
the street. After rising to the position of restaurant chef at the Fairmont
Waterfront, in 2007 Rob rejoined chef Casavant as pastry chef at
the Sonora Room, the restaurant at Burrowing Owl Estate Winery
near Osoyoos.

MELISSA CRAIG, BEARFOOT BISTRO Following the rigorous three-day black box and wine-pairing contests, Melissa topped the podium at 2008's Canadian Olympic Gold Medal Plates competition, the first woman to do so. At Whistler's Bearfoot Bistro, she has tightened supply lines and unleashed a passion that shows on the plate and is in keeping with the restaurant's extraordinary wine cellar. A graduate of Malaspina College, Melissa was National Champion at the 2001 Canadian Federation of Chefs & Cooks National Junior Cook Competition, the first Canadian woman to do so, and at just twenty. Further training and exposure to local ingredients followed at Sooke Harbour House and King Pacific Lodge, where she indulged guests with her twist on indigenous preparations.

QUANG DANG, C RESTAURANT Quang, the son of a Vietnamese professor of engineering and a Canadian mother of Scottish descent, was born and raised in Calgary. His rise up the culinary ranks is proof of the meritocratic nature of the restaurant industry. In a few short years, he went from being a refreshment vendor at the Calgary Stampede to a senior line cook at Coquitlam's Joeys. He then signed on with chef Chris Mills at Vancouver's Diva restaurant at the Metropolitan Hotel, then as sous chef at Rare, where he cooked with Brian Fowke. Two years ago, at the age of twenty-seven, he became chef de cuisine at C, arguably Canada's most forward-thinking sustainable seafood restaurant.

LAURENT DEVIN, BISTROT BISTRO Laurent's love of hospitality began as a teenager in France. After graduating from hotel and catering school in 1990, he and his wife, Valerie (who runs the front-of-house at their Kitsilano eatery), moved to England, where he worked for the Chez Gerard Group and the Marriott hotel chain. Emigration to Canada followed, and after working stops in Montreal, Windsor and Toronto, Laurent and his young family finally landed in Vancouver in 2005. Their much-loved neighbourhood restaurant, Bistrot Bistro, renowned for its devotion to rustic French cooking and personal service, was launched in 2007.

ANDREY DURBACH, LA BUCA AND PIED-À-TERRE Andrey Durbach is a no-nonsense operator and uncompromising cook. Best known for simple, classically inspired dishes, he layers rich flavours and plates without fuss. His flagship restaurant, Parkside, opened in 2003 and has since replicated his La Buca restaurant both in name and rusticated Italian menu. Andrey and his partners also operate the Pied-à-Terre bistro on Cambie. Both his dedication to high-quality ingredients and his avoidance of culinary trends have won him a devoted following among the food-obsessed, as well as the respect of his peers.

ROB FEENIE, CACTUS CLUB CAFES Canada's first celebrity chef and also its first Iron Chef, Rob is a graduate of the Dubrulle Culinary Institute. After apprenticing extensively overseas, he trained under Michel Jacob at Le Crocodile in Vancouver. He opened his iconic Lumière restaurant in 1995 to critical and popular praise. It was soon regarded as Vancouver's best restaurant, winning Relais Gourmand, Mobil and AAA 5 Diamond awards. He has published three cookbooks and starred in a long-running television cooking series on Food Network Canada. From his kitchens have sprung some of the province's top young chefs, many of whom now command their own rooms. In 2008, Rob joined Cactus Club Cafes to direct the menu development and chef-training programs.

MANUEL FERREIRA, LE GAVROCHE Veteran restaurateur Ferreira is a legend in Vancouver's food and beverage community. He is recognized as much for his international experience and knowledge of fine wines (his cellars are unparalleled on the West Coast) as for his prowess in the kitchen, and his smooth personal style and grace at the table have cemented his reputation as one of B.C.'s top independent operators. His two restaurants, the long-established French-themed Le Gavroche in the city's West End, and the newer Portuguese-flavoured Senova in Kerrisdale, are known for their fealty to tradition and sharp service.

TINA FINEZA, THE FLYING TIGER Tina has worked at many of Vancouver's most popular restaurants, among them Lumière, Diva at the Met, Star Anise, Bin 942 and George Ultra Lounge. On a Les Dames d'Escoffier scholarship, she went to the Napa Valley to study at the Culinary Institute of America and spent a working holiday at Ridge Vineyards of Santa Cruz and Sonoma. In 2004, Tina joined the Relais & Châteaux Ryland Inn in New Jersey, followed by a working holiday in Chicago with chef Charlie Trotter. Next, Tina explored the culinary traditions of Thailand, the Malaysian flavours of Penang and Kuala Lumpur, and the fabled hawker stalls of Singapore. She opened at The Flying Tiger, an exploration of Asian street food, in 2006.

DOMINIC FORTIN, BEARFOOT BISTRO Raised in the small Quebec town of Beaupré, the twenty-six-year-old Fortin began working in restaurants at the age of fifteen, training at the nearby L'Auberge La Camarine for three years. But it was at Vancouver Island's Sooke Harbour House that Dominic discovered his love of pastry, a passion he pursued up-island at the Wickanninish Inn in Tofino with pastry chef Bruno Feldeisen. Dominic has been resident at Whistler's Bearfoot Bistro for the past three years, working as head pastry chef under renowned chef and 2008 Canadian Culinary Champion Melissa Craig.

FRANÇOIS GAGNON, CINCIN Gagnon brings years of experience to CinCin's wood-fired kitchen. With a culinary mantra of "simplicity is the hallmark of genius," he believes that "fresh ingredients should speak for themselves in order to allow natural flavours to stand out on the plate." He graduated from Quebec's Centre Integer en Alimentation et Tourisme program in culinary arts, continued his training in France under Roger Verger at the Relais & Chateaux property Le Moulin de Mougins, then worked with Joel Garault at Monte Carlo's Hôtel Hermitage. After arriving in Vancouver and working at Lumière, he became executive sous chef at Blue Water Cafe and in 2008 became executive chef at its sister restaurant, CinCin.

WARREN GERAGHTY, WEST After stints at several Michelin-starred restaurants in the U.K., including one as chef at Marco Pierre White's famed L'Escargot, the disciplined and highly pedigreed Geraghty came to Vancouver in 2008 to take over the kitchen at South Granville's multiple award-winning West. Always pushing Vancouver's regional cuisine to the next level by building bridges between its kitchen and our farms, West has evolved into an iconic powerhouse. It's the perfect fit for Geraghty, who has quickly acclimatized to our terroir, striking up friendships with suppliers and plating with a confidence that states West's regional and seasonal goals are in very capable hands.

THOMAS HAAS, THOMAS HAAS FINE CHOCOLATES AND PÂTISSERIE A fourth-generation chocolatier and chef de pâtisserie, German-born Thomas emigrated to Vancouver in 1995 but moved to New York as the opening pastry chef at Daniel Boulud's Restaurant Daniel. He returned to Vancouver to raise his family, working at the Metropolitan Hotel and Sen5es. In 2001, he won all four major categories at the U.S. National Pastry Team Championship. After launching a line of specialty chocolates, he opened his own premises in North Vancouver. Now, Thomas Haas chocolates are available near and far. Thomas believes that success is "knowing what you're doing, loving what you are doing and believing in what you are doing." He is also a director of the Chefs' Table Society.

DAVID HAWKSWORTH, HAWKSWORTH AT THE HOTEL GEORGIA David launched at West seven years ago after a decade of cooking in Britain beside such luminaries as Marco Pierre White and Bruno Loubet. His reconnection with his native Vancouver led him straight to the top of the city's culinary pyramid; in just its second year, West and Hawksworth won the Restaurant of the Year award from *Vancouver* magazine and continued to win it during the balance of his tenure. David's kitchen has turned out some fine young chefs, now working across the city, and he has made valuable contributions to the Chefs' Table Society. After a year of research and development, he will open his eponymous Hawksworth restaurant at the Hotel Georgia in 2010.

CAMERON HOCK, TERRA BREADS BAKERY CAFÉ Cameron began his adventures in food by growing heirloom rhubarb that had been handed down by his grandmother. His journey was given a solid foundation when he graduated from Stratford Chefs School in 1998. Today, he continues to learn and explore a food philosophy that revolves around local, seasonal and whole foods simply prepared, allowing the quality of the ingredients to take centre stage. Before joining Terra Breads, Cameron developed recipes and managed the regional kitchen for Capers Community Markets.

TODD HODGINS, PAIR BISTRO Todd's family sparked his love of cooking, with explorations of his grandparents' farm and his mother's dedication to sourcing seasonal ingredients. His interest turned into a passion, and while enrolled in the sommelier program at Dubrulle Culinary Institute, Todd and his wife, Janis, created Pair Bistro. An intimate restaurant focussing on locally harvested products from the open waters, vineyards and farms of B.C., since 2004 Pair has fully integrated this all-B.C. concept with daily visits to Granville Island Public Market, produce delivered from the University of British Columbia farms and strong friendships with local fishermen, farmers and vintners. In 2005, *enRoute* magazine name Pair Bistro one of the best new restaurants in Canada.

STUART IRVING, COBRE An ardent culinary polymath, Irving is always searching out new flavours and cooking styles that reflect his love of the world's cuisines. As the opening chef at the Crosstown area's game-changing Wild Rice, he and proprietor Andrew Wong created dishes for Vancouver's first modern Chinese bistro. In the summer of 2007, Stu and two partners launched Cobre (Spanish for "copper"), a Gastown restaurant fronting Nuevo Latino cuisine: a blend of Cuban, South and Central American flavours and traditions married to fresh, local ingredients, light textures and modern presentations.

STEPHANE ISTEL, DB BISTRO MODERNE Istel's cooking career, which began in his native Alsace, has since taken him across France, then to the Caribbean and New York. Last year, he landed in Vancouver to become executive chef at Daniel Boulud's newly launched DB Bistro Moderne. "I have seen Stephane demonstrate a real care for his craft as well as the discipline it takes to cook at a consistently high level of quality," Boulud said about the young chef who had worked with him for three years prior to the appointment. "Now my mission is to practise my passion and my love of cooking," Istel says, "with all the incredible foods the farmers and fishermen of this region have to offer."

MICHEL JACOB, LE CROCODILE From Alsace, where Michel trained with the great Émile Jung at Strasbourg's Michelin three-star Au Crocodile, he journeyed via Umberto Menghi's Il Palazzo to Denman Street, where he opened Le Crocodile in a tiny storefront in 1991. Chef Jacob (for he will always be a chef first and a proprietor second), now ensconced in grander digs, welcomes the bright and the beautiful nightly to his classic, determinedly French restaurant. But the athletic Michel's story is also written in the quality of the chefs that he has trained in his kitchens, perhaps most notably Rob Feenie and David Hawksworth. "My real claim to fame," he says of Feenie, "is that I stopped him from becoming a fireman."

SCOTT JAEGER, THE PEAR TREE Canadian-born Jaeger trained under Bruno Marti and subsequently worked at the Waldorf Hotel in London, then in France, Australia and Switzerland. He is Vice Conseilleur Culinaire of the esteemed La Chaîne des Rôtisseurs, a member of the Canadian Culinary Federation and a director of the Chefs' Table Society. Pear Tree, which Scott owns with his wife, Stephanie, has perennially won the *Vancouver* magazine award for Best Suburban Restaurant. A past competitor for Team Canada at the Bocuse d'Or, he continues his coaching and management work with them. His honours include the B.C. Restaurant Association's Restaurateur of the Year, the B.C. Chefs' Association Chef of the Year and *Vancouver* magazine's Chef of the Year.

DON LETENDRE, ELIXIR RESTAURANT AT THE OPUS HOTEL
Executive chef of the Opus Hotel and its award-winning Elixir Restaurant, Don has cooked in kitchens as diverse as Tokyo's Domani Cucina, England's L'Odeon and Le Manoir aux Quat' Saisons, and Vancouver's much-missed Mustache Café. More recently, he opened the three-hundred-seat Koko at the Opus Hotel in Montreal. Known for his deft, far-reaching flavours, including those of Asia and North Africa, Don is also a patient and knowledgeable mentor to many aspiring cooks and apprentices.

NICHOLAS LIM, GUSTO DI QUATTRO Nicholas took on the leader role at Gusto di Quattro in 2008 at the age of twenty-five, the youngest executive chef in the Lower Mainland. He has since divided the menu into two sections: Quattro Classics and Quattro Seasonal. "It just makes sense," he says. "We have guests who visit us weekly for their Spaghetti Quattro and radicchio-bocconcini fix, as well as diners who want to experiment with new, market-fresh dishes. This way we still hold on to our classics while emphasizing backyard cuisine with Italian flair." Before joining the Quattro Restaurants group as sous chef at Gusto in 2007, he was executive sous chef at Caffé dé Medici and executive sous chef at Hart House.

DALE MACKAY, LUMIÈRE A native of Saskatoon, Dale returned to Canada after spending six years abroad cooking under Gordon Ramsay at the Conrad Tokyo Hotel in Japan, London's Claridge's Hotel and the three Michelin-star Restaurant Gordon Ramsay. He was most recently executive sous chef at New York's Gordon Ramsay at the London. He joined the Lumière team as chef de cuisine in 2007, just prior to the restaurant's renovation and reimagining in collaboration with celebrity chef Daniel Boulud. MacKay is now Lumière's executive chef and is thrilled to be working with Boulud—and the ingredients of the West Coast.

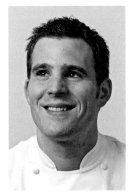

MARY MACKAY, TERRA BREADS BAKERY CAFÉ A driving force behind the Chefs' Table Society, Mary had been head baker at Terra Breads for six years when she became a co-owner of the bakery-café, famous for its crusty breads made from natural starters. After graduating in 1987 from the Dubrulle Culinary School, Mary was fortunate to meet and work with people in the food industry who inspired, trained and cultivated her sense of the importance of food. She was recognized by the Dubrulle Culinary School in 1993 with an Award of Excellence. Mary is the author of the bread-making video *Rolling in Dough* and a contributor to three popular cookbooks: *The Girls Who Dish, Seconds Anyone?* and *Inspirations*.

BRUNO MARTI, LA BELLE AUBERGE Marti is the most honoured chef in Canada. He has been inducted into both the American Academy of Chefs and the B.C. Restaurant Halls of Fame, and has been awarded the *Vancouver* magazine Lifetime Achievement Award for Culinary Excellence. His restaurant, La Belle Auberge, in suburban Ladner, pays homage to classic techniques enlivened with the freshest produce, fish and game. Bruno has also trained many young chefs to international standards. An international culinary competitor (in 1984 he captained Team Canada to victory in the Culinary Olympics in Frankfurt), he has managed local teams and Team Canada for events such as the Bocuse d'Or, where he is now a judge. Bruno has also served as head of the Canadian Culinary Federation and of the B.C. Culinary Arts Foundation.

WAYNE MARTIN, FRAÎCHE RESTAURANT After cooking for sixteen years at Four Seasons Hotel properties in the West Indies, Texas, Georgia and Vancouver, Toronto-born Wayne Martin struck out on his own in 2006 to open Crave on Vancouver's gentrifying Main Street. Its well-executed comfort food and genuine neighbourhood feel made it an instant success, and Martin has since opened two more restaurants: the locally inspired Fraîche in West Vancouver—recently named one of the "Top 10 New Restaurants in Canada" by *enRoute* magazine—and Crave Beachside, an encore of the original, in Ambleside village.

COSMO MEENS, MO:LE RESTAURANT Rising through the ranks of Victoria's restaurant scene after getting his start washing dishes at the age of twelve, Meens grew up to launch Mo:Le Restaurant. Now one of the city's most popular breakfast and lunch venues, it reflects Cosmo's active support of Vancouver Island farmers and producers. His focus on local, organic, raw and vegan foods and juices put him into the international spotlight when he was named executive chef at Santa Barbara, California's Raw Spirit 2008, the largest raw food festival in the world. That same year, he was named team chef for the Canadian Triathlon Team, cooking for them at the 2008 Olympic Games in Beijing.

NICHOLAS NUTTING, THE POINTE RESTAURANT AT THE WICKANINNISH INN Nutting graduated on the dean's list from the SAIT Professional Cooking Program in Calgary and went on to earn top honours at the Knorr CFCC Junior and La Chaîne des Rôtisseurs cooking competitions. After stints in Montreal at award-winning restaurants Garçon and Truffert Bistro, he brought his talents westward to the Wickaninnish Inn on the wild west coast of Vancouver Island, where he runs the kitchen with co-chef John Waller, extolling Tofino's virtues in the province's most spectacular dining room, "where nature is still in charge."

YUJI OTSUKA, YUJI'S JAPANESE TAPAS A man of many smiles, Otsuka brings Western and Japanese flavours together to create his own personal style of tapas at Yuji's, his eponymous Kitsilano restaurant. While as playful and innovative as any izakaya chef, he is also well known in the local cooking community for his discipline as a skilled sushi master. Eschewing farmed fish in favour of fresh and wild, he is continuously creating new dishes that are unique to the restaurant.

FRANK PABST, BLUE WATER CAFE + RAW BAR Pabst came to Vancouver in 1993 after working in several Michelin-starred restaurants in Europe, including La Becasse (Aachen), L'Hôtel Negresco (Cannes) and Restaurant de Bacon (Antibes). He led the kitchen at Lumière as chef de cuisine before opening at Pastis in 2000, which won Best New Restaurant at that year's *Vancouver* magazine restaurant awards. As executive chef at Blue Water since 2003, Pabst is a leader in celebrating local producers and sustainable-savvy fishermen. His Unsung Heroes menu salutes lesser-known seafood every February. Frank took the gold at the 2008 Vancouver Gold Medal Plates culinary competition and silver at the Gold Medal Plates national competition.

ALANA PECKHAM, CRU RESTAURANT Vancouverite Alana studied cooking at the Art Institute of Vancouver, earning her culinary certificate in 2002 and pastry certificate in 2003. Upon graduation, she worked at Feenie's and then the more formal Lumière, before joining the brigade at West Broadway's wine-forward Cru Restaurant, where she rose to become the executive chef. Her cooking style is influenced both by her training in traditional French techniques and by her cultural heritage as a Chinese Canadian. Alana shops for the restaurant at Granville Island Public Market every day and is a regular patron of the University of British Columbia's organic farm.

ADAM PEGG, LA QUERCIA After receiving a culinary diploma from Victoria's Camosun College, Adam spent the next twelve years cooking and baking at various restaurants in B.C.'s capital before taking two years off to work stages across northern Italy. He studied at the Higher Institute of Gastronomy in Jesi, returning home to the kitchen line at Vancouver's La Buca, where he was reunited with an old friend, Lucais Syme. In 2008, the two chefs opened their first restaurant together, the Italian-themed La Quercia ("The Oak Tree"), to critical and popular acclaim.

SINCLAIR PHILIP, SOOKE HARBOUR HOUSE Sinclair's tenacity in sourcing virtually all of his ingredients (except for coffee and citrus) within a tight radius of his renowned Sooke Harbour House is legendary. Extensive herb gardens, local fruits and vegetables and nearby foragings supply the kitchens daily, and he can even be spotted walking up the beach with some freshly speared salmon and a bucket of oysters. One of B.C.'s true pioneers in the ethic of sustainable aquaculture and agriculture, Sinclair's example has inspired many younger chefs and proprietors. He has received innumerable awards, including induction into the B.C. Restaurant Hall of Fame, and was also the first Canadian president of Slow Food Canada.

CRISTIANO POSTERARO, CIOPPINO'S MEDITERRANEAN GRILL Toronto-raised Cristiano started helping out at his father's restaurant, Celestino's, when he was just thirteen. After training at George Brown College's culinary program, and on the line by his uncle, chef Pino Posteraro, he worked at the Four Seasons Hotel and Truffles before moving to Vancouver and the demanding pasta station at Il Giardino. By the time Pino opened Cioppino's in the Yaletown area in 1999, Cristiano had proven his mettle and became its junior sous chef. Since then he has worked his way up to chef de cuisine; with his uncle and their skilled brigade, they oversee the main restaurant, private dining rooms and the adjoining Enoteca.

PINO POSTERARO, CIOPPINO'S MEDITERRANEAN GRILL Born in Calabria, Pino's first interest in cooking came in his mother's kitchen. After leaving medical school, he moved to Toronto to help out at brother Celestino's newly opened restaurant. He later taught at George Brown College, but in 1990 returned to Italy. Pino got his big break when he was appointed chef of the Ristorante Bologna at the Marina Mandarin Hotel in Singapore. After stints at Toronto's Borgo Antico and an encore in Italy, Pino moved to Vancouver to helm Il Giardino's kitchens. In 1999, he opened Cioppino's, perhaps the finest Italian restaurant (with southern French inflections) in the country. In addition to winning many awards and critical accolades, he has trained a number of fine young chefs.

ALESSANDRA QUAGLIA, PROVENCE RESTAURANTS While gaining hands-on experience in the kitchen of Toronto's acclaimed Fenton's restaurant, Alessandra worked towards her diploma in culinary management at George Brown College, moving on to apprentice at the famous Windsor Arms Hotel. She then moved to France, where she staged in fine kitchens across the Côte d'Azur. In Nice, she fell in love with a young chef de partie tournant: Jean-Francis Quaglia. She returned to Canada with him, and they launched their first restaurant together, Provence Mediterranean Grill, in 1997, following it up with Provence Marinaside in 2002.

JEAN-FRANCIS QUAGLIA, PROVENCE RESTAURANTS Jean-Francis's mother is the acclaimed French chef Suzanne Quaglia (for whom, at age eight, he made his first tarte au citron) of Le Patalain in Marseilles. After graduating from the École Hôtelière de Marseilles, he apprenticed at the Hôtel Sorbitel and Le Patalain before gaining further experience in the restaurants of the Côte d'Azur and Monte Carlo, including Eze's famed Château de la Chèvre D'Or and the Hôtel Negresco. He met his future wife, Alessandra, at the latter, and moved with her when she returned to Vancouver, where they launched their two highly successful restaurants.

DINO RENAERTS, DIVA AT THE METROPOLITAN HOTEL Executive chef of Diva at the Metropolitan Hotel, with a background that includes stints at some of the city's best kitchens—the William Tell, Bishop's, Bistro Pastis, West and Fairmont Hotels—Dino is also serving as president of the B.C. Chefs' Association. The winner of a number of international cooking competitions, his appreciation for wine led him to become western Canada's first chef to attain his sommelier certificate. His role in the B.C. Chefs' Association now sees him travelling across the province, mentoring younger members.

SEAN RILEY, GLOWBAL RESTAURANT GROUP Sean's kitchen prowess has won him several local and national culinary nods, including Ontario's prestigious Tony Roland Hot Award. He has cooked in the Vancouver kitchens of Joe Fortes Seafood & Chop House as executive sous chef, Brix Restaurant and Wine Bar as executive chef and Cioppino's Mediterranean Grill as executive sous chef. Today, he oversees all the kitchens of the Glowbal Restaurant Group as corporate chef, creating new dishes and mentoring his team at Glowbal Grill & Satay Bar, Coast, Sanafır, Italian Kitchen and Trattoria Italian Kitchen.

PETER ROBERTSON, RAINCITY GRILL After training under chef Tony Bilson, a champion of Australia's local cuisine, the Sydney-raised Robertson staged at Berkshire's Fat Duck and London's Tom Aitkens restaurants before making the move to Canada. Mentored by chef Rob Clark at Vancouver's C Restaurant, he became its sous chef and took over the chef de cuisine role at sister restaurant Raincity Grill last year. Renowned for its dedication to local, seasonal, organic and sustainable foods, Raincity now offers a special "100-Mile Menu" all year round.

JOSEPH SARTOR, NU RESTAURANT Joseph, a Humber College Culinary Management honours graduate, was born and raised in the Ontario town of Niagara-on-the-Lake. He trained there at the Prince of Wales Hotel and staged for six months at Oxford's Michelin-starred Le Manoir aux Quat' Saisons under chef Gary Jones. Returning to Canada in 2005, he gained further experience in Vancouver at Bin 941 and the Wedgewood Hotel's Bacchus Restaurant. Now chef de cuisine at Nu and through working closely with executive chef Rob Clark, Sartor feels quite at home. His personal food philosophy of freshness and simplicity mirrors that of the restaurant's; his classical French preparations and clean flavours are a fine marriage.

NICO SCHUERMANS, CHAMBAR BELGIAN RESTAURANT A chef of exacting standards, Nico studied at the prestigious CREPAC school of culinary arts in Belgium. After apprenticing at the Michelin-starred La Villa Lorraine, he took on the chef de partie position at Comme Chez Soi, Belgium's finest restaurant. From there, it was on to the Savoy Hotel in London, where he completed his professional training before moving to become head chef at Sydney's Alhambra. Since making the move to Vancouver and opening the award-winning Belgian- and Morrocan-themed Chambar in 2005, and the next-door Medina, he has established himself as one of our top chefs.

MERRI SCHWARTZ, GROWING CHEFS!/QUATTRO ON FOURTH
Merri attended the Baking and Pastry Arts Program at Vancouver Community College, then trained at Sweet Obsession Cakes & Pastries before starting at C Restaurant as assistant pastry chef, rising quickly to pastry chef. She apprenticed at Cocoa West Chocolatier, on Bowen Island, then on a scholarship from Les Dames d'Escoffier, she went to France to attend workshops at the Valrhona Chocolate School and to Italy and Switzerland to develop her pastry technique. Formerly the pastry chef at Quattro on Fourth, she is the founder and director of Growing Chefs! Chefs for Children's Urban Agriculture, a non-profit organization that pairs elementary schoolchildren with chef volunteers who help them to plant, grow and cook their own vegetables.

LUCAIS SYME, LA QUERCIA The Edmonton-born Syme moved west in 2003 to work and train at many of Vancouver's better restaurants, among them Cioppino's (where he worked with the Chefs' Table Society's current president Pino Posteraro), La Buca and Parkside, where he learned the robust flavours of chef Andrey Durbach. He opened the popular La Quercia ("The Oak Tree") in 2008 with chef Adam Pegg. Their culinary collaboration is centred on the cuisines of northern Italy and is based on the belief that "simple ingredients treated properly create the most satisfying experience." Though scarcely a year old, La Quercia has become one of the most popular neighbourhood restaurants in the city.

YOSHIHIRO TABO, BLUE WATER CAFE + RAW BAR A native of Japan, Yoshi began his lengthy apprenticeship in Osaka more than thirty-five years ago. Landing in Canada in 1972, he worked at Kaede and later for the original Koji Restaurant before going independent, first with the popular Shijo in 1986 and then with his award-winning, eponymous sushi restaurant, Yoshi, in 1998. He has been impressing diners with his precision knife skills and artful presentations at Blue Water Cafe's Raw Bar since 2002, demonstrating how to prepare and serve B.C.'s fresh, wild and sustainable ocean harvest.

NEIL TAYLOR, CIBO TRATTORIA At age sixteen, Taylor, born and raised in the U.K., knew that his true passion in life was food. After high school, he enrolled in a culinary apprenticeship program and began working in the kitchen at a local hotel. In 1997, he moved to London and worked his way through the kitchens at some of the city's top restaurants. Three years later, he was offered a position at the Michelin-starred River Café—a restaurant renowned for its authentic, market-fresh Italian cuisine, and where celebrity chef Jamie Oliver also cut his chops. Recently arrived in Vancouver, Neil's remarkable Italian-inflected food at Cibo and Uva Wine Bar has already attracted a critical and popular following.

HIDEKAZU TOJO, TOJO'S Since arriving in Vancouver in the early 1970s from Japan, where he learned the traditional basics of Japanese cookery (and, if legend can be trusted, memorized some two thousand recipes), Tojo-san has helped shape the city's culinary culture. Sometimes called "the Elvis of Sushi," this master transforms the ocean's freshest products into intricate and always innovative plates. His rigorous apprenticeship of sixteen-hour days taught him that hard work and honesty would deliver his dreams. Today, in his beautiful new restaurant on Vancouver's West Broadway, Tojo is "training a new generation of chefs to follow in my footsteps, to step out of the traditional cooking methods and be creative."

ESTHER TSO, THOMAS HAAS FINE CHOCOLATES AND PÂTISSERIE
Esther's ardour for pastry art led her into an intensive ten-month culinary training program. She began her apprenticeship under Thomas Haas at Sen5es and the Metropolitan Hotel in Vancouver. In 2003 she placed in the top three in each category at the Salon du Chocolat competition, in 2005 she joined Thomas at his new (and soon to be award-winning) chocolate and pastry shop in North Vancouver, in 2006 she taught alongside Thomas at the World Pastry Forum in Phoenix, Arizona, and in 2007 won her first culinary competition at the Quady Winery Dessert and Wine Pairing competition in Vancouver. Esther is now Thomas's valued assistant, creating distinctive and innovative works of pastry while also managing production and special events.

MASAAKI TSUJIMOTO, HAPA IZAKAYA Born and raised in Wakayama, Japan, Masaaki began cooking professionally at the age of twenty. After six years of training in a kaiseki-style kitchen in Osaka, he realized his dream of working overseas when he moved to Vancouver. Masaaki started at Hapa Izakaya in 2006 and is now the executive chef at Hapa's Robson Street location, where he seamlessly weaves both Western and traditional Japanese ingredients in an assortment of dishes that define the cacophony of modern izakaya cuisine.

EDWARD TUSON, SOOKE HARBOUR HOUSE More than two decades ago, Sooke Harbour House gained an international reputation for its local, seasonal, organic and wild cuisine. Rated the "Best Restaurant in the World for Authentic, Local Cuisine" by *Gourmet* magazine and "Best Restaurant in Canada" by the *Globe and Mail*, it remains a locavore's dream. Tuson has been at the helm for the past twelve years, crafting inventive daily menus using edible flowers, native plants and herbs organically grown in the inn's own gardens. Combined with the fecundity of the local inlets (proprietor Sinclair Philip frequently brings home the catch), Edward also zealously sources from nearby gardeners, forest foragers, seaweed harvesters and artisan food producers.

RHONDA VIANI, WEST A high school teacher first sparked Rhonda Viani's passion for the kitchen. After apprenticing at Michel Jacob's Le Crocodile, she worked for four years under chocolatier-pâtissier Greg Hook at Chocolate Arts before rising to the pastry chef positions at Lumière and Sooke Harbour House. Landing at West in 2002, she has become one of Vancouver's sweetest—and most sought after—pastry chefs. Her dessert menu changes with the seasons, often showcasing fresh fruits and chocolate desserts that include a whisper of fresh local herbs.

VIKRAM VIJ, VIJ'S Born in India, Vikram moved to Austria in 1984 to study hotel management, settling in Canada five years later. He worked at Vancouver's Bishop's and Raincity Grill before opening the internationally renowned Vij's in 1994. The forward Indian menu (which he constantly retools with his wife, Meeru, to reflect the local seasons) is designed to pair with wine. Vij's has been featured in several North American television broadcasts and publications, including the Food Network, CNN, *The Globe and Mail*, *Washington Post*, *Travel + Leisure*, *Food & Wine* and *Bon Appétit*, and was described in the *New York Times* as "easily among the finest Indian restaurants in the world."

JOHN WALLER, THE POINTE RESTAURANT AT THE WICKANINNISH INN Waller started his career in Toronto as one of the youngest Red Seal Certified chefs in Canada, achieving the distinction at the age of just twenty-one. He has since worked at some of the best restaurants in Toronto and Victoria, and has also owned two restaurants on Vancouver Island. Together with co-chef Nicholas Nutting, he enjoys managing the food program at the Wickaninnish Inn on the west coast of Vancouver Island and is known to wax effusive when local seafood, game and produce suppliers drop by to sell their wares.

JAMES WALT, ARAXI Gordon Ramsay's favourite B.C. chef, James Walt of Whistler's much-lauded Araxi restaurant is spontaneous and inventive. His résumé, which includes several of B.C.'s top restaurants, features a one-year appointment as executive chef at the Canadian Embassy in Rome, and three performances at New York's celebrated James Beard House. As a resident of Whistler's nearby farming community of Pemberton, James has built direct relationships with area farmers and ranchers whose produce and meat products are regularly highlighted on his locally driven, sustainable menus.

ANDREW WONG, WILD RICE Andrew's roots in the hospitality trade run deep. His grandfather, Wong Wam-Fung, was the owner of Vancouver's Lotus Hotel, and his father served tables for years. Andrew's first restaurant job came at thirteen, and by twenty, he was working at three jobs while completing the hospitality management program at Dubrulle Culinary School. In 2001, he made his dream of creating a modern Chinese bistro a reality with Wild Rice, located next door to his grandfather's old hotel. Using local and sustainable ingredients to create Wild Rice's unique cuisine, Andrew is a charter member of the Ocean Wise Program and the Green Table Network, and has developed a wine list featuring West Coast labels.

NEIL WYLES, HAMILTON STREET GRILL British-born Neil is a Yaletown institution, having launched his popular, steak-focussed Hamilton Street Grill in 1996, long before the neighbourhood emerged as Vancouver's premiere restaurant locale. He studied music at UBC and is self-taught in the kitchen, claiming, "My passion for food comes from a passion for eating." He is the treasurer of the Chefs' Table Society and president of the Yaletown Business Improvement Association.

KOJI ZENIMARU, KINGYO IZAKAYA The young Japanese chef at award-winning Kingyo is one Vancouver's most exciting izakaya innovators. Koji's loud, open kitchen—a sushi-free zone—crowds Western notions with izakaya inventions from the late-night cauldrons of inner city Tokyo and Osaka. Notorious for his fun-loving antics at cooking events (he and his kitchen crew often dress up as Mexican wrestlers, complete with masks and dragon wings), Koji offers much-appreciated whimsy in both his cooking and in his attentions to his guests.

Index

Photos are referenced in italics.

aïoli, chipotle, 80
aïoli, mint, 31
albacore tuna togarashi with
    buckwheat soba noodles and
    candied ginger–three citrus
    vinaigrette, 82, *83*
almond(s)
    cream, 214
    melon gazpacho, 146–47
    pear tart, 214–15
apple(s)
    and bulgar wheat salad,
        60–61
    and French sorrel sorbet, 48
    in port wine gelée, 198
apricot purée, 149–50
arctic char à la Provencal,
    100, 101
artichokes, 119
avocado purée, 162

BACON
    crisp, with chanterelle open-
        faced ravioli, *206, 207*
    double-smoked, with chicken
        orecchiette, 126–27
    emulsion, 188
    in horseradish sauerkraut, 138
    maple-smoked, and hazelnut
        dressing, 165
    and pea purée, 14, *15*
    smoked, vinaigrette, 185
    wild boar, with scallops, 29
Baja-style fish tacos with jicama
    slaw and chipotle aïoli, 80
balsamic glaze, 135
balsamic zabaglione, 164
barbecued Peking duck soup
    and homemade won tons with
    lime, chili, ginger and green
    onion, 180, *181*
barbecue sauce, chili, 166
barbecue sauce, spicy, 22–23

BASIL
    in bull kelp salad, 161
    oil, 146–47
    in terrine of sardines,
        heirloom tomatoes and
        zucchini, *16, 17*–18
    and tomato salad, 143
B.C. albacore tuna ceviche
    with avocado purée, pickled
    red onions and chili lime
    chips, 162, *163*
B.C. Honey mussels with thyme
    and Gruyère frites, 154, *155*
bean, cannelloni, topping for
    bruschetta, 152–53
béchamel sauce, 68
BEEF. *See also* veal
    oxtail, red wine-braised,
        with sugar pumpkin
        gnocchi, shallots and
        pancetta, 196–97
    rib-eye steak, dry-aged, with
        morels, nugget potatoes,
        144, 145
    tagliata di manzo, 96
BEET(S)
    glazed, 39–40
    pickled, 208–09
    and vodka-cured hamachi,
        156–57
Berkshire pork duo: tender-
    loin and crispy belly with
    sauerkraut, horseradish
    coleslaw and mustard pork
    jus, 136, 137–39
beurre blanc, tarragon, 74–75
bison burgers, 124–25
bison tenderloin with bison
    goulash, *178, 179*
blackberry pie, SoBo's, 45
black currant jam, 214

Blue Heron Farm squash agno-
    lotti with chestnuts, brown
    butter and sage, *34, 35*–36
boneless Cornish hens with
    bread stuffing and escargot
    ragout, *184, 185*
bouillabaisse du Pacifique,
    58–59
brandade, sablefish, 37
bruschetta sampler, 152–53
bulgur wheat, apple and
    fireweed honey salad, 60–61
bull kelp, candied, salad, 161
burgers, bison, 125
BUTTER
    brown, 32–33, 35–36
    gentleman's, 145
    maple salted, 171
butterflied leg of lamb with
    herb jus, 97

cake, honey sponge, 62–63
calamari, spicy curry, 109
candied bull kelp salad, 161
carnaroli risotto on heirloom
    tomato and basil salad, 143
carpaccio, halibut, 183
carrot and pear salad, 46
cauliflower, celery root and
    Jerusalem artichoke soup
    with black truffle cream
    and fried sage, 24
celery root and cauliflower
    and artichoke soup, 24
celery root purée, 182
ceviche, tuna, 162
Chantilly cream, 171
chanterelle open-faced ravioli
    with crisp Berkshire bacon,
    206, 207
chard, rainbow, in minestrone
    verde, *128, 129*
chard, Swiss, and artichokes
    with seared salmon, 120
charred tomato achiote sopa
    (soup), *78, 79*